THE MAKERS OF CHRIST

A THOUSAND YEAR STORY

By

Michael Stannard.

For my Grandchildren,
Steven, Daniel and Christopher
The Generation of the 21ˢᵗ Century.

© Michael Stannard 1999

ISBN 1 897 887 22 1 (Paperback)
ISBN 1 897 887 23 X (Hardback)

Published by Natula Publications
5 St Margaret's Avenue, Christchurch, Dorset BH23 1JD

British Library Cataloguing-in-Publication Data.
A catalogue record for this book is available from the British Library.

The publisher is grateful to the following for permission to use their illustrations:- Bookends; British Museum; The estate of Kathleen M. Chilver; Christchurch Borough Council Archives; Christchurch Borough Council; Christchurch Priory; Daily Echo Bournemouth; DERA Land Systems; Dorset Record Office; Cecil Gardner; Michael Oram; Red House Museum, Hampshire County Council Museums Service; K.C. Tullett.
Drawings on pages 25, 65, 89 and 132 are by Tom Lovell.
Other drawings are by Jane Martin and based on original illustrations.
Photographs on pages 137, 177 and 187 are by Zoë Martin.
Other photographs are the authors own.

Front Cover Illustration
> Top left: ancient town seal of Christchurch-Twynham.
> Top right: ancient Conventual seal c. 1260.
> Bottom left: coat of arms of the Borough of Christchurch.
> Bottom right: cross and salmon of Christchurch Priory

Back Cover Illustration
> Original medieval document granting lease of property in Castle Street to John Kene.

PREFACE.

Much is being written at this Millennium time about the great events and famous men and women of Wessex and England that have made Britain Great.

Though there have been some notable national figures who have had close links with the burgh called Twynham that later became known as Christchurch, this book prefers to concentrate more on the ordinary men and women of the town and the part they have played in England's history. They are the Yeomen of England who have always formed the basis on which the greatness of the country has prospered. Most, though not all, were honest and industrious in their endeavours and all in their turn have made their contribution not only to the wellbeing of their families, but also to the community of which they were part. It is these people and their deeds, the lifeblood of this country, and the events in which they took part or witnessed that forms the main theme of this book. Humility would prevent most of them laying claim to fame for themselves. Yet in sum, they have made a considerable contribution to the prosperity and greatness of the country as well as helping to create a place where many others would wish to live because of its numerous advantages.

There was an ancient settlement, that came to be known as Twynham, that occupied a small area of southern England, which today lies on the borders of Hampshire and Dorset and was centred round the confluence of the rivers Avon and Stour. Originally the place had probably been called "Tweoneam", meaning the place between the two rivers. Much of the surrounding land was composed of infertile compacted river gravels on a bed of ironstone that made it initially unsuitable for cultivation, though the river valleys themselves are more fertile. There had been a settlement on a promontory about a mile away since the Bronze Age that contained the chief port connecting the Normandy peninsular and what later became known as Wessex. Through this place passed the goods brought down from the areas of Salisbury Plain, Cranborne Chase and beyond, to be exchanged for goods shipped from Normandy, Brittany and the Channel Islands. Since the site was well defended by a system of earth banks and ditches that successfully kept out unwanted invaders, it prospered considerably not only from trade and the trans-shipping of goods, but also from the smelting of various metals.

It was not until the 7th century that the area a mile further inland where the two rivers meet, was considered as a suitable site for a new settlement. Then it was only because the new arrivals were not so much interested in trade as in converting the scattered heathen population to Christianity. This great Faith had started at the eastern end of the Mediterranean, then spread throughout much of continental Europe having two often contending centres in Constantinople and Rome. This Faith was now having an impact upon England. The small settlement of Tweoneam was initially established, not as the usual trading place to which a church or temple would later be added. That already existed a mile away on the edge of the harbour. Here the reverse happened. The little church was built first with the priests' hovels beside it and the settlement grew up around the church. From the 7th century, the church here has played the main part, first, as a missionary centre with its church and nine chapels, and then with the dominating Priory round which the town gradually grew and developed.

This book does not pretend to be an in-depth study of the town's history. That must be left to more qualified scholars who have the time and skill to dig deep into the extensive archive that the town is so fortunate to possess. Much of this is now on microfilm in the Dorchester Record Office though there are many other detailed sources too. Rather it is an attempt to give an overview of the story of this small south coastal area and the settlement at its centre, that has a documented history stretching back over 1,000 years. It can do no more than highlight some of the more interesting people and events of its long history. Like most ancient towns, it was originally dependant upon agriculture. However, being a coastal town, it was also sustained by fishing and boat building. Being at the outflow of two rivers, the town also grew into a trading post, connecting the continent of Europe with the hinterland of southern and central England. In addition, for the last 900 years, its great Priory Church has been a place of pilgrimage, the effects of which would in modern parlance be termed tourism. Cut off by a great royal hunting forest from the capital of the region and at one time of the country, and also from other major centres of population, the Burgh of Twynham, later to be known as Christchurch, has nevertheless sometimes played a part in national events far in excess of its size. Though the town has not yet grown to 50,000 souls, it has had an interesting and at times important history, producing men and women who have played notable if often unrecognised parts in the life of the nation. In such a story, it is inevitable that only a sample of people and events can be included and some will unfortunately feel that the deeds of other worthies have been omitted. This is not to slight the contribution they may have made to the life of the town, but is due either to ignorance on the part of the author, or lack of space in the text, for which he apologises. Let others correct the omissions.

Since events have both a cause and an effect. I have tried. where it seemed relevant. to put things into context. Sometimes the causes have been national and the effects local. sometimes the reverse.

Though each chapter is an entity in itself. there is a theme that runs through the whole. Each chapter deals with an event or person that has had a marked effect on the town. Some may ask why therefore there is no chapter devoted to the Church or to the Town. The answer is that Church and Town are so closely intermingled that it is impossible to separate them. The first chapter shows how the new settlement at the junction of the rivers was built to support the little church that was the reason for the new settlement. Similarly the building of the Priory was the reason for the growth of the town - and for its change of name. When the Leper Hospital was built. it was on Priory land and run for centuries by the canons. Even the town's bridges owe their early care and maintenance to Indulgences granted by the Church. For over 300 years. from the reign of Edward I until Tudor times. the churchwardens supervised the archery practice undertaken by all men of the town between the ages of 16 and 60 after Mass on Sundays. This took place on land between the North Transept and North Porch of the Priory Church on what is still an area of unconsecrated ground in the churchyard. Likewise. the school in the town was originally housed within the Priory precincts. More recently. when other schools were founded. often by other denominations. the Priory School continued. keeping its close links with the Priory. whose vicar is ex officio a Governor. Even after the suppression of the Priory. when it might be assumed that the Church would be driven from its dominant position. the Priory Church was returned to the Town to be its parish church. The body set up to run the church. known as 'The Sixteene' consisted largely of the town's burgesses. Today. as always. the Mayor holds his Civic Services in the Priory. The ancient ceremony of Beating the Bounds. which always involved choirboys. is now seldom held as it used to be on a Rogation Day. However on Rogation Sunday the priest of the daughter church of All Saints at Mudeford 'Blesses of the Waters' at Mudeford Quay. in the presence of members of the Council. He prays for the safety of the fishermen. sailors and those who man our lifeboat. and for a good harvest from the sea. for the town still depends greatly on the sea.

Probably the greatest attraction for tourists is the magnificent Priory Church. and many enterprises in the town use the name 'Priory' in their name. Nor should we forget that the seal of the Borough that was used for centuries. depicted the figure of Christ seated in majesty. holding the scriptures in his left hand with his right hand raised in benediction. while the Borough's modern coat of arms is surmounted by the 'Chi-Rho' monogram standing for Christ. above which rises the

Priory's tower. The old Priory seal displayed the original Priory Church with its central tower while the new Priory symbol is a cross and the famous Christchurch salmon. These are but a few examples of how Church and Town have always been inseparable - and long may it continue since neither would prosper so well without the other.

A note needs to be added about the spelling of names both of people and places. Until printing had become widespread and education had reached the stage where most of those who wished to do so could learn to read, spelling was a haphazard affair. Even Shakespeare spelt his name in many different ways. To give a consistent spelling of names in the early centuries of 'Twynham' is not possible, since it is found in many forms. Names of people vary similarly, though sometimes it was deliberate. One of Henry VIII's Lord Chancellors, Thomas Worsley, who was for a time lord of one of the manors here, decided to spell his name 'Wriothesley' because he thought it looked more aristocratic. In later centuries, men sometimes took on the surname of a relative when they inherited an estate. This can lead to confusion when trying to trace a direct line of descent.

I have had recourse to many sources of information, the main ones being:- The *Domesday Book* of 1086, compiled for William I, and its ecclesiastical equivalent the *Valor Ecclesiasticus*, compiled for Henry VIII, in both of which the town has full entries; the *Christchurch Cartulary*, of which approximately only the first 250 charters, painstakingly translated by Austen Willson, are as yet available; the many charters and other documents that comprise the archives of the Borough of Christchurch; and the archive records of the Leper Hospital of St Mary Magdalen, Christchurch. Where appropriate, I have also relied heavily on contemporary documents, often translated from their original Latin some centuries ago, some of which are in the Cotton Library, the British Library and Public Record Office, as well as the local archives now in the Dorchester Record Office, the Red House Museum and with the Christchurch Local History Society. I also owe an inestimable debt to many people. Some I have been able to interview. In other cases I have drawn on the published works of nationally recognised authorities as well as local people who have written about events that affected the town. To all of these, I humbly acknowledge my debt. In particular I would mention Hugh Jaques, the Dorset Archivist, and Caroline Edwards the Hampshire Archivist, also J. Barker, Kate Bennett, Norman Davies, Taylor Dyson, Keith Feiling, David Fox, Rev. G.N. Godwin, Roger Guttridge, Alastair Hoare, S.F.Hockey, Michael Hodges, J.Hunter, Col J.H.Joiner, M.D.Knowles, H.Mayr-Harting, Sir George Meyrick, G. Morley, B. J. Pickering,

Michael F. Powell, D. Richardson, Olive Samuel, Eric N. Spreadbury, Roy Stride, Ken Tullett, O. G. Vernon, Allen White, Leslie R. White, David Williamson, Brian Woodifield, J.A. Young, and Philip Ziegler.

I am also indebted to several of the Borough Council's officers, who have given me invaluable assistance; in particular Michael Allen, Miss. S. Bessant, David Fairbairn, Peter Jones, Michael Turvey and Frank Tyhurst. Nor would this book have seen the light of day without the care and attention given to it by its publisher, Jane Martin, to whom, as always I owe an immense debt.

Finally I am most grateful for the generous financial support provided by the Red House Museum Christchurch Archives and Local History Fund towards the publication costs of this book.

I offer this book as a personal contribution to the Millennium celebrations of this ancient town that was once a Royal Burgh and is now a distinguished Borough. It is my hope that it may help future generations to better understand their past and perhaps encourage them to seek out much of the information that exists but has not yet been uncovered. May it also help the citizens of Christchurch and those who come to visit the area, to understand why we say that this town, whose documented history reaches back over 1,000 years, is a place "Where Time is Pleasant".

Michael Stannard.   Christchurch, 1999.

About the Author.

Michael Stannard was born in London in 1926 and educated at Marlborough College and Christ Church, Oxford, where he gained a Master of Arts degree. Commissioned in 1945 into the Coldstream Guards, he served for a time in Nigeria. By profession, a schoolmaster, he was for some years headmaster of a well-known preparatory school. For over 30 years his home has been in Christchurch, where he sat for many years as a Justice of the Peace and has been closely involved with a leading Housing Association for some time. His interest in local affairs led him to bring to light some of the town's ancient documents and to publish two historical novels and numerous historical articles on early Christchurch-Twynham.

Michael is the third generation of his family to be a Freeman of the Worshipful Company of Gardeners of the City of London. His 18th and 19th century ancestors were Freemen and Worsted Weavers of Norwich. His other interests are sailing and gardening. He is married with two sons, both of whom live and work abroad.

By the same author:

HUGH OF TWYNHAM
*
JOHN DRAPERS TREASURE

Contents

Contents (cont)

Illustrations.

Illustrations (cont).

Chapter 1.

Saint Birinus d. A.D.650.

When St Birinus, who was the first Bishop of Dorchester near Oxford, sent his missionaries into Wessex, he can have had little idea what this simple act would lead to. Not much is known about Birinus, except that he was sent over by Honorius I, who was pope from A.D. 625-638, to try to convert the central part of England to Christianity. He obviously had some success since in A.D. 635, he baptised the heathen King Cynegils and some, though not all of his family, but he had to struggle to persuade the kingdom to accept the new religion. Perhaps because of this, he sent some of those who had accompanied him to the more southern parts of the kingdom. If so, then it seems that those who were sent to the lands to the south of the king's great hunting forest came upon a strategically important site. The harbour that we know as Christchurch held an important settlement that had long been one of the main trading ports linking Britain and the continent. The Romans had improved the harbour that had existed since the Bronze Age on the north side of what is now known as Hengistbury Head. The headland, which was then twice its present width, was well protected by a double line of fortifications. However it was little used as a site from which to preach a new gospel, since those who used it were bent on shipping goods and trading. Because of the low lying and marshy nature of the immediate surrounding land, any habitations would have had to be built some little way inland, and so out of sight and reach of the events at the port. Presumably the whole site had originally been chosen because, once its double dyke defences had been constructed, it was particularly easy to keep out marauders.

Far more suitable for these first missionaries was a spit of land that lay about a mile further inland at the junction of two rivers, the Avon and Stour. Here the land rose a few metres above the river level and was drier, being composed of compacted river gravels. The site had several other advantages. It was surrounded on three sides by the water of the two rivers that formed the main trade routes inland. In the case of the Avon, trade came down from as far afield as the ancient temple of Stonehenge and its nearby encampment of Sarum. It was also near the location of the lowest possible crossing points of the two rivers, so that any traffic between the old Roman port of Hamworthy and the capital of Wessex at Winchester would have to pass near it. The site was obviously easy to defend, because of its watery barriers, but at the same time presented a more friendly aspect to visitors.

Finally, and probably of considerable importance to the missionaries, anyone travelling inland along the trade routes, would be able to take such knowledge as the missionaries were able to instil into a very wide area of inland Wessex. Certainly the site had many advantages over the then existing port under Hengistbury Head and it appears that these early missionaries were soon blessed with success, despite the natural opposition they would have met from the heathen – and no doubt cynical – traders and travellers.

St Birinus blesses the first church at Twynham

Before too long, the missionaries would probably have made contact with those who were already established at Bosham to the east and Wareham to the west, particularly by sea, as well as with the communities in Normandy and Brittany. However for the most part they would have had to be self-reliant and would soon have felt sufficiently confident to replace their original wooden and thatch church with a more substantial stone structure. That the Saxons were competent builders in stone we can assume from their work at Bosham, where the church is considerably larger and higher than anything they built at Twynham. Tradition has it that ultimately there was built here a stone church and two stone chapels, and also seven other chapels, probably of wood. This implies that there must have been a considerable colony of priests. It also means that the settlement itself must have flourished, since, even in those early days, as many as perhaps a dozen and a half priests would have been required to serve it and the other small outlying settlements that grew up in the neighbourhood. These would have looked to the main settlement at Twynham for protection and trade.

This can be assumed from the fact that by about A.D. 900, with the still present threat of attack from the sea by the marauding Danes, King Alfred considered Twynham to be of sufficient importance to be nominated as a burgh. It thus became one of the series of defensive settlements that were established, each about twenty miles apart, spread along the coast from the Kent-Sussex border in the east, to the Cornish border in the west and provided refuges for all the population in time of attack. In all probability, there was also built a small defensive mound that would have been surrounded by a timber palisade and which would have acted as the last line of defence within the settlement. Into this would have huddled as many of those who survived the initial assault, where they would have put up their last desperate defence against the brutal and gory death that would have awaited any who were unlucky enough to be captured. One particularly unpleasant fate that was sometimes meted out by these ferocious warriors was to split open the chest of their victim with their axe and then throw the wretch's lungs over his shoulders to resemble a flying angel. No wonder the inhabitants welcomed the presence of the defensive walls of the settlements and were willing to help in its protection. In view of the known length of the boundary defensive walls, the population of the burgh and its surrounding settlements must have been considerable, since every adult male was responsible for the defence of about two yards of wall. As the community grew and became more of a trading post, so probably did the old port on Hengistbury Head decline and then fall into decay. The new settlement would also quickly have acquired its taverns to supply not only beer and other drinks, but also food, somewhere to sleep, though probably not beds as such, and the other comforts required by sailors and travellers.

An additional advantage that would quickly have become apparent to the inhabitants of Twynham over those still occupying the harbour area behind Double Dykes, would have been a good water supply. This could have been obtained from either of the two rivers, and would have been far superior to that available on Hengistbury Head. Streams appear to be lacking there, and water taken from the harbour, even on a falling tide, would at best have been brackish. At Twynham, the river water would almost invariably have been fresh, except perhaps at the highest spring tides. Once the millstream had been constructed, the Avon would have remained largely unpolluted, since the river lay on the far side of it. Much of the burgh's drinking water would therefore have been of better quality than that found in those parts of the world nowadays where wells are still dug next to cesspits. The millstream would have been used as a sewer, to carry away most of the rubbish and excrement from those whose houses lay against it.

3

No doubt the miller at Place Mill by the Town Quay, complained regularly when the smell became more pungent than usual, though equally surely it was to no effect. It is however worth noting that in the mid 19th century, before main drainage was laid in the town, a lease for the mill contained an undertaking that the Mill Stream had to be kept clear throughout its length. We should remember that even today in some third world countries, the women still gather up the fresh animal dung in their hands in order to collect it for drying into one of their main sources of fuel. Though unacceptable by the standards of present day western civilisation, the ever-present filth and excrement, both human and animal, was taken as part of life in those days. It is little wonder therefore that life expectancy was so short.

Ploughing and sowing.

It is hard to know exactly what trades would have been practised in early Twynham. One of the first would certainly have been milling, though this was controlled by the priests who, as the initial driving force of the community, had probably overseen the construction of the millstream. They were probably the only people with sufficient intelligence and expertise to undertake such a large task, since it is at least one kilometre long. It is further remarkable in that the water is taken from the Avon but is returned to the Stour by the Clay Pool, just before it joins up with the Avon. Considering the extremely flat nature of the bed of the Avon, it meant that the construction of the stream had to be carried out with the minimum of fall if there was to be any head of water at the site of the mill wheel. However, since it is known that the southern part of England is dipping downwards at the rate of over 1 mm. per year, it is probable that when the mill stream was first constructed, about 1.200 years ago, the level of the land would have been over a metre and a half higher than at present. This would have given sufficient fall for the mill wheel to turn successfully at almost any state of the tide, which is not the case now. It would then have been a very valuable mill, bringing a handsome profit to the priests who worked it. This could well have helped finance the building of their first stone church and chapels.

Other trades that would have sprung up were leatherworking, woodworking of all sorts and of course spinning, which would have been practised in every household by the womenfolk, and no doubt weaving too. This would have included the wool already woven in the home, as well as other materials. One of the most common was nettles, whose fibres are particularly strong and could be woven into a variety of hard wearing cloths to be used for sacks and aprons for example. There was also a considerable amount of fishing. Some of this was carried out at sea, but most of it was from the rivers, especially where the two flowed out into the open sea. From time immemorial it seems that salmon have been plentiful, particularly in the Avon. The fish were usually caught with nets that would be rowed out across the entrance in coracles. These small but remarkably versatile craft were made to different designs throughout the country and are still made today at Ironbridge in Shropshire. Their basic materials were willow withies, because of their flexibility, and a cowhide which would be stretched over them. The size of the craft was inevitably limited by the size of the beast that was available, but it was possible to have two people in such a craft. Other forms of fishing involved the use of traps made of withies, or in the case of eels, skewered with special multi-pronged forks. Net making and boat building would therefore have been well known crafts locally. Other trades would have been associated with what we would now call tourism. Brewing small ale and the provision of food and other comforts in the inns for travellers; baking in what would at that time have been the common bread ovens; and of course subsistence farming with all the crafts that went with it. Some of this would have been done in the home by the labourers themselves, though specialist craftsmen would soon have acquired the skills to improve the quality of the tools required.

Like all early settlements, most of its inhabitants would have travelled little. Few probably went further than a mile or two from their home. There was no need. Their contact with the outside world was through the crews of the vessels that came into the harbour and those who brought goods down river from the inland areas of the rest of Wessex. The settlement was particularly cut off from the east and towards the north, by the great royal forest that stretched for more miles than most men cared to walk. Nor would they wish to be found in the royal forest less they be accused of taking the royal deer, which carried unpleasant penalties. To the west, the land was for some miles mostly blasted heathland, before one reached the more fertile area by Wareham.

The settlement needed to be self sufficient, being unable to rely on any quick help in case of attack from the sea. That this could happen they were all too well aware, or they would not have been called upon to become a burgh with all that this entailed in self-defence. One consolation they did have was the fact that any attacker would provide them with plenty of warning. The threatening ships would be visible from several miles out to sea, and their proposed point of attack easily identified. Either the ships would enter the harbour, or else they would sail by to threaten some other settlement, in which case the inhabitants of Twynham would heave a sigh of relief and return to their labours. Were the attack to threaten Twynham, it would take several hours for the invading ships to reach the settlement. Such craft, like the more peaceful trading vessels, had first to negotiate the difficult entrance. At that time it was probably not the narrow Run we know today, but much more of a delta through which the locals, but few others, knew the best channel. Once that was negotiated, there was then the problem of making the lengthy passage of almost two miles to the settlement itself. This gave those who lived in the vicinity, and to whom the settlement was their place of refuge, time to round up their families and even their livestock and hurry them inside the defensive walls of the burgh. It also presented an opportunity for the defenders to mount harassing attacks from the shoreline and river banks onto the passing vessels, perhaps firing them with aid of flaming arrows. The result was that in the main, the settlement was left largely undisturbed and was able to pursue its own ends of farming and trading.

It also appears that quite soon Twynham acquired a reputation for healing the sick. Often this was said to be miraculous, though it was probably more due to the cleanliness of the water supply and perhaps a few simple herbal remedies than anything else. What is certain is that there were soon discovered a series of remarkably pure wells in the area, which probably flow down from the higher land of the New Forest. It is said that the Romans were aware of one or more such wells on the northern shore of the harbour in the area now known as Purewell, though this name may owe more the Saxon word for a pear tree than clean water. Although some of these wells are within a very few feet of the harbour's edge, it seems that they still retain remarkable purity. Even today, in spite of the vastly increased pollution of our rivers, the Avon is regarded as being a particularly clean river. In its passage from the Wiltshire downlands, it passes

6

through many different types of soil and probably picks up traces of various minerals that are beneficial to mankind. Those wells that draw their water supply from the great royal forest are likewise supplied with similarly beneficial water. There have always been those who are particularly skilled with herbal remedies and it is likely that the combination of pure water and abundant herbs encouraged any local practitioners to follow and perfect those arts. Indeed, as will be seen later, such practices became increasingly important at Twynham.

There is an interesting comparison to be made between the various early settlements of Bosham, Portchester, Twynham, Wareham and Corfe Castle along the Hampshire-Dorset coast. Bosham, situated near the Roman palace of Fishborne, was perhaps the earliest Christian settlement along this part of the coast. That it failed to prosper may in part have been due to the conservatism of the local population and their isolation from other larger centres of population, or the silting up of its harbour. Even Chichester was the other side of the inlet that leads up to Bosham and as such would have had little effect on its inhabitants who would rarely have had contact with those sailing up to Chichester. Portchester was well defended, being secure within the particularly strong walls of the Roman fort and remained occupied until about A.D. 370. Its walls still present a formidable obstacle and would always have kept out both friend and foe alike. Wareham, built on a low ridge between the two rivers Piddle and Frome – much as Twynham is situated – was an important Anglo-Saxon port and frequently took the brunt of ferocious Danish attacks. Like Twynham, it was an early Christian settlement and contains the oldest surviving church in Dorset, dating from about 1030. That the town did not grow to any great size may be due to the lack of trade that came down its small rivers as well as the long journey necessary to reach the open sea beyond what is now Poole Harbour. Corfe Castle, a massively strong defensive site set in a gap in the hills on the Isle of Purbeck, is likewise forbidding to any wishing to approach. Even friends could suffer at the hands of those who held it, as the 18 year-old King Edward discovered in 978. He was stabbed to death there while quenching his thirst after a long ride, at the instigation of his mother, Queen Aelfryth, so that she could control the kingdom. From this tragic event was born the ceremony of the 'loving cup', when a friend stands with his back to the one who drinks a toast to his neighbour, to prevent a similar treachery from occurring. Both Corfe and Wareham probably had little trade beyond the Isle of Purbeck. Bosham and Portchester, though in a more fertile area, lacked the good river routes inland that so favoured Twynham. None of the four grew to any size, or achieved more than local fame.

Only Twynham seems to have prospered and grown somewhat in

importance. Unlike the other places, it had excellent river communications with the hinterland and a good crossing of the two rivers dividing east from west. But most of all, it seems to have presented a welcoming aspect to those who approached, either from the sea, from which angle the small church would have been the first building to be seen, or from across the rivers, which formed the main barrier to the settlement. Today's much larger Priory Church can be seen from as far out to sea as the Needles. Though inevitably there would have been a low protective embankment, surmounted by a timber palisade, it would not have appeared to present a threat to an approaching friendly traveller. With the presence of a particularly good water supply, the possibility of prosperity becomes apparent.

So with the passage of the years, the priests sent by St Birinus started a train of events which were to lead to things of which they could have had no concept. From the foundations laid by those first adventurous priests has grown a community that has continued for over 1,000 years. They chose their site wisely, more wisely than they could have known, and thus sowed the seeds of our present town, "Where Life is Pleasant".

Chapter 2

Sulfric circa A.D.930 – 990.

Christchurch is very fortunate to possess its Cartulary. This is a resumé of the several hundred then known charters and other documents connected with the Priory up to 1362, which was the year that the monk who compiled this record completed his work. Approximately the first 250 documents out of something like 600, have been painstakingly translated over a period of several years by Austen Willson and give us an unusually clear insight into events connected with the development of the Priory and its pre-Norman church.

The three earliest charters are all Saxon, the first two being grants of land to a man called Sulfric. The earliest, dated A.D. 956, which is a grant of land by King Edwy, reads.

'Edwy, king of the English, grants in perpetuity to the famous huntsman, Sulfric, a 'mansa' and a half at Seale and a 'mansa' only at Dunnyngtherd, with unrestricted right of bequest. His grant, dating from A.D. 956, the first year of his reign, is free of all royal dues, save those of military service, bridging, and fortress-work: witnesses, the donor himself, Archbishop Oda, Eadger the atheling, bishop Elfsige, and bishops Osulf, Oschitel, and Daniel'.

'Seale' or Zeals, and 'Dunnyngtherd' or Donhead, are two extant villages in Wiltshire, and a 'mansa' was an area of land sufficient to support a family. The 'atheling' was Edwy's younger brother, who ruled after him from A.D. 959-975. Osulf was Bishop of Ramsbury, which with Sherborne combined to become the see of Salisbury a century later. Daniel was Bishop of Selsey, which in the next century became the see of Chichester.

The second charter, dated A.D. 985, is a grant of land by King Ethelred and reads.

'Ethelred, Basileos of all Albion, has given to the priest Sulfric a whole mansa, a half being at Borstealle, and the rest at Haestandic and at Cnolla, with pastures, meads and woods with right of bequest and free from all secular demands, save for military service, bridging and fortress-work. Dated A.D. 985: confirmed by Dunstan, archbishop of Canterbury, Oswald, archbishop of York, Elfstan, bishop of London, Elfheh, bishop of Winchester.'

'Borstealle' is probably Bosley Farm, which lies between Fairmile Road and the River Stour, and is mentioned in the Domesday record. 'Cnolla', which appears in other charters, would appear to be part of the Portfield, later to become an area of over 125 acres stretching from the Barrack Road recreation ground towards the Stour.

Both these charters were obviously of considerable importance, since not only were they grants made by the kings themselves of land held in their estates, but they were witnessed by an impressive assembly of bishops in the southern part of England. Since Donhead in the earlier charter is at least 30 miles from Twynham, with Zeals being a further 10 miles distant, the immediate question that arises must be what connection the 'famous huntsman' had with Twynham. Secondly, what had he done to deserve the grant of more than enough land to keep his family? Had he perhaps been particularly successful in providing boar and deer for the king to hunt, or had he saved the king from being gored by an angry charging beast, be it boar or wolf? We do not know, but for whatever reason, the king seems to have been grateful to him. Nor do we know in which forest he was a huntsman. It was probably not the great forest of Andret, later to become the 'New Forest', but may have been part of the extensive Clarendon Forest in Wiltshire. Since all the Cartulary documents refer to lands held by the church at Twynham at the time that the Cartulary was assembled, one must assume that the 'Sulfric' of the first charter had come to Twynham at some later date. Did he perhaps retire from his post as royal huntsman and move to Twynham with his family while he continued to draw rent and receive produce from his lands in Wiltshire? Did he then change his profession and take the tonsure to become a canon at the church at Twynham, which by then already had several little chapels, and probably its first stone church? Such a change in lifestyle was far from uncommon, particularly as a way of preparing oneself the afterlife if one felt that ones sins were particularly burdensome.

The second charter also presents problems. Why should a second king also make a grant of land to a man who on the face of it was no more than a priest in a small town, albeit that Twynham had been a Royal Burgh for over half a century. Ethelred, who reigned from A.D. 979 to 1016, styles himself as 'King of the whole of England', despite the continuing Norse attacks and invasions in the north of the country. Was he, perhaps, still troubled by the death of his half-brother Edward the Martyr, who was murdered at Corfe Castle apparently at the instigation of his mother on 18th March A.D. 978 – a matter to which he was no doubt privy? Only 5 years before the A.D. 985 charter, Ethelred had caused Edward's body to be translated from Wareham where it had been buried, to Shaftesbury where it was re-interred with great pomp by Archbishop Dunstan. There followed miracles at the dead king's new tomb that resulted in a movement to have him declared a saint and martyr, which finally occurred in 1001. Was Ethelred perhaps trying to secure his place in heaven by this grant to Sulfric, whom he could well have met at Shaftesbury, which is only 3 miles from Donhead and who could have been visiting his lands there? Or was Ethelred concerned about the state of agriculture in A.D. 985, for the Anglo-Saxon Chronicle tells us that the next year '*A great murrain first occurred in England*'. This decimated the livestock of the country and Twynham would not have escaped the pestilence, losing both sheep and cattle. Such plagues take time to spread, but the first serious sheep losses might well have begun the year before. We do not know, but the king's conscience may well have been sufficiently troubled for him to try to make amends.

What does seem certain is that the Sulfric of the first charter is the same man as the Sulfric of the second. Why else should the first charter be part of the Cartulary which only contains documents referring to matters related to Twynham and then Christchurch? Most priests were then married - the idea of celibate priests had not yet been adopted - and many of them owned land. However on his death, because Sulfric had 'right of bequest', he may well have given all his land both in Wiltshire and at Twynham, to the church that he was then serving. It would not have been the first such gift to the church at Twynham, since it had always been the custom to bestow goods and lands on the Church in return for Masses being said for one's soul to ensure its speedy passage to heaven. These particular acres, even though some were situated more than a day's ride from Twynham, would have been a useful source of income to the small Christian community and may perhaps have enabled it to build one of the two stone chapels.

The small royal burgh by this time would surely have replaced the once thriving port a mile further downstream. It would also now have had its mill beside the Clay Pool that would have belonged to the church community. The corn from Sulfric's Portfield and Bosley acres would have been quickly ground into flour, whatever the state of the tide. With farmers bringing in their corn to the mill, other trades would also have started to spring up so that there would soon be a more balanced community.

There is a third pre-conquest charter in the Cartulary, dated 1053, which reads:

'*Edward, ruler of all the English and of neighbouring people, grants in perpetuity to his thegn Lutrise, with right of bequest, held a 'mansa' at the place called 'Bageslucesleia' with its fields, pastures and meadows and woodlands, free from all service, save bridging, fortress-work and military service. Granted in 1053, with agreement of bishops Stigand, Hereman, Leofric, Sulsise and Eldred.'*

Saxon kings at this time claimed lordship over both Scotland and Wales, who were the 'neighbouring people'. Stigand had recently been elevated from the Bishopric of Winchester to be Archbishop of Canterbury. Hereman was the last Bishop of Ramsbury before it combined with Sherborne to form the See of Salisbury. Leofric and Eldred were bishops respectively of Exeter and Worcester. Sulsise appears to have had no see, but may have been a suffragan bishop. 'Bageslucesleia' can be identified as 'Bashley' on the edge of the New Forest. Since the Domesday record shows that one of the priests at Twynham held 150 acres and also 16 acres of meadow during the reign of King Edward, it may well be that part of the land granted to Lutrise was soon afterwards given to the church. Alternatively, the priest, named Alsi, may have himself inherited part of Lutrise's lands. Again, we do not know, but since this grant is also in the Cartulary, it seems to imply that at least part of the royal gift came to the church before 1086.

Part of the Christchurch Cartulary

The importance of some of the details of these three gifts of land will become apparent in future chapters. Certain aspects of them would appear to provide a direct link with events several hundred years later, and to give a clear indication of the duties men owed to their overlord. It also seems that Sulfric is the first person who can be positively identified by name as having lived in and owned land in and around Twynham. His exact position in the hierarchy of the burgh is not known, but in view of his association with royalty and as a priest - perhaps even their leader - he appears to have been a man of some consequence. He is also the first man whom we may name as having almost certainly celebrated Mass in the stone church and chapels whose walls form the three crypts that lie beneath the Great Quire and north and south transepts of the present Priory Church.

For a town to have documents that enable it to trace its history continuously back for so many centuries is surely the envy of many greater cities.

Chapter 3.

The Domesday Record of Twynham 1086.

There are, fortunately, lengthy entries in the Domesday Record that give considerable detail of the land holdings in and around Twynham. The importance of the record that William the Conqueror had compiled is threefold. It lists who owned what in 1086; what major changes had taken place since pre-conquest times under Edward the Confessor from 1042; and finally the immediate recipients of land after Duke William of Normandy was crowned King of England at the end of 1066. The original purpose of the record was to enable William to discover the value of the tax revenue he could obtain from his newly conquered lands. For us today, it means that place names can be identified, the distribution of the population can be assessed and even on occasion the present ownership of land traced back to those distant times. In the first place we know that the Hundred in this area comprised four distinct areas, namely Egheite, Shirley, Roderic, and Bovre which later became the New Forest Hundred. For us, the most important of these is Egheite. Over the years, the original names have been corrupted but the places can still be easily identified. They are Tuinam, Thuinham, other spellings of 'Tweoneam' (Tweoxneam) that later became corrupted to Twynham, Holeest (Holdenhurst), Herne (Hurn), Chenap (Knapp), Stanpeta (Stanpit), Hoburne (Hoborne), Bailocheslei (Bashley), Bovre (Boldre) and Bortel, which is probably Bosley.

Godric listing the church lands in 1086.

14

It is important to remember that Twynham was a royal burgh, having been owned by successive Saxon kings until it fell by right of conquest to William the Norman. Hence the first part of the entry gives details of his property. For ease of reading, certain Saxon words have been modernised, since spelling even of place names in those days, and for several more centuries, was far from consistent, as can be seen from this first entry.

'The King holds Tuinham in demesne. It belonged to King Edward's ferm and was then and now assessed as one virgate of land; there is land for 13 ploughs; in the demesne are 2 ploughs; 21 villeins and 5 bordars have 12 ploughs; there is 1 serf, 3 coliberts and 4 radknights have 2 ½ ploughs; there is a mill worth 5/- and 61 acres of meadow; the woodland is now in the King's forest; in it there were formerly 5 villeins with 3 ploughs. In the burgh of Thuinam are 31 messuages paying 16d. land tax each. In King Edward's time and afterwards it was worth £19 by tale; now it is worth £10 by weight of 20d. to the ounce but it pays £12.10s.0d. The part which is now in the Forest is valued at £12.10s.0d.'

'Villeins', 'bordars', 'coliberts', and 'radknights' were different categories of landholders cultivating various quantities of land. It is usually reckoned that a 'virgate' was about 30 acres, and a 'hide' about 120 acres, though these areas varied in other parts of the country, largely depending on how much land could be ploughed in a day. A 'plough' refers to a plough team of 12 oxen, which would usually have been assembled by several households. The site of the mill mentioned here is not known, but it was neither that at the town quay nor the mill at Knapp. Since the 31 people listed were all heads of families, each of which probably contained on average of 5 people, we can estimate the total population of the royal estate to be about 170 souls.

The next part of the entry concerns the secular canons of the church of the Holy Trinity Twynham. By this time, it is estimated that there were besides the little stone church, 2 stone chapels and 7 other wooden chapels. All these buildings would almost certainly have had wooden roofs covered with thatch made from the abundant supply of reeds in the rivers.

'The Canons of Holy Trinity Thuinham hold in the vill 5 hides and a virgate and a hide in the Isle of Wight; these hides have always belonged to that church. There are 5 ploughs in the demesne; there are 11 villeins and 13 bordars with 1 plough, there are 2 serfs; there is a mill worth 30/- and 108 acres of meadow land; there is woodland

for 2 swine; there are 6 messuages worth 13/4d. To this church belongs the whole tithe of Thuinam and one third of the tithe of Holdenhurst; in King Edward's time it was worth £6; now £8. This church formerly had 8 acres in Andret in Bovre but they are now in the Forest.'

From this it can be seen that the church had 630 cultivated acres, some of which would have been that part of the Portfield originally given to Sulfric, and 108 acres of meadow, much of which may have been the land on either side of the rivers. Since it would flood regularly, it would produce good early pasture and be of particular value for feeding cattle.

However, this is not the total land holdings of the canons, for three are named as owning estates personally.

'Alsi the priest holds from the King, Bashley; he held it in King Edward's time; then assessed at 1 hide and 3 virgates; now at 3 virgates only; there is land for 1 plough there are 2 serfs; 1 villein and 1 bordar; half share of a mill worth 3/-; 16 acres of meadow; it was and is worth 20/-.

Alsi seems to have been a wealthy man and may, like Sulfric, have entered the church late in life. However he lost 120 acres of probably not very good land, which was appropriated by the new king, William, to enlarge his Forest. He would however have been compensated for the loss of this land.

There is also Alnod.

'Alnod the priest holds of the King, Bortel. He held it in parage of King Edward; then assessed at 1 ½ virgates; now the same; there is land for half a plough; there are 2 serfs; also one third part of a mill worth 25d.; there are 10 ½ acres of meadow. This Alnod also had 2 messuages in Tuinam'.

It appears that by 1086 Alnod had become the sole owner of Bosley, rather than being a shared owner as in King Edward's time, though whether by inheritance or purchase is not known. However it is likely that part of the land was the half 'mansa' given to Sulfric by King Ethelred. It is however clear that by 1086 the Church and individual canons between them owned large estates which would produce considerable income in addition to the eight 'messuages' or properties with their surrounding outhouses and gardens within the burgh itself. What a long way the little missionary community first established by St Birinus had come in 400 years. In ownership of land, the Church community at Twynham already came second only to the King.

Finally there is a reference to 'Godric Presbyter', who is discussed in the next chapter. He is listed as holding an estate at Prestpiddle, now known as Bryants Puddle.

There is also a record of who held other land in the immediate area that formed part of the local Hundred.

The King himself holds Holdenhurst; Earl Tostig held it; it was assessed at 29 hides and half a virgate. When 'Hugh de Port received it there were 22 hides and half a virgate and they never paid tax. The other 7 hides are in the Isle of Wight. There are now 18 ½ hides and ½ a virgate as 3 ½ hides are in the Forest. There is land for 20 ploughs; in the demesne are 4 ½ ploughs; there are 37 villeins with 19 ploughs; there are 14 serfs; there is a chapel, a mill worth 15/- and 3 fisheries for the use of the hall. There are 181 acres of meadow and woodland for the 6 swine from the pannage. On the hides that are now in the Forest dwelled 13 villeins and 3 bordars with 8 ploughs and with these hides now detached from the manor there is woodland for 129 swine from the pannage. In King Edward's time it was worth £44, afterwards £34. It is now worth £24 paid by tale but it pays £25 of 20d to the ounce. That part which is now in the Forest is valued at £2.10s.0d.

This entry shows that the Manor of Holdenhurst which, though it still looked to the burgh of Twynham for its defence, was of far greater size than the burgh. The chapel and a small parcel of land at Holdenhurst would have come under the control of Twynham and will be mentioned later in connection with leprosy that was brought into England by some of those returning from the first Crusade. It also demonstrates the sort of changes that were taking place as a result of the Conquest. Tostig, who was King Harold's rebellious brother, had been killed at Stamford Bridge, shortly before the Battle of Hastings and his lands would have reverted to the King. Consequently William would have acquired them after 1066.

Hugh de Port was one of the great Norman barons who acquired much of Hampshire from the previous Saxon owners as a result of the Conquest. Besides the lands already listed, he had other local estates.

Hugh de Port holds Hurn of the bishop of Bayeux and 2 tenants hold it from him. Then as now it is assessed at 1 hide; there is land for 1 plough; there are 3 bordars and a serf; half a fishery worth 2d.; in King Edward's time it was worth 20/- now 36/-. The same Hugh holds 1 hide at Knapp. In King Edward's time it was held by 3 tenants but it was given to bishop Odo who granted it to Hugh. Then it was assessed at 1 hide; there is land for 1 plough; there is 1 serf; there is a mill worth 20/- and a fishery worth 50d.; there are 16 acres of meadow; formerly there were 3 halls; In King Edward's time it was worth 20/-, now 30/-.'

The Bishop of Bayeux, Odo by name, was a half brother of the Conqueror, and like Hugh de Port was given vast tracts of land as a result of the take-over of England by the Normans. There is no record of what happened to the 3 halls that had belonged to the previous Saxon owners. In the turmoil that followed the redistribution of land after 1066, they may well have fallen into decay, since they would have been only wooden buildings with thatched roofs. This was particularly likely if the Saxons who had held them had been killed either during the battles at Stamford Bridge or Hastings, and the new owners had more profitable acres to occupy their time.

Other less important new landowners in the area are also mentioned. Some of the estates they held were in absolute ownership as an 'alod', rather than under feudal ownership with its accompanying duties. This was a great advantage to the landowner, since he could concentrate on farming his land without having to spend days working for his overlord. Inevitably this would have been at a crucial time, such as harvest or sowing, when every man needed to make the most of the favourable weather. The normal tenant often found that his own meagre harvest had to be neglected while he gathered in the much larger crops of his wealthy overlord. Such a system could easily lead to bad relations between the two.

'William son of Stour holds Sopley. Edric held it of King Edward as an alod. Then it paid tax for 7 hides, now for 1 hide and a virgate; there is land for 2 ploughs. In the demesne is 1 plough; 3 villeins and 6 bordars have 2 ploughs; there is 1 serf and a mill worth 10/- which also provides 875 eels; there are 30 acres of meadow. In King Edward's time it was worth £10, afterwards £2, now £2.10.0d. but it pays £5. The King has 5 hides from the manor and all the woodlands in the forest valued at £5.10s. Waleran the huntsman holds Winkton of the King and Robert holds it of him. Earl Tostig held it of King Edward as an alod. It them paid tax for 7 hides, now for 3 hides and a virgate; there is land for 4 ploughs; on the demesne are 1 ½ ploughs; 14 villeins and 7 bordars have 4 ploughs; there are 2 mills for the use of the hall and 450 eels come from the mill. Bishop Walchelin of Winchester holds Highcliffe in demesne and it has always been the minster's. In King Edward's time it was worth £10 but it is now all in the Forest except for 8 acres of meadow. Sauf's wife holds Hoburne of

*the king; Sauf had it of King Edward; then assessed at 1 hide now at
1 virgate; there is land for 1 plough; there are 2 bordars; also 6 acres
of meadow; In King Edward's time it was worth 20/- now 15/-.'*

It seems that Highcliffe was never part of Twynham and its
inhabitants may well have used the chapel at Bashley or Hinton rather
than the church at Twynham. The 120 acres owned by Sauf and his
wife would have more than covered the present Sauflands area.
Another area to appear in Domesday is Stanpit.

*Hugh de Port holds Stanpit. He had two estates there, one of which
had been held by Wislac in King Edward's time and the other by
Godwine the priest. Then as now assessed at 2 hides; in the demesne
is half a plough with 2 villeins and 2 bordars; there are 8 acres of
meadow. In King Edward's time worth 20/-, now 40/- but it pays 60/-.'*

It seems that much of Stanpit changed hands shortly afterwards, in
the reign of William Rufus, since he granted land there to the 'Church
of the Holy Trinity'. Unusually it would appear that the estate that had
belonged to Godwine the priest ceased to be connected with the
church. Did it however return shortly afterwards to the Church? There
is also a charter in the Cartulary by which Witro the falconer and his
wife Adeline, who appears to have been a noted healer, granted 1 hide
and 1 virgate in Stanpit to the church in Twynham. This could have
referred to the same estate.
Less than five miles from the centre of Twynham lie Avon and
Ripley. Both were largely granted to Hugh de Port, though part of
both places were kept by William who incorporated the woodland into
his New Forest. The Saxon Wislac, who had held Ripley in absolute
ownership under King Edward, seems to have lost all his lands.
Perhaps he died at Hastings. Another Saxon, Ulvict, fared a little
better. As one of King Edward's huntsmen in what was then part of
the forest of Andret, it seems he held his land absolutely. Under
William, he owed service to the King but lost about 65% of his land
when it was incorporated into the enlarged New Forest. However the
presumption is that he continued as a huntsman, though he had to pay
tax of 50/-, increased from the 8/- that he had paid under Edward the
Confessor. It is also stated that the land incorporated into the forest
was worth £5, for which, as was customary, he would have been
compensated.
From these various entries it is possible to obtain a fairly clear idea
of how land in and around Twynham changed hands during the
turbulent years immediately following the Conquest. Inevitably much
of the land was given to William's relatives and the barons who
accompanied him, but it is also clear from the names that many of the

estates remained in the hands of the Saxons. This was obviously wise, since it would make the control of the country far easier if many of the previous and surviving Saxon lordlings, who knew the ways of the people, could be kept friendly. It is also clear that the little stone church at Twynham with its attendant chapels was not only becoming increasingly wealthy, but also would have exerted considerable influence on the surrounding hamlets and groups of hovels. All these villages and even Holdenhurst, would have looked towards Twynham as the only defensible burgh within a day's travel.

It is difficult to picture what the countryside must then have looked like. Away from the river valleys, the land would be largely poor scrub. There would be scattered groups of dwellings, each self-sufficient and where possible situated near a stream to provide water for both people and animals. Many also had a mill and fish ponds, often stocked with eels. Surrounding these groups of dwellings would be cultivated acres divided into strips, with each household being allotted strips on the good and less fertile land. There would also be a common meadow. Each settlement might scarcely be within sight of its neighbour, the only link being perhaps a narrow track that wound its way through the scrub-land. There would have been little to disturb the silence.

This empty land would have resembled the open spaces that can still be seen between Bransgore and Burley, and other largely treeless stretches of the New Forest. Once one moved away from the fertile river valleys there was neither cultivation nor habitation. Families led isolated lives, concerned largely with scratching a living and making ends meet if possible. When harvests failed, usually through bad weather, and starvation threatened, the only place to which to turn was the Church. Twynham was therefore fortunate, since its little church was already well endowed, so that the starving and sick could be sure of some relief. Few people would have seen the lord of the manor, who had other far larger estates elsewhere, nor were they concerned with what went on in the great wide world in such distant places as Winchester. Such news as did reach them, probably came more by ship than by land, for the King's Forest cut them off from the rest of the country. Folk preferred not to enter there without good reason, lest they be caught and accused of poaching the deer, the penalty for which was often the loss of a hand, particularly if they were "caught red-handed", i.e. with the blood of the deer still on their hands. Their dogs would have been crippled by the removal of two toes to prevent them hunting down the royal deer.

When the King's clerks came to compile the Domesday Record, it would have been a talking point for a few days or weeks, partly because it was rare for so many of the scattered householders to come together in one place. Once those literate priests had left, life would have returned to the normal daily grind. It probably mattered little to ordinary folk who owned what estates or how much each was worth. Though the King might now be pleased to know how much he could expect to receive in taxes, the ordinary folk still had to pay them as they had always done. For them, nothing had really changed.

Lord of the manor entertaining on the eve of Domesday.

Chapter 4.

Godric the Priest and Ranulf Flambard 1093-1096

It seems that from their first contact, Godric and Flambard were at cross-purposes. The records give little detail about the life of Godric except to say that he was accepted as the leader amongst the secular canons who were responsible for running the church of the Holy Trinity at Twynham and the religious community that served it. He seems to have been at Twynham from about 1050, so that by the time he met Flambard, he would have been an old man. Certainly he could not have known his predecessor, Sulfric, except perhaps by name and reputation. More importantly however, he was accepted by his contemporaries as a man of considerable experience and wisdom. Unlike some of the other Twynham priests, Godric is not named in the Domesday record as owning land in the close vicinity of the burgh. However, Sir William Dugdale, in his 1661 translations of the *Monasticon Anglicanum* that were in the Cotton Library, gives considerable detail both of Godric and Flambard. A certain Canon Godric held at 'Pidele', which would appear to be in the vicinity of Puddletown, a large estate of about 600 acres, which included about 44 acres of meadow, woodland and pasture. He also had 7 slaves, 2 servants, 3 cottages and a mill, all of which was valued at £4. He was therefore a man of considerable substance, holding more land than either Alnod, Alsi or Godwine, the three canons mentioned in Domesday who held land in the vicinity of Twynham. It is also worth noting that the church at Twynham seems to have had land and indeed the benefice of a church at Puddletown from before the Conquest until the Suppression of the Priory in 1539. 'Godric' was a common Saxon name and indeed Dugdale consistently refers to 'Godric the elder', implying that there was another canon by the same name. There could not have been many who were also canons and it seems likely that 'Godric the elder' was indeed the leader of the Twynham canons, perhaps as an elder statesman and also the largest landholder.

Dugdale states that *'By the relation of the ancients, well informed fathers, grandfathers and great-grandfathers, as well clerks as laymen, to their successors concerning the church of the Holy Trinity which is situated in the town which is called Twynham, and concerning the convent of the same church, such an account is handed down as most true'*. He says that in the time of William Rufus, *'there ruled over the aforesaid church of Twynham a certain clerk named Godric, famed for his life and honour, together with 24 canons who after their custom completed the hours of the night and of the whole day each day at the point of dawn. This Godric however, was reverenced by his clerks at that time not as dean, because they were ignorant of that title, but as elder and patron'.* Godric's income appears to have been considerable, for all the offerings at morning Mass and High Mass were his. Offerings made before other masses were divided impartially between the rest of the canons, as were *'the lands adjoining the church, to wit, Hurn, Burton, and Preston'* on the Isle of Wight. In addition, *'any canon who celebrated mass had all manner of offerings of the same mass after the offering of his cope until he put it on, without sharing it with anyone, this being his good fortune'.* It seems therefore that the church at Twynham was already well endowed even before 1066.

This was one reason why Flambard asked *'for this church with the town from King William, on which since God there worked many wonders in many persons, he bestowed many kinds of riches and precious relics of saints'.* Another reason was probably that Flambard was aware of Twynham's position as a trading and trans-shipping port for goods passing from Normandy up the Avon to the Salisbury area and vice versa. The lord of the manor could expect to exact tolls on such goods. Flambard was successful in that he was granted the church and its lands, though he was not the Lord of the Manor. This remained as before in the hands of the King, who likewise would have been well aware of the revenues that the tolls would generate.

Flambard is given the church lands by William II.

From what has been described, it appears that the community at Twynham did all that was necessary to care for the souls of those who lived in and around the burgh. Though most of the canons lived in the burgh itself and served the church and its nine chapels, some of them lived further away in the outlying villages such as Sopley,

Holdenhurst, Brockenhurst, Hordle and Boldre, caring for the churches and people there. Though they came under the jurisdiction of the church at Twynham, they liked to remain separate from it. Puddletown was also linked to Twynham Church, though it seems not to have been under its direct control.

There is a fair amount of information available about Ranulf Flambard. He was apparently the son of a poor Norman priest and a local lady, the implication being that he was illegitimate. Exactly when he came to England is not known, but it was probably quite soon after the Conquest. It is however clear that he managed to become attached to the royal household in a clerical capacity at an early age, perhaps even as a companion to the Conqueror's son William Rufus. It is clear that Flambard was ambitious and made use of every opportunity that came his way to further his own interests. Since the Domesday record was compiled largely at Winchester, it is probable that Flambard was able to study some of its contents, particularly concerning areas near at hand such as Twynham. He may even have been one of the clerks whose task it was to transcribe parts of the record. He was certainly aware of the wealth of the Twynham community, situated as it was only on the other side of the King's greatly enlarged New Forest and decided that he could use its revenues for his own aggrandisement. According to Dugdale, Flambard *desiring and designing to pull down the aforesaid church of the Holy Trinity of Twynham to the ground and to build a better and more beautiful one for some order, agreed with Godric the elder of the same place and the whole convent in these words that for the completion of the church to be built they should grant to him merely the ecclesiastical offerings of pilgrims and of the whole parish as well of the living as of the dead (except those which should be in the form of food and drink, and except their foreign lands),until he should restore to them the church whole and complete and dedicated to God with the offerings he had received; in the meantime however he would find them in addition a sufficient livelihood'.*

The majority of the canons apparently agreed to this arrangement. However, Godric was more far-sighted and realised that Flambard was effectively making a take-over bid with all the usual redundancy implications that would inevitably follow. He rightly appreciated that to build this new church would take many years, by which time all the present canons would be dead and there would be none to claim back their lands, rights and benefits. As Dugdale says, *'To his wish and arrangement the rest of the canons yielded, but Godric the elder stoutly opposed him and so long gainsaid him, until he was driven from the church and persecuted throughout England, obtaining the favour and aid of neither the King nor his bishop herein'.*

24

Godric therefore fled to France. There he probably went to Bec. whose abbot was one of the most powerful clerics in northern Europe. If so, then no doubt he obtained some satisfaction from the abbot, possibly in the form of an instruction to Flambard, to treat Godric more kindly and in accordance with his considerable status as the ex-head of a community of some fame in southern England. Dugdale continues *But returning he besought the pity of the bishop Ranulf who appointed him to his earliest place among the canons instead of their chief as he was before. But the bishop of that place broke down the primitive church and nine others which had stood within the churchyard with the house of certain canons near the place of the churchyard, to make both a more suitable place for the offices and a fitting place for the canons of the town, as their lord appointed'*. Since the town itself had not been given to Flambard, but remained in royal hands, it may be that the King had some say in the arrangement.

Work begins on building a larger church.

It is hard to establish how much influence Flambard had on Twynham once his initial 'take-over' had been accomplished. We know that he quickly became one of inner circle of powerful men who surrounded William Rufus and as such would have had little time to oversee the building of his new church or the accumulation of the revenues due to the old one. Indeed, before long, Flambard became Chief Justiciar in England, and as such virtual regent when Rufus was out of the country. Legend has it that Flambard was unable to build his new church on his chosen site, the top of St Catherine's Hill a mile outside the town. Apparently this was because every time stone was taken up to the site on the top of the hill, it was returned by night to the site of the old church and its chapels. Had Flambard been present in Twynham at the time, he would probably have investigated the occurrence to discover the true reason, though the townsfolk attributed

25

it to the hand of God. Whatever the reason, the church was eventually built on the spit of land between the rivers Stour and Avon, on the site where the original mission church had been built.

However Flambard's instructions continued to carry weight even in his absence. When Bishop Carilef of Durham died on New Year's Day 1096, there is little doubt that Flambard set his heart on becoming his successor. That northern see was not only vast, but also powerful and effectively independent. It was to be 3½ years before his ambition was fulfilled, probably because the King felt he could keep his Chief Justiciar under better control so long as the prospect of Durham was dangled before him. It also meant that the King could appropriate the revenues of the vacant see to himself, though this could not be done indefinitely for fear of angering the Pope. With his other heavy duties, Flambard was therefore absent from Twynham almost continuously after about 1095. Like the King however, he ordered that *upon the death of any of the canons, he retained his benefice in his power giving it to no one, desiring to give every single prebend to another order, if the fortune of death should remove them all in his time*.

The canons at Twynham therefore decreased in number and the burden of caring for the folk in the burgh and surrounding villages became more onerous on the increasingly elderly few remaining canons. Godric for his part struggled on, fighting what must have seemed a losing battle. The church area was little more than a builders' site, crossed by trenches for the foundations and full of stone and other materials, while the wooden chapels had long since been torn down. It seems probable that he was able to retain at least the stone church and chapels for use by the parish, though it must have been difficult to pick one's way through the debris to reach them. Even his wisdom and standing must have been called into question by these who came to worship.

Eventually Godric himself died and Dugdale tells us that *not long afterwards ten canons out of the convent likewise died, whose prebends the bishop granted to the fourteen remaining ones who survived for the increase of their livelihood*. It is probable that at least some of these fourteen had been appointed by Flambard himself, carefully chosen to do his bidding and ensure that as much of the revenues of the community were transferred to him. There is plenty of evidence that Flambard was ruthless in the exploitation of his influence and power, even in such a small place as Twynham. When in 1100, Henry I succeeded Rufus on his death in the New Forest, *he seized Flambard against whom many made serious charges to him, and after seizing his, thrust him into prison at London, and his church of the Holy Trinity of Twynham into which the bishop had previously conveyed all his riches, by force and violence he despoiled, and gave it from that time in perpetual alms to a certain clerk named Gilbert de Dousgunels, solitary and destitute of all its canons save five'.*

Thus, by the time Godric died, despite all his efforts, the religious community at Twynham had been reduced almost to extinction by the depredations of Flambard, though it is doubtful if he personally knew much of it. Fortunately Gilbert de Dousgunels took up the work of building the new church again and also ensured that the remaining canons received their full dues. The building work would naturally have provided much needed employment for men in the burgh. As the building work progressed, he journeyed to Rome to petition for the establishment of a Regular Order of Canons to be established. Though he died on the return journey, and the order was not established for another 50 years, his initiative set the process in motion, for the ultimate great benefit of the town.

Flambard on the other hand suffered, as he should. Henry imprisoned him in the Tower of London, partly to bring to heel one of the most powerful and wealthy men in the land. It was also to help curb any opposition there would inevitably be to his accession to the throne, besides being a just reward for Flambard's misdeeds that were many and various. Though he was able to engineer his escape from the Tower – about the only person ever to do so – he was later summoned to Rome to answer various serious charges before the Pope. Even this he was able to overcome, by persuading 20 bishops to act as character referees and thus counteract the charges laid against him.

It should not however be thought that everything that Flambard did was to the disadvantage of Twynham. Had he not decided to build the new church, there would be no Priory here today. His errors were in his methods to achieve that aim, which were both ruthless, for his own aggrandisement and harmful to the hardworking local canons. For the community at large, there would inevitably have been some advantage in that there would have been an almost insatiable demand for labour of all sorts including that of skilled craftsmen. All the local trades would likewise have prospered, as would have agriculture, since the increased population would have created considerable demands for goods and services. It was Flambard's personal ambition and greed that Godric tried to counteract so far as he was able. Within his limited experience and power, he did what he could. It was left to the succeeding king, Henry I, to wisely give both church and town to Richard de Redvers, a distant kinsman. Under him and his family, the proper function of the newly built Priory could be established and the enlarging town could begin to prosper.

Chapter 5

The Augustinian Canons Regular - established 1150.

After the death of Gilbert de Dousgunels, Richard de Redvers, as Lord of the Manor, appointed Peter de Oglander, one of his clerks, to be Dean of the few remaining canons. Though he presumably had good reason to trust Peter, this turned out to be an unfortunate choice, since he did not act as intended. In spite of the generosity of Richard de Redvers and others, Peter de Oglander seems to have been more in the stamp of Ranulf Flambard than Gilbert de Dousgunels. He kept most of the church's revenues for himself and lived a life of luxury quite out of keeping with his position. As Dugdale says, *'For Richard de Redvers gave to that church for its and the canons' advancement a certain land in the Isle of Wight which is called Ningweda. A certain one of his tenants also gave another land by name Absa. The parishioners also gave all their tithes, as Gilbert appointed. For Gilbert himself completing the daily and nightly service, as now, settled the convent. Now the aforementioned Peter, filled with an ill-omened ambition, alas, withdrew from the building of the church everything which had been promised for that purpose after the custom of those of old time, five canons being found for the oblations appropriated to the completion of the church; he granted to himself and the clerks he brought with him a court-like table during his life by converting it to his own uses he distributed the money not canonically but by the rule of might'.*

There can be little doubt that the inhabitants of Twynham would have been angry. Not only were they deprived of their old places of worship but the new and supposedly magnificent church they had been promised was now lying part-built and derelict, gathering weeds. Meanwhile the dean and his canons lived luxuriously, probably ignoring their offices and paying little heed to the spiritual needs of their parishioners. It was probably some time before either the Bishop of Winchester or the Lord of the Manor became aware of this state of affairs. The former was largely occupied as one of the king's chief advisers and the latter had many other large estates stretching from Devon to the Isle of Wight, with others across the Channel in Normandy. The situation may not have come fully to the notice of either until Peter died and the need to appoint a new dean became apparent. However before a new dean could be appointed, the remaining canons whom Peter had brought with him, in the words of Dugdale, *'the stranger clerks expelled the others from their company and council and amongst themselves seized the said altar, the offerings appointed for the building of the church they cleverly filched away, each bearing witness to the other as of a matter settled and by the dean granted and confirmed'.*

Presumably the remaining secular canons at Twynham made both Richard de Redvers, as Lord of the Manor, and Henry of Blois, Bishop of Winchester, well aware of the situation on the death of Peter de Oglander. Bishop Henry then suggested to the remaining canons that one of his own clerks, Hilary by name, should be the new dean. He was a suitably strong man and good organiser, capable of taking matters in hand and re-starting the building work. No doubt Richard de Redvers was more than willing to agree, particularly since any enquiries he might have made as to his suitability would have produced glowing reports. Though of humble origins, Hilary had acquired a considerable reputation in ecclesiastical circles. Not only had he accompanied Bishop Henry, by then appointed a papal legate, to Rome to act as an advocate at the papal curia, but while he was there, he had got to know several other leading clerics. Two of these later became popes under the names of Eugenius III and Alexander III. Hilary was also highly regarded by Archbishop Theobald of Canterbury, who used him more that any other cleric as a legal assessor. Appointed as Dean of Twynham in 1140, he appears therefore to have been an excellent choice. He has been described by Professor M.D. Knowles as being "an extremely quick-witted, efficient, self-confident, voluble, somewhat shallow man, fully acquainted with the new canon law but not prepared to abide by principles to the end. His talents were great but he used them as an opportunist". Certainly he used his abilities for the benefit of Twynham. Though Hilary was appointed to the See of Chichester in 1147, he continued to act as Dean of Twynham and to oversee the continuing building work there for a further three years until Reginald was appointed as the first Prior in 1150.

Hilary was also instrumental in establishing the financial security of the parish of Twynham, as opposed to monastic community. It was becoming increasingly common for absentee rectors of churches to appropriate most of the income of a parish to themselves, while leaving a resident priest to struggle in poverty to cope with the daily needs of the parishioners. Twynham was no exception. The Second Lateran Council in 1139 had forbidden churches to be committed to stipendiary priests and had also decreed that every parish with sufficient resources should have its own priest. The Burgh of Twynham should certainly have been able to afford a parish priest, as is made clear in the charter quoted below. The Council at Rheims, which Hilary attended in 1148, quite possibly as advisor to Archbishop Theobald, but also as the recently installed Bishop of Chichester, went further. It explicitly stated for the first time that the two main principles of perpetual vicarages were that priests should have the permanent security of the benefice, and that part of the revenues of a church was to be set aside as payment for the resident vicar. The result was that over the next ten years, Bishop Henry of Winchester, aided by Bishop Hilary of Chichester, who still maintained his interest in Twynham, instituted this system in all the parishes that came under the control of the great church there. Though Hilary was not to know it at the time, securing the position of the parish priest at Twynham was to have an important effect in Henry VIII's reign. Though, as will be explained later, Henry suppressed the Augustinian Convent, he was persuaded to return the church to the people for use as their parish church, complete with its parish priest, who was one of the Augustinian canons, and with his recognised income.

St Augustine of Hippo.

The growing wealth of the community at Twynham becomes apparent from the charter of Baldwin de Redvers, who inherited his father Richard's estates during the 1140s. By then, not only was the church building progressing well but both the community of canons and the burgh had become far more wealthy and important, as the translation of his charter by Dugdale shows.

'Baldwin de Redvers to all men, French and English, and to the rest of the faithful of Christ to whom the present writing shall come, greeting. Know ye that I for the love of God and for the health of my soul and for the souls of my ancestors and successors and of my friends have granted and by this my present charter have confirmed to Hilary the dean and to all the rest of those serving God and to serve him in the church of Christ at Twynham, the churches, tithes, church scots, lands, rents, men and their tenements and their families, all as well ecclesiastical possessions as secular tenures and all things, whatsoever belong and ought to belong to them upon my fee, of which the church is seised, or whatever they reasonably claim and ought to have my fee, as in lands, men, meadows, pastures, in waters, in all other liberties and free customs and acquittances, and that they may hold well, in peace, freely and quietly of me and of my heirs, all things which are theirs and which ought to be theirs, that they may have all things wholly in free, pure and perpetual alms, that they may always possess them fully, as best, most fully and most freely they can be possessed, so that they may have their full dignity and their free customs in all things with honour as of old time they were always wont to have; - to wit the school of the town itself their free court with Soc and Sac, Tol and Team and Infangenethef as fully freely and quietly as king Henry granted them to my father Richard de Redvers to hold, when he first bestowed the whole fee on him to hold by hereditary right, namely Christchurch of Twynham with all its appurtenances, in which they serve God; all the land which they have in the two villages of the same town of Twynham, with the messuages and curtilages, with the men and their families, reaching up to the water of Stour; the land which they have next to the churchyard of the gift of Aluric de Brochleia; all the land thence to the water of Avon, which is between the churchyard and the castle ditch; the messuage upon the castle ditch which they have of the gift of Gamelin; the messuage with appurtenances which they have opposite 'la borram'; the church at Boldre with its chapel at Lymington and of Brockenhurst; the church of Hordle and of Milford with its appurtenances, the church at Sopley with everything that belongs to it one virgate of land with the appurtenances in the same town of the gift of Godwin the earl, of which Orricus de Stanton forcibly deprived the

same church of Christ; the chapel of Holdenhurst, the church of Piddletown with all things belonging to it; the prebend which they have from old time in the town itself of Piddletown; all the tenement which Alsi the priest held in Bashley and which Alnod holds in Bosley; the whole land of Hurn; the grove with Bosley itself, Bradefelde and Richedon with their appurtenances; Hedenesburia [Hengistbury] with all things which adjoin there to; the land at Stanpit and of Hoburne and of Prestetone with all their appurtenances in the Isle of Wight of the gift of Richard de Redvers, the manor of Ningwode with Hamstede Presteton and with a certain land in Southampton with their appurtenances; all the land of Apsa of the gift of Roger de l'Estre; the tithe of the lordship of Alurich de Brochle in Ernemua; the tithe of the toll of the ferry of Christchurch; the tithe of Wreck whatever it be that shall happen upon my fee in their parish except of great fish [whale?] of which they ought to have the left side; of ancient rights, the first salmon each year, the tithe as well of salmon and of every catch of fish as of all my new-born beasts yearly within the town and without; two carts each day going for heath upon my land; a hundred carts yearly of turf for the kitchen from my fee, if they have it not on their land; that everywhere upon my land they be free from toll whether they sell or buy; the right of first purchase of all things in the town of Christchurch, if I or my heirs be absent, but if we be present, they ought to have right of second purchase. My reeves ought not to suffer any merchandise to be bought or sold there to the damage or discharge of the church for the sake of gain to me or my heirs nor at any time throughout the year to receive a toll from merchandise in the church. The servants of the church of Christ shall fish wherever they will, but because of my salmon below Twynham where two waters, namely Avon and Stour unite. Because of the testimony of many they have had all these things with their appurtenances before my time, I have granted and by this my present charter and by my seal have confirmed them to be held freely and quietly of me and my heirs and to be held wholly to them and to their successors, firmly enjoining the reeves of me and my heirs that no one shall molest them therefor or permit any contravention to be committed against them. These being witnesses:- Hubert de Vaus, Stephen de Mandevill, Jordan del Estre and many others.

Where possible, the place names have been modernised to make their identification easier. However in some cases their location is in doubt, and the original spelling has been retained. Some old terms require explanation. 'Soc' - the area where 'Sac' - the liberty of court granted by the King to try causes and receive fines can be held. 'Tol' - imposition of payment for goods bought or sold in the market.

32

'Team' - the right to take and keep bondmen from one generation to another. *'Infangenethef'* - the right to try and judge a thief taken within the burgh. *'Outfangenethef'* - the right to try a thief taken outside the burgh. It is interesting to note that the first privilege that was confirmed to Hilary and his canons was the right to continue to run "the school of the town". This would have been held in some part of the monastic buildings and run by the canons. The syllabus would have been largely Latin and a little mathematics, though it is to be hoped that the canons sometimes took the children into the surrounding country and taught them a little about the abundant wildlife of the area and some herbal medicine, as described in 'Hugh of Twynham'.

It is clear from the amount of property and the number of churches that are under the control of the canons of Twynham, that it had become a wealthy and therefore important establishment. However Pope Honorius II was surely justified in not establishing a Regular Order at the request of Gilbert de Dousgunels, not only because the church was only part built, but also in view of the problems created by Peter de Oglander. He would naturally have sent over an emissary to investigate the situation before he was prepared to make such a grant. He would have needed to be satisfied that the community was sufficiently well endowed to be self-sufficient. By 1150 however, under the guiding hand of Hilary matters had advanced sufficiently for a new approach to be made. By then not only was the major part of the original church complete, but also the monastic buildings were well advanced. A fresh approach to a new Pope, Eugenius III, was therefore made. This was backed not only by Dean Hilary, now Bishop of the neighbouring see of Chichester who already knew Pope Eugenius, but also by Baldwin de Redvers as the Lord of the Manor and a great benefactor of the community at Twynham. In addition, the petition had of necessity the support of Henry of Blois, Bishop of Winchester, in whose diocese Twynham lay, and perhaps most importantly of all, the backing of his elder brother King Stephen himself. This petition, so formidably supported, was successful and a Convent of August-inian Canons Regular was established at Twynham in 1150. However, because of the amount of work that the papal clerks and scribes had to accomplish and the slow means of travel, it was 18th May 1152 before the Papal Bull, with its leaden seal or 'bulla' attached, was finally despatched to Twynham. Nor should it be forgotten that the second Crusade was then raging in the lands at the eastern end of the Mediterranean. This would have occupied much of the attention of the Pope since it involved not only the constant fighting against the Mohammedans but also the equally difficult problems that had to be faced with the Eastern Christian Church. The supposedly Christian princes battling for possession of the lands came not only from both parts of the Norman clan, those in England and those who controlled the kingdom of the Two Sicilies, but also from the French and German principalities. To keep them working in some sort of concert would tax the ingenuity of even the most astute Pope. Approving the establishment of a new Regular Augustinian Convent would therefore have been low on the Pope's list of priorities, particularly as a convent, albeit a secular one, already existed.

By 1151, Hilary had been succeeded at Twynham by Reginald. It was logical therefore that he should be appointed as the first Prior. Richard de Redvers also issued a further important charter. It confirmed what no doubt had already been granted by Henry of Winchester, the right of the canons regular to choose their own prior and also the right to hold a court, both of which had previously been granted to the secular canons. It seems therefore that the influence of the secular canons in the town was already considerable, bearing in mind that they already ran the school. It should be noted also that although the parish altar was still dedicated to the Holy Trinity, with its own parish priest, the High Altar in the Great Choir used by the canons and the centre of their worship was dedicated to Christ the Saviour. It was because of this, that the town was soon to acquire its new name of Christchurch. A précis of this and several other Papal Bulls, like many other charters concerning the church, are to be found in the Cartulary.

Writing to Reginald, prior of the church of the Holy Trinity at Twynham with his brethren vowed to the Regular Order, Pope Eugenius declares that since under God he must be a harbinger of justice, shining as a mirror of the apostles Peter and Paul, he has hearkened to the petition of those serving God in the same church by taking them under the protection of the apostles through his present charter, firstly he confirms the perpetual establishment there of the Order of Augustinian Canons, and secondly that their goods and possessions, both present and future, whether grants of kings, nobles, or others, shall be theirs forever, and in particular the following: the vill of Ningwode in the Isle of Wight; the land of Bosley with two virgates belonging to Holdenhurst vill, and the vill of Hurn; the land of Bashley and a hide and a virgate belonging to Stanpit; Puddletown church with its chapels, lands, and tithes; Boldre church with its chapels at Brockenhurst and Lymington; the churches at Hordle, Milford, Sopley and Holdenhurst; lands at Hoburne, Apse and Preston, 10 shillings worth of land in Hampton, some Winchester lands [at Wilton, Porton, Whaddon and Ramsbury] and a virgate at Bulnore; right of burial is to be open to all wishing to be interred at

Christchurch, unless excommunicate or under interdict; all privileges and lawful dues of that church are confirmed; when a prior dies there is to be a fair election of whomsoever the canons shall choose according to their Rule. The Pope has also decreed that no man may damage, annex, withhold, diminish, or encumber the said priory or its property, but they are to be preserved unimpaired, saving the authority of the Holy See and the rights of the Diocesan. Let no man, lay or cleric, knowingly infringe this Bull; as for those who after due warning fail to make amends for their misdeeds, let them know that they are in danger at the last judgement; but those who maintain the priory — may they reap the fruits of their righteousness in this world and find the reward of eternal rest.

Granted at Segni, [30 miles south of Rome] *by the hand of Bozo, clerk of the Holy Roman Church, 18th May, indiction 15, A.D.1152, in the 3rd year of Eugenius III'.*

The effect of this Bull and the other charters issued at the time probably had little immediate effect on the citizens of Twynham, though this would have become more evident over time. It did however consolidate the position of the canons and as Henry II was to find a few years later, it would have increased the power and influence of the Church. This came to a head with the conflict between Henry II and Thomas à Becket, who was by then Archbishop of Canterbury. It was a conflict that Hilary became closely involved in, though not always on the same side. The papal decree in the Bull, that "no man may damage, annex, withhold, diminish or encumber the said priory or its property", was not something that Henry VIII was prepared to acknowledge, as will be seen in a later chapter.

In a town like Twynham, even though by 1150 there was a stone built castle and constable's house, the greatest building was still the Priory with its conventual buildings and the largest employer was the Church. It would be surprising therefore if the ordinary citizens did not already feel the effects of Mother Church on their everyday lives. No doubt the enthusiasm of the recently arrived Regular Augustinian Canons brought a new focus into the lives of the townsfolk with a heightened emphasis on attendance at Mass. One noticeable difference would have been the withdrawal of most of the canons within the conventual buildings themselves. Partly this was because the regular canons were celibate whereas the secular canons were mostly married. Though the seculars were naturally allowed to keep their wives, it seems likely that there would be friction between the two groups of canons, which was almost bound to lead to pressure to conform to the stricter disciplines of the regulars. No doubt also, the new arrivals drew attention to the generous gifts from both Richard and Baldwin de

Redvers. It would be only human nature if they felt that such patronage, backed as it now was by the authority of the Holy See itself, did not lead to some arrogance amongst the newly arrived clergy. There also seems to have been an increasing number of 'miraculous' cures carried out in or near the Priory. Many of these were apparently cures for failing eyesight for which the Priory continued to be famous for some centuries. One reason for this may have been the particularly pure water to be found in the wells and rivers in the area. This not only increased the fame of the church and attracted a growing number of pilgrims but also brought with it a growing number of gifts from the cured and faithful.

Attending Mass.

Thus the town prospered from the presence and influence of the Priory. Trade of all kinds flourished, and the citizens tended to enjoy greater prosperity, while the Priory also grew in wealth from the many pious gifts bestowed upon it. As always, Town and Church benefited each other.

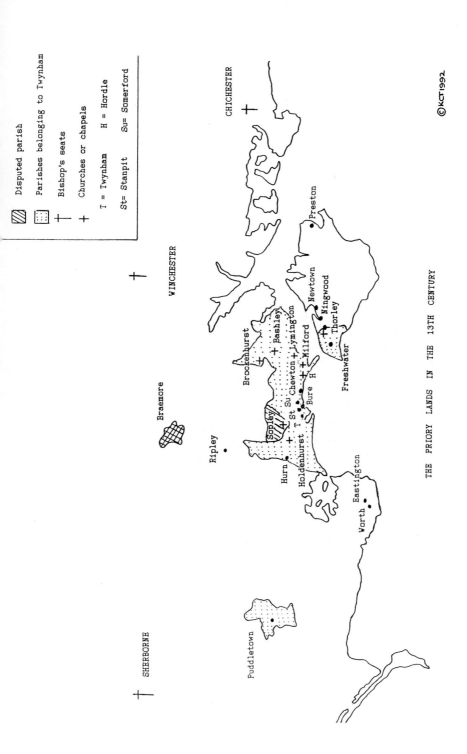

THE PRIORY LANDS IN THE 13TH CENTURY

Disputed parish

Parishes belonging to Twynham

+ Bishop's seats

+ Churches or chapels

T = Twynham   H = Hordle

St= Stanpit   Su= Somerford

CHICHESTER

WINCHESTER

SHERBORNE

Braemore

Ripley

Puddletown

Brockenhurst

Bashley

Sopley

Hurn

Holdenhurst

T

St Su Chewton Lymington

Bure H Milford

Worth Eastington

Freshwater

Thorley

Ningwood

Newtown

Preston

©KCT1992

37

Chapter 6

King John 1199 – 1216.

An event which would strike terror into the hearts of the smaller as well as larger land-owners was a visit by the royal household. Not only was this likely to lead to a more thorough investigation into crimes that may have been committed in the area, but it also meant horrendous additional expenditure that would have to be met by the local magnate. All kings made a habit of making a 'progress' round their kingdoms, partly to show their face to their subjects and partly to keep their more powerful nobles under control. Since all free men had the right of access to their sovereign, it was important that they should be able to exercise it locally, for this was the only redress that they were likely to have against an oppressive overlord. Naturally the overlord resented this, but it helped to keep the worst abuses of power in check, so long as the king himself was powerful and unwilling to be influenced by the ambitions of his nobles. For King John this was particularly important. During the time he had to act as regent while Richard was away fighting in the Crusades, it was more than usually necessary for him to exert his authority. Because he tended to abuse his own power, he found that he had stiffer opposition to overcome from his greater magnates.

One way of doing this was to spend as much time as possible touring the country and accepting the hospitality from the most powerful in the land. Though this could be portrayed as bestowing singular favour on whoever he stayed with, it also had the beneficial effect of impoverishing a recalcitrant nobleman. This could be increased or decreased according to the size of the royal entourage and the length of stay. The country had as yet not fully recovered from the depredations of the civil war between Stephen and Matilda, so that even the most wealthy magnates would be hard put to it to entertain a large royal party from their own resources. That would not have been possible until later Tudor times, when the country was increasingly prosperous and the greatest in the land could vie with each other to produce the most magnificent hospitality for their sovereign. Some then even went so far as to virtually re-build their houses to out-do their rivals.

There was another reason for these 'progresses'. Imagine a party of anything up to 200 people, all mounted on horseback, and accompanied by a wagon train of many dozen carts also drawn by horses. Without adequate stabling, properly equipped with drainage and the means of disposing of the piles of dung that would inevitably accumulate, the immediate vicinity of the property would quickly deteriorate into an Augaean stable. Add to this the general lack of personal sanitary arrangements, particularly if it should rain, and the site would soon resemble a badly organised point-to-point ground or a County Agricultural Show-ground with no adequate latrines after a downpour. Mud would be everywhere, and the smell intolerable. Disease was also likely to spread fast, and it was not unknown for epidemics of dysentery and other unpleasant ailments to break out. The King therefore had every reason to move on from manor to manor, only staying in one place so long as he could stand the deteriorating conditions. In some respects, winter was a preferable time to make his 'progress', since the frost not only kept the ground hard, but also kept down the smell and helped to prevent the spread of disease. Life at court could have its disadvantages.

King John felt that he needed to tour his realm for several reasons. While he acted as regent for his elder brother King Richard, the nobility needed to know that, even though the King was absent, his influence was still present. Besides, John knew that in the event of Richard not returning, he would assume the crown himself. It was therefore in his own interest to stamp his authority on the country. However popular Richard might be, when he had to be ransomed from captivity - as romantically portrayed in legend - vast sums of money had to be raised from all levels of society. No doubt the common folk were keen to have their rightful King back amongst them and the unpopular regent replaced, yet they could justifiably complain about the necessity of the ransom by blaming Richard for having been captured in the first place. The exploits of Robin of Loxley, or Robin Hood, probably portray the general resentment in the country with fair accuracy, even if the hero's exploits rely more on glamour and romance than historical accuracy.

It is recorded that King John visited Twynham no less than seven times in his 17 year reign, far more than any other monarch. Though other monarchs must have visited the town occasionally, records of such visits are extremely sparse. Though the de Redvers family were Lords of the Manor of Twynham, it was not their major headquarters. They had large castles at Exeter and Carisbrooke on the Isle of Wight. Frequent appearance with a large train of followers and a quantity of armed men would be a pointless exercise if it were merely to impress the citizens of what was quite a small town. Certainly Twynham had a strong stone built keep set on the usual earth mound and surrounded by a ditch. There was also a stone built hall-house for the use of the constable, but neither of these presented such a threat as to need a frequent show of force to keep the place in order. There must therefore have been other reasons for the frequency of the visits.

King John hunting in the New Forest.

The main reason was almost certainly the hunting in the New Forest, a sport of which John was particularly fond. Sometimes this was centred on Brockenhurst, where there was a royal hunting lodge, sometimes at Kingston Lacy, where later John of Gaunt had a hunting lodge and at other times it was centred at Christchurch, where the King would stay in the Constable's House. Since there is no record of how long the royal party spent in the town, it may be assumed that the visits were short. One reason for this assumption is the lack of any detailed record of his visits. Had they been protracted, then they would surely have left an impression on the townsfolk.

Fortunately for King John, the Constable's House had its own 'garderobe', or privy, which emptied into the millstream. Such a luxury was not to be found in all the houses in which he stayed. Many of the rest of his party would have been housed in the outer bailey of the castle, while his men-at-arms probably took over the castle itself for their quarters. Because of the lie of the land and its nature - largely river gravel - the usual problems of drainage and sewage would have been to some extent reduced. It may also be that some of the senior members of the royal party found accommodation in neighbouring manors, such as Somerford and Hurn, which lie little more than a mile or two from the town. Quite when these two manors came into the possession of the Prior at Christchurch, is not known. However, if indeed he did own them at that time, it would be natural for the prior to offer members of the royal household lodging in his comfortable manors. It was always advantageous to be seen to be accommodating to the king and his entourage since any favour granted could always, if necessary, be called in at a later date. Priors, though holy, were also worldly wise. Finally, if the main reason for the visit was hunting, then many of the party and their horses would be absent from the town for most of the day. This would further reduce the sanitation problems.

There is however, another reason that might explain the unusual number of royal visits during this one reign, particularly if they were of short duration. The castle at Corfe, only a day's journey from Christchurch, was extremely strong and particularly easy to defend against outside attack. During the Civil War of the 1640s, it was considered "the impregnablest fort in the kingdom". It is recorded that Lady Bankes, aided by a mere handful of defenders (mainly women), kept out a considerable and well-armed attacking force. In all its long history, Corfe Castle has never been taken except by treachery. It was therefore a suitable place for the king to use as a repository for his treasure chests as well as a secure royal residence. It was certainly a safer place to lodge the crown jewels and other treasure than the Wash, where John is reputed to have lost them, sunk without trace in the soft mud. Furthermore, he used its dungeons to confine many prisoners, including his nephew, Arthur, Duke of Brittany, whom he subsequently murdered. Nor did he endear himself to the aristocracy of England by starving to death 200 French knights in the Corfe Castle banqueting hall. Apart from any humanitarian considerations, it was generally considered to be a terrible waste of 200 ransoms, which could have filled the royal coffers for some time and saved the need for raising taxes on the English magnates. Such actions would naturally sour his relations with the English nobility and may well have been a contributory factor leading on to Magna Carta. To King John, however, Corfe might have increasingly been considered a safe refuge from his numerous enemies. There was, therefore, every reason for him to make frequent visits there, where none could reach him. And the constable's house within the bailey of the castle at Christchurch-Twynham would have been a convenient stopping place between Winchester and Corfe, where he could rest over night in safety.

Since these royal visits would appear to have been quite short, it seems that they did not interrupt the normal life of the town too seriously. At least Christchurch-Twynham did not have to use what may well have been a ruse adopted by the village of Kingsclere that nestles under the Downs on the Hampshire/Berkshire borders. There, it appears, King John curtailed his visit after a very short time, since his sleeping quarters were apparently infested with bed bugs. So viciously did these creatures attack the Royal Person that the King ordered his party to pack up and leave immediately, it is said never to return. The town's finances as well as its health were thus saved. To commemorate this happy event, the good people of the village have erected a golden bed bug on the top of their church tower as a weather vane. It looks down on the village to this day as a reminder of their happy deliverance many centuries ago.

Twynham, however, probably found their deliverance from pestilence more in the presence of its rivers and mill stream that would carry away much of the effluent created by a large royal party, and the composition of its well drained soil. Perhaps the hunting in the nearest part of the forest to the town may have been a contributory factor. For this the local huntsmen may also deserve some credit, by not always being too assiduous about ensuring a plentiful supply of game. Assuredly the local inhabitants did what they could to look after themselves. Some of the king's visits may have been towards the end of his reign, when he was finding the opposition of the barons growing increasingly vociferous and Magna Carta was being drawn up. If so, then it may well have been that the lord of the manor was himself not over keen to receive his sovereign, making little or no effort to provide the sport for which his royal master had come. Certainly the town seems to have weathered the visits well, without too much interruption to the lives of its inhabitants or drain on their pockets.

So it may be that the local inhabitants preferred even then a life that was pleasant to the expensive notoriety of entertaining their sovereign. This is not to imply that they were anti-royalist; merely that they were realistic in their assessment of the situation. And who can blame them, particularly in those early days when the lot of the ordinary citizen was hard and he did most of the giving while the king did much of the taking.

Chapter 7

Isabella de Fortibus. c.1230-1293.

It is only in comparatively recent times that women have been generally accepted as being able to take an active part in important affairs, whether in the home or the country. When such a person comes to our notice, such as Boudicca in Roman times, the Empress Matilda during the reign of King Stephen, or the Queens Mary, Anne and the two Elizabeths, one may be sure that they were people of more than usual importance.

There can be little doubt that Isabella de Fortibus falls into that category, particularly as regards events in Christchurch-Twynham. She was also the first of only two ladies to be appointed Constables of Carisbrooke Castle, the second being Queen Elizabeth the Queen Mother. However, like so many famous people, it is not known exactly when she was born. But since her eldest child and only son, Thomas, died at the age of 16 in 1269, it may be assumed that she was probably born about the year 1230. She may therefore have been over 60 years of age when she died. Her importance to Christchurch is that she was the last of the line of the de Redvers family, who had been granted the Manors of Twynham during the early Norman period.

Isabella was the younger sister of Baldwin, the 8th Earl of Devon, who died without living issue in 1262, at which date she inherited the title, but only part of the widespread lands that went with it. This was because both the widow of the 7th Earl, Amicia de Claire, and the 8th Earl's widow, Margaret of Savoy, were still to live for another 21 and 30 years respectively, and each held considerable estates as their dowers. Despite this, Isabella was probably the richest woman in the country, owning the Lordship of the Isle of Wight, large tracts of Dorset and the West Country, and much land in the locality of Christchurch. This included the Manor of Christchurch, the Borough of Christchurch, the Manor of Westover, and the Hundred of Holdenhurst, besides the lands inherited from her husband, William de Fortibus, Earl of Albemarle, including much of Holderness. It appears that she did not inherit the Manor, or Honour of Christchurch until 1292, a year before her own death, since until then it had been held by her brother's widow. No doubt, however, she had kept a close eye on that estate, since it bordered her other lands and she knew that it would ultimately come to her. It was a manor that enjoyed a series of 'liberties', such as a free court with several rights, that had been granted to the 1st Earl by Henry I. There was also the liberty of wreck from the sea, which could be of considerable benefit to the inhabitants and which was a liberty Isabella already enjoyed in full on the Isle of Wight. Some estimate of her wealth may be gained from the fact that she owed Edmund, Earl of Lancaster no less than 3,000 marks for the wardship of part of the Aumale Estates in Holderness. Much of her life was spent at Carisbrooke, on the Isle of Wight, which she made her headquarters, so that she would have been in close touch with Christchurch-Twynham and aware of all that was happening there. More especially was this so because the Prior of the Augustinian Convent also held several estates on the island. Indeed there was considerable trade between the two, which must inevitably have led to a close knowledge of each other's problems and needs.

The power and influence of Isabella can be assessed from several events. Her elder daughter, Aveline, married Edmund Crouchback, Earl of Lancaster, and son of Henry III in 1270, eight years after Isabella inherited the Earldom of Devon. Details of the dowry that was paid to Edmund probably three years previously, show that it was an unusually large amount, so that Edmund, and perhaps more importantly his father Henry III would have been mightily pleased to receive it. Though Aveline died four years later when only 15, and probably before the marriage had been consummated, such a royal connection would be important for her influence at court.

Isabella was important to the King for other reasons too. The Isle of Wight had long been one of the most important defensive areas against attack from across the Channel. Indeed, William the Norman had intended originally to land there to make his invasion of England in 1066. Only adverse winds blew him off course so that he had to make his landing in the region of Hastings. With the loss of much of Normandy during and after King John's reign, it fell increasingly to the inhabitants of the coastal regions of Hampshire, Dorset and the Isle of Wight, to provide the defence against any possible sea-borne attack. Though this fell particularly heavily on the islanders, it also meant that the inhabitants of Christchurch were likely to be called upon to provide men and sometimes ships to defend their country.

Isabella de Fortibus also had an interesting and profitable additional source of income. Normally all 'wreck' formed part of the royal income, as did the ownership of any whales, though it was common for the local magnate to be granted half the benefits. It is clear from the early de Redvers charters in the Cartulary, that the Earls of Devon had the benefit of these rights from the coastal region either side of Hengistbury Head. The charters also make clear that a tithe of these rights of wreck, as well as half of any whale, or 'great fish', was granted by the de Redvers family to the Priory at Twynham. On the Isle of Wight, however, Isabella had claimed the full rights of wreck in 1280. This was because although the safe custody of wrecks had, in

1277, been vested in the king's coroners, an earlier court in 1229 had already found that there should be no coroner on the Island. As always, it was very difficult for the king or overlord to enforce his full claim. Inevitably this led to local people making little effort to save either ships or their crews from wreck, since there were profitable pickings to be had as a result. Nor would the overlord necessarily take effective action to try to save either ships or crews or cargoes, since he stood to be the main beneficiary from the wrecks. Being but a few miles from the Island, Christchurch men were frequently involved in the benefits of salvage, to their considerable advantage, quite possibly with Isabella's connivance. Later, in 1336, there is a record of a ship being driven ashore, from which much of the cargo was removed by men of Christchurch, Milford, Lymington and Portsmouth. Nor should it be imagined that this was the only occasion. It is clear therefore, that those who lived along the coast took clear advantage of any disaster that happened within reach. The inhabitants of Christchurch therefore seem to have found some profit over the years from the rights of wreck on the Island, as well as along their immediate coastline.

The importance of the Island became apparent once more in 1266 when there was yet another threat of invasion from the continent. Piracy has always been rife in the Channel, and Isabella was apparently harbouring one of the more notorious of them, by name Henry Poun. Isabella de Fortibus, *'Countess of Albemarle and Lady of Insula'*, was appointed *'to defend the Isle of Wight against the king's enemies and rebels who were holding out at sea and committing depredations and other grave offences'*. All the men of the Island, both religious and others, were ordered to aid her *'on pain of disherison* [being disinherited] *and loss of all their goods'*. Shortly afterwards, Edward of Lancaster, who had been married to Isabella's daughter, took over the Island, and entrusted it to John de Insula the next year. Though it was later returned to the countess, she was warned that she might well lose it for ever if she did not take sufficient care to guard it against invasion. It may well be that this threat was as much a warning to her not to harbour pirates who were preying on the King's ships, as to prevent any possible invasion. There was a constant need for kings to keep a check on their most powerful magnates, and Isabella de Fortibus certainly fell into that category. Whatever the reason, it is clear that Isabella took the necessary steps to secure the Island. All her sub-tenants had to provide for its defence, according to their ability. The Prior of Christchurch, who owned Ningwood, had to provide four armed horses, one more than was provided by the Constable of the Island himself. Whether the full cost was borne by Ningwood, or whether some part of it came from the other estates of the Priory near to the town itself, is not known, but that may well have been the case.

Certainly in 1377, the Prior had to pay over the considerable sum of 100 marks, to go towards the wages of 100 men-at-arms, so that Christchurch would almost certainly have had to provide at least part of that sum.

For all her power, Isabella de Fortibus seems to have been unusually devout. Certainly it was the custom for great magnates to found and endow abbeys and large churches, and Isabella was no exception. Though she tried to exert perhaps too much influence on the monks at Carisbrooke, partly no doubt because she spent so much time living close to them, she nevertheless bestowed great gifts upon them. The prior and canons of the Augustinian house at Christchurch also benefited greatly from her charity. In 1263, the year after she inherited the lands belonging to her father, she gave part of Hinton to the Priory at Christchurch. In 1272, she also gave the Manor of Somerford, which included the hamlets of Bure, Chewton and Street, to the Priory. Almost 300 years later, the last Prior, John Draper, had reason to be grateful to her, for it was the Manor of Somerford that was given to him as a home for the rest of his life, after he was turned out of the Priory. And in 1292, the year before her death, she confirmed the grant of the Manor of Ningwood on the Island to the Priory. This included the right to enclose the land 'with dykes and hedges', except that 'doe and fawn should have free passage'. This is an interesting exception, not unlike that found in the New Forest, where deer were permitted to roam freely. Another interesting benefit that she bestowed on the Priory in the same year, was the tithe of rabbits on her Manor of Thorley, whether they were caught for sale, or gift or for any other purpose. During the Middle Ages, rabbits were an important source of food, for all classes of society - they were sent to the Bishop of Winchester and even the King - and their skins were similarly put to good use for clothing, so that there are frequent references to 'rights of warren'. From the considerable gifts Isabella made to other abbeys and churches, it seems that she was unusually generous to the Church.

There remains something of a mystery surrounding the last days and hours of Isabella de Fortibus. Since she had no surviving children, the many great estates that she possessed, even after the large gifts she had made to the Church, not least the Priory at Christchurch, would have to pass to her nearest, though distant relative. This was Hugh de Courtney, who was a grandson of Mary de Redvers. According to one source, Isabella is supposed, on her death-bed, to have granted all her lands to the King, Edward I, because, as one account of the event suggested, she was prompted to do so '*from the consideration that her next heir, Hugh de Courtney, was so remote in blood that if he were of age she might have married him without a dispensation*'. There is little doubt that Edward I would have been pleased to receive such a gift, with its considerable revenues. The Isle of Wight alone produced over 1,000 fleeces a year besides large quantities of grain. He was also keen to ensure that the Island was securely defended, since, after England was severed from France, it presented a continual threat as a possible site for invasion from across the Channel. Certainly this was in part mitigated by the fact that the inhabitants of the Island paid 'scutage' direct to the Crown, and the tenants that held their land direct from Carisbrooke Castle were responsible for its defence. Even so, there was good reason for the King to make sure that he had proper control of the Island. Another account states that the King bought the countess's estates on her death. There may be some confusion here since he would inevitably have had a say in the disposal of her lands, since, if according to the quotation above, Hugh de Courtney was a minor and would therefore have been a ward of court. It would have been necessary to appoint guardians to administer the estates, and clearly the King would have been able to determine who they should be. This was particularly relevant, since Magna Carta, not so many years before, had laid down strict guidelines regarding the appointment of honest guardians of minors. Certainly, it is known that in 1299, six years after Isabella's death, Edward granted the Castle, Manor and Hundred of Christchurch and also the Manor of Westover, all of which made up the Honour of Christchurch, to his second wife, Margaret, who was the daughter of Philip III of France. No doubt part of the reason for this was to reduce the threat of invasion, of England, particularly via the Isle of Wight. It would have been an embarrassment to a French king to invade what was in effect the neighbouring estate to his own daughter.

Isabella hands over the Manor of Christchurch to Edward I.

47

There is however a third account, that Edward acquired the estates fraudulently. There appears to be good reason to suppose that the charters granting the estates to the King were probably forgeries produced by a notorious Chamberlain of the Exchequer by name Adam de Stretton. He had apparently been imprisoned fourteen years earlier, when he had deliberately destroyed one of Isabella's charters in which she had granted lands to the abbey at Quarr. We also know that when in 1315, Hugh de Courtney, who by then had attained his majority, petitioned for the return of his estates, there was a full enquiry that included much episcopal and other evidence, the majority of which seemed to suggest that there had been no foul play. But in those days, that should certainly not be taken as conclusive evidence, particularly as the current owner was the King's wife. Two further petitions by Hugh and his son Hugh in 1347 and 1364 achieved a similar unsatisfactory result for the de Courtneys, so that the Manor of Christchurch with all its surrounding lands remained in royal hands of the first three Edwards or their wives. From the town's point of view, it did however have the advantage of keeping the lands together under one owner for a long time.

Whatever the final truth of the matter may be, Isabella de Fortibus might not have been too unhappy at the outcome. Certainly, knowing the amount of time she spent in litigation over her various estates, she would probably have approved of the fact that they were to remain together. The people of Christchurch were probably not unhappy to revert to being under the protection of the sovereign or his wife. As for the canons at the Priory and particularly the priors, they would have ample reason to say Masses for the soul of their generous benefactor who had granted them so much land and so many benefits.

Chapter 8

A Property in Castle Street.

Christchurch is fortunate to have a large collection of ancient documents, many of them beautifully written on parchment, and some with their seals still intact. To be able to handle such ancient and beautiful parchments and to hold the seals that were impressed upon them so many centuries ago, cannot fail to stir one with a deep sense of history. Many of these documents refer to properties in the town. From them it is possible to trace much of the history of particular properties, who owned and lived in them, for how long and even what occupation was carried on in them. One of the most interesting, though there are many others of almost equal interest, concerns a property in Castle Street. Currently known as the Old Perfumery, it is reckoned to be the oldest inhabited property in Christchurch, and is situated on the south side of Castle Street, next to the pathway leading to the castle mound. Though not the original building to stand on the site, parts of the present structure probably date back to Tudor times.

The first document relating this property is thought to be the earliest known parchment in the Borough's archives. Written in particularly clear script, it is unusually well preserved and intact and is probably dated sometime between 1290 and 1310. This beautiful document, measuring 16 cm wide by 12 cm long, complete in all its parts and with its green wax seal still attached by a parchment ribbon, is remarkably clear to read, provided one can understand medieval Latin. In translation it reads:-

'Know present and future that I Ralph Kene, have given, granted and by this my present charter confirmed to John Kene my brother for his service, half of the entire tenement in the town of Christchurch Twynham with the houses built upon all its appurtenances, which John Cole once held and which is situated next to the castle moat between the messuage of Roger de Warham and the castle gate, that is the east part of the aforesaid tenement, is nearer the gate of the aforesaid castle. To have and to hold from me and my heirs and assigns, freely, quietly, well and in peace with all liberties and free customs pertaining to that amount of land in the same town. And if it should happen that the said John does not have an heir of his flesh legitimately, the said half of the said tenement with all its appurtenances will revert to me or my heirs or assigns. The aforesaid John and his legitimately procreated heirs rendering thence annually to me or my heirs or assigns one pair of gloves of the price of one penny or one penny on the Feast of the Holy Trinity for all secular service and every kind of exaction. And I, the aforesaid Ralph, and my heirs or assigns will warrant the said half of the tenement to the aforesaid John and his legitimately procreated heirs against all mortals forever. In witness of which matter I have confirmed the present charter with the impression of my seal. These being witnesses, Walter de Feringeford, then constable of Christchurch, Richard Tyrenach, Robert Punch, Henry the Long, John Harold, Dionisius the clerk and many others. '

The seal is vesicle shaped and shows a scorpion in the centre and has the letters "+s' RADUS KENE" around the edge. It is the seal of the grantor, Ralph, or Radulphus (shortened to Radus) Kene. To handle such a document is awe inspiring, when one realises that it is about 700 years old. One can imagine its author standing in the presence of many of the important men of the town who acted as witnesses, and solemnly impressing his seal on the wax attached to the document before he hands it to his brother. Such an event brings history to life and makes one wonder how each brother felt and what each said to the other on that occasion. For young John Kene, it probably meant that he could establish himself as a tradesman in the town since he now had a workshop of his own. He appears not to have been married, but was probably considering taking that step now that he had a house in which to raise his family. It was the first great step in enabling him to be independent and self reliant - to become a Yeoman of England. The elder brother, Ralph, may well have been a burgess by this time and the head of the family. If so, then he may have felt that young John was now mature enough to make his own way in the town, having presumably completed his apprenticeship as a worker in leather. There is a suggestion that young John may have been a bit of a lad in his youth, perhaps inclined to sow his wild oats too freely. This may be one reason why the lease specifically states that only John's legitimate heirs may continue to hold the property. If Ralph was a respected burgess and perhaps straight-laced in his views, he may not have relished the prospect of a host of illegitimate children laying claim to his valuable house and workshop.

The annual rent paid by John Kene seems at first sight to be remarkably low. A penny at that time equated approximately with a day's wages and it is not unreasonable to suppose that a man could cut out and stitch a pair of ordinary gloves in less than a day, the balance of the cost being the leather. Gloves were in common use by all sections of society. Soldiers, particularly archers, and agricultural workers needed them to protect their hands. The nobility required gloves for a different purpose. They frequently took the form of heavily tooled and embossed gauntlets, often with jewels sewn onto them or elaborate embroidery. Such gloves were more for show and as an ostentatious display of wealth. When not being worn, the gloves would be looped over the belt at the waist, with the gauntlet part, on which the most elaborate decoration was displayed, hanging outwards for all to see and admire. The fingers of such gloves would be of the thinnest possible kid, so that the wearer could slip his largest rings over the outside of the glove for all to see. However we may assume that John Kene was a more humble worker in leather and probably spent most of his time producing leather goods of all sorts, mostly of cow hide, for everyday use. His work would have included saddlery, bridles and other accoutrements for working horses, household buckets, 'blackjacks' or leather jugs to hold the ale, and other domestic articles. However in view of the amount of rabbit skins that would have been available from the warrens in and around the town, it is likely that some of the articles he made would have been made from that material. Since Ralph Kene was able to transfer the property with 'with all the liberties and free customs pertaining to it', the assumption must be that he was a man of substance, certainly a free man in his own right, and perhaps a burgess. The date for the payment of the rent due was the patronal festival of the parish altar in the Priory, which would be a day that could not easily slip the memory in those days. As in many other documents, the rent days are nearly always fixed by reference to an important day in the Church's calendar, since those were the days that people knew about and which tended to govern their lives.

The reasons for the apparently low rental are probably twofold. In the first place, since Ralph was leasing the property to his younger brother, he had an incentive to keep the rental low in order to give John a good start as an independent man. Secondly, it was not permitted for a property to be sub-let for a sum greater than the head lease. By setting a low rental, Ralph could make certain that he both helped his brother and prevented him from making a profit from the property by sub-letting it.

It is also interesting to compare the rental of this property, one penny a year, with the rent of a tenement between the two bridges in 1304. It is not known how the two properties compared for size, but the one in Bridge Street was rented at 2 shillings and 3 pence per annum and there was also a consideration of 20 shillings demanded. Even allowing for Ralph Kene's generosity to his young brother, there was presumably some other factor to be taken into account. Perhaps the owner of the Bridge Street property had certain rights such as charging tolls on those who used the bridge. If so, Roger Calfs who owned it and whose seal is attached to the document, would have been able to farm out the collection of the tolls to William le Pessoner' (or should it have been pensioner? an old French word,) and his wife Alice, being the couple who took on the lease. They would probably have been able to recover their costs within a reasonable period and thereafter derive an income on which to live.

The lease also stated that Ralph Kene's property was 'next to the castle moat'. The moat has long since been filled in, being no longer required. However it seems unlikely that it could ever have held water. The height of the river at that point is 0.9 m above ordnance datum, and the millstream is higher at 1.2 m above datum. However Castle Street is 3.9 m above datum and the Church Lane/Castle Street corner is 5 m above datum. The land therefore rises almost 4 m between the millstream and Church Street, where the backs of the houses towards the castle are close to the bottom of the castle mound. There is therefore a minimum difference in height of about 2.7 m between the millstream, from which any water for the 'moat' would have had to come, and the lowest part of the base of the castle mound. It would appear therefore, that the 'moat' must have been a dry ditch. It would certainly have collected any rainwater that ran down from the castle mound, but this would have quickly drained away. Probably the ditch was filled with rubbish thrown out from the houses that abutted it. That it was regarded as a 'moat' or ditch is reasonable, since it was presumably dug to present a further obstacle to anyone attacking the castle, since they would have to go down into it first, before starting to climb up the castle mound. It would also have been bridged opposite the entrance to the castle itself, thus further creating the impression of a 'moat'.

Although there are obviously some gaps in the long story of the property, it is possible to trace most of its history. Many of the names on the documents contain peculiar spellings and sometimes need free interpretation in order to identify them. For example, 'Walter Lone' in the following document may well be a relative of 'Henry Long' in the previous document. Medieval spelling was notoriously unreliable and the lettering on the documents is often difficult to interpret with certainty. So far as one can tell from the names on other early leases, it appears that this property has been owned by the mayor and burgesses of Christchurch-Twynham since at least 1416, a period of about six centuries. There are probably few towns that can boast of holding a property for longer. Such documents help to record the continuous history of this ancient borough and emphasise the heavy burden of responsibility that is placed on the shoulders of the present Mayor and Council.

On the Monday after the feast of St John the Baptist, in '8 Ric. II' (the eighth year of Richard II's reign) i.e. 27th June 1384, *'Richard Lyon granted to Richard Averay and Adam Oncel, son of Richard Lyon's wife, 'A house and outbuildings, once in the tenure of Richard Bosyngyr on the eastern half, and Walter Lone* [or Long] *on the western half, on the east side of Castle Street'*. The grant also contains a reference to the customary services that are due. The property is to be held *'freely quietly well and in peace for ever of him his heirs and assigns during the services to the chief lords of that fee thence owed and of right accustomed to'*. One is reminded of the three Saxon Charters in the Cartulary already discussed in an earlier chapter, where the land was granted with somewhat similar conditions, namely *'free of all secular dues save those of military service, fortress work and bridging'*. The witnesses were *'John Barbour, Richard Alayn, Philip Helyer, John Walteres, William Smyth, Thomas Sohypman and Walter Doget'*. There is a circular red seal attached, which shows a plant between two heads in the centre, surrounded by a flower. Also visible are the initials 'V.P.' between two petals, but the other initials are worn and illegible.

The fact that 'Henry Long' witnessed the Ralph Kene lease would make sense if he, or more probably his like-named father, was the owner of the neighbouring property that is part of the 1384 lease. It may also be relevant that a 'Richard Doget' was Mayor in 1415 and we find a 'Walter Doget' witnessing the 1384 lease. Walter may perhaps have been the father of Richard and himself either a burgess, or even mayor, though the town's list of mayors is silent on this point.

1416 was a busy year for this property. On the *'Sunday after the feast of the translation of St Thomas the Martyr, 4. Henry V.'* [i.e. 12th July 1416] *Thomas Couk* [whose name was more likely Cook] leased to *William atte Wode and Robert Frensshe 'a messuage situated between the Castle gate, to the east of the messuage of Peter Smyth to the west Christchurch; a messuage bounded by a messuage of the Prior to the west of a lane leading to the place called the Portmulle to the east, Christchurch.* In addition there was also leased 2 ½ acres of meadow in East Marsh. The lane leading to the place called 'Portmulle', or 'Portmill' may be along the site of the present Convent Walk, which leads to what is now called Place Mill, situated near to the site of the old town quay; in other words, the mill beside the town's port. The witnesses were William Jacob, John Everard, John Bakere, Robert Bauche and Henry Gladhayt. The same day John Couk appointed William Jacob, the first witness, to be his attorney to deliver possession of the property to William atte Wade [or Wood] and Robert Frensshe. Both these documents have red circular seals showing a horned creature in the centre. It is interesting that Thomas à Becket, who was murdered on the steps of his cathedral in Canterbury in 1170 and subsequently made a saint, was still after almost 250 years sufficiently regarded to have documents dated by reference to his saint's day.

On *'Sunday after Michaelmas, 4 Henry V'*.[i.e. 4th October 1416], Robert Frensshe granted the same properties to *'Richard Brym, chaplain, Richard Stouche, Henry Whetacre, John Everard and William Jacob,* the witnesses being *'John Westwode, John Baker, Robert Bauche, William Gardiner and Henry Gladhait'.* The same day Robert Frensshe renounced his claim to the properties, most of the witnesses being different people, namely *'John Fremane, John Ponchardon, Thomas Ponteys, Thomas Westwode* [who was presumably a close relative of John Westwode] and *Thomas Gardiner.* Both documents have red circular seals with the letter 'R' in a hexagonal shield in the centre. The next day, Richard Brym, chaplain, and the other new owners, leased the property back to *'Agnes Couk, late the wife of John Couk'* for her lifetime *'and after her death to John and Christine her children by John Couk and after their deaths to their two sons, or one son if they have no other'.* This lease contains certain covenants. The new tenants agree *'to repair the premises at their own cost without waste and if they neglect to do so or make waste it will be lawful for the said Richard Brym etc.* [the new owners] *to enter and take possession'.* This appears to be the first occasion that such a covenant was introduced for the property and seems to show a considerable advance in the law of property ownership. Most of the succeeding leases contain a similar covenant. Some of the witnesses are the same: *'John Westwode, John Baker and William Gardiner,* but two are different, namely *'Richard Smythe and Richard Trenechenytt'.* Since the seal on this document depicts Christ in Majesty in its centre, it is probably an early example of the borough seal. Because on this lease and on the grant executed the previous day, the first lessor is listed as 'chaplain', and not 'prior', 'canon' or 'vicar', it seems that this cleric was not part of the establishment of Priory. However, the mayor and burgesses would probably have had a priest to act as their chaplain. Taken together with the seal, it seems reasonable to conclude that the purchasers of the previous day and the following day's lessors were burgesses. It seems logical to assume therefore, that in 1416, the property came into the ownership of the town where it has remained ever since. The fact that the lease was for effectively three lifetimes - the first long lease since the days of Ralph Kene - may also suggest that it was granted by the town rather than a group of independent men. The rent was 12 pence, to be paid at Christmas. Though this may seem to be a twelve fold increase in about a century, it is not strictly comparable, since it was for the whole house and also some of the pasture in East Marsh.

Twenty two years later, *'Thursday next before the feast of the Holy Trinity, 16 Henry VI'* [i.e. 23rd May 1438], William Jacob, one of those who leased the property to Agnes Couk and her two succeeding generations, granted the properties to *Roger Bryght, John Dany, Richard Hammond, Thomas Baker* [probably a relative of John Baker who witnessed the 1416 documents], *John Bonvyle* [who was Mayor the next year], and *William Covent* [who had been Mayor the previous year]. One is led to wonder if one of the other lessees was Mayor in 1438, though unfortunately this is not stated and the list of Mayors in the town hall does not help. Nor is it known if the others were all burgesses. Certainly the witnesses: Walter Hyder, the Vicar, Thomas Covent, the Reeve and probably a close relative of William Covent, one of the lessees, and Richard Wyse, John Rygge, Thomas Broun, Richard Shyrley, and John Wynter-borne, were unusually important men. Unfortunately the seal is missing, since this might have provided conclusive evidence that the town was by that date the owner of the property. There is also the mystery of why Agnes Couk surrendered the lease. Perhaps she found that she and/or her daughters were not able to manage the pastures or the rent. Possibly, when the daughters came into the properties, their husbands decided that they were unwilling to take them on. Unfortunately, we shall probably never know.

We next come across the property in Castle Street at Michaelmas in the first year of the reign of Richard III (29th September 1483). Then *'William Peynter, John Vytrok,* [who had been Mayor in 1471], *and John Shory,* leased to *'Walter Arnold of Christchurch, butcher and Isabelle Arnold, his wife,'* for a term of two lives at a rental of 10 shillings a year, during their lifetime. The property is described as

'*A tenement on the south side of Castle street, between the gate and the castle bridge on the east side in Christchurch,* formerly *held by William Peynter, John Vytrok and John Shory with William Clavile, John Frank, William Hykkys and Robert Bright (now deceased), of the gift of Robert Bright and William Covent.* The witnesses are '*Richard Lowen,* [Mayor in 1483 then Reeve of Christchurch] *John Ryder, John Carpenter, Robert Baker* [mayor in 1488] and *Francis Hamell'.* There are two red seals attached. One has the letter 'W' in its centre and the other, though broken shows in its centre, the Star of David. Does this suggest that one of the parties was a Jew? This lease was for only part of the property mentioned in the earlier documents, but because of the names, it seems that it was still owned by the borough.

The next lease is dated 28th November 1527 and like the previous document refers only to the tenement to the eastern side of the property. It is for a period of 20 years at a rental of 10 shillings per annum According to the lease '*The tenement on the western side of the property is owned by Margaret Countess of Salisbury'.* There can be no doubt that the property was still owned by the borough, since by that date the lessors are '*John Benett* [or Bevell], *mayor of Christchurch, Thomas Mooreman, Thomas Brandenham, Thomas Hancock* [Mayor 1556] *Robert Farrant* [Mayor 1526 and 1537], *John Frayle* [Mayor 1550], *Richard Genge* [Mayor 1539] *and William Colgell, burgesses'.* The tenant was *John Plowman,* who covenanted '*to repair one kitchen appertaining to the aforesaid tenement'.* It seems that this was also a full repairing lease. It is not known what trade John Plowman practised, but it could have been butchery, as Walter Arnold before him. Alternatively he might have been a glover, like the next known tenant, since the Countess of Salisbury would probably not have been too keen to have a butcher's shop next door to her property, whereas glove-making was at that time a highly respectable trade. Since the Countess was the Lord of the Manor, she would have been able to exert some influence on the mayor and burgesses regarding who took a tenancy of the property next to one of hers. This lease also contains the following clause. '*If the rent be unpaid for one month after Michael's in any year an no sufficient distress found, the lessors may enter and take possession'.* Could it be that the clause was inserted because Agnes and her family, the tenants of the 1416 lease, had been unable to pay the rent and had therefore had to surrender the property? In return, the lessors also covenanted to allow the tenants '*quiet enjoyment'* as in the previous deed.

There is a gap in the records at this stage, though there is some evidence that Pancheridge Genge, who was probably a descendant of Richard Genge, Mayor in 1539, leased the property from 1573. Pancheridge was Mayor in 1584 and presumably a burgess for some years before that date. However, he must have surrendered the lease after nine years, since on 18th September 1582 the tenement was let to *'Matthew Dixsonne of Christchurch, glover'* by *'Thomas Pettey, mayor of Christchurch, Henry Pawsonne* [Mayor 1559] *Richard Colgell* [Mayor 1582 after Pettey] *Richard Inwood* [Mayor 1578] *and William Nutkune* [Mayor 1583] *burgesses of Christchurch'.* The term was for 21 years at an annual rental of six shillings with a consideration of 40 shillings.

It is thought that members of the Pitman family were tenants of the property between 1601 and 1635, their occupation is not known. They too were a family of some importance in the town, since one of their number, John, was Mayor in 1606. It is likely that he was a burgess in 1601 when the family first leased the property.

Some time later, but the lease has not survived, the property was leased by the burgesses to Arumnell Hayly and Elizabeth Hayly. However for reasons that we do not know, Thomas Stevens bought them out at his own cost in the sum of 40 shillings. The document is dated 20th August 1665, by which time Charles II was on the throne and all the troubles of the Civil War and the sacking of Christchurch were long past. The document shows that *'Henry Rogers, gent, mayor of Christchurch and the burgesses of Christchurch lease to Thomas Stevens of Christchurch, yeoman'* for a term of 99 years at an annual rental of 11 shillings and a consideration of 40 shillings. The property leased comprised, *'A messuage to the north of the Castle and to the west of the way leading to the Castle Green, Christchurch; two halves of arable land in the Portfield, one lying in the West Marsh and one lying on the way leading to Knapp Mill'.* Both the land at Portfield and that on West Marsh had long been owned by the town, though earlier records show that at certain times the mayors and burgesses had not always been scrupulous about letting the lands for the benefit of the town. Other records in the town's archives show that the chief citizens had sometimes appropriated the lands for their own benefit. On this occasion, however, all seems to have been well.

For some reason that is not at first clear, on 18th November 1687 when there were still 77 years of the lease to run, the same property and lands were leased again to John Stevens, now referred to as a gentleman rather than a yeoman. The rent was the same, namely 11 shillings, but the consideration was only 20 shillings. Once again, the rent had to be paid regularly *'at Lady Day and Michaelmas in equal portions after which days if the rent be unpaid for ten days and no sufficient distress found the lease to determine. The lessees covenant to pay rent and to repair the premises'.* It may be that because of the political troubles towards the end of James II's reign it was felt advisable to re-affirm the lease. Alternatively, since John

Stevens had been Mayor in 1680, and was to be Mayor again from 1689-91, and also because John Blake was Mayor from 1685-88, it was felt advisable for the burgesses at large to re-affirm the lease, lest others in the town should think that these two men were acting to their mutual advantage.

There is now a gap of 125 years before the next surviving document. It is dated 1812, in the 52nd year of George III's reign and is between *Thomas Beckley, Mayor, and the burgesses, on the one part, and Meshach Pike of Christchurch, Cooper, of the other part'.* The property is described as a dwellinghouse with a garden or yard *bounded on the north by the King's Highway, on the south by way leading to the Castle Green and on the west by land of the Right honourable George Rose which premises were formerly in the tenure of John Stevens and then were possession of the said Meshach Pike.'* It seems therefore that the continuity of known ownership is almost unbroken. This lease was for 21 years at an annual rental of £10.10s.0d. The lessee covenants to pay *'rent, rates and taxes to repair and not to assign without consent in writing of the lessors under their common seal.'* This appears to be the first mention of a liability to pay rates. There is a further interesting clause in the lease. *'Except and always reserved out of this demise and grant unto the said Mayor and Burgesses and their Successors for the time being and assigns from time to time and at all times during the said term free use of the small Back Parlour in the said house hereby demised and the Court or Yard adjoining the same together with the free use of the Right of Way to the same for the Town Clerk and Voters for the time being to attend for the purpose of taking and pooling the several votes for the choice and election of the several officers of the said Borough according to ancient custom (in later deeds)'.* So it appears that the property was used as a polling booth for local elections. Since the date of the lease is before the great Reform Bill of 1832, which disposed of the rotten boroughs like Old Sarum, it may be that the small room was also used for the very few voters then eligible to vote at parliamentary elections. Records also show that the rear section of the western part of the property was where the Manor Court was held, until it was demolished in 1884. For centuries this Court had dealt mainly with market and trading matters. There is a photograph of the whole building, dated 1873, in Allen White's booklet on Church Street and Castle Street.

However, the lease was cancelled by the deputy mayor on 3rd July 1826, probably on the death of Mary Pike's husband, Meshach. *'Joseph Hannaford, deputy mayor of Christchurch'* took over the remaining six years of the lease held by *'Mary Pike, James Pike, Abraham Pike, Meshach Pike, Samuel Bayly, Mary Bayly and Joanna*

Pike', paying them £3 a year for five years and releasing Mary Pike from her liability to carry out repairs, on condition that Mary Pike paid the outstanding rates and taxes and the remaining three quarters' rent, amounting to £7.17.6d. Another matter of interest is that Joseph Hannaford, described as 'deputy mayor' to Charles Philip Rose who was Mayor that year, did not, as one might assume, become Mayor the next year, but had to wait until 1832 to be elected First Citizen. Was there some internal power struggle in the council, or was it from personal reasons? Whatever it was, Joseph Hannaford seems to have carried out his duties properly, since he was re-elected in 1839.

It may be that with the death of Meshach Pike, about the year 1826, the family business declined. If he were indeed a butcher, then his death might well have caused the business to decline, particularly if his sons were less skilled than their father or perhaps more interested in the farming side. We find that in the next year, 1827, the property and pastures are leased afresh by *Charles Philip Rose, mayor of Christchurch and the burgesses of Christchurch to Edmund Domone of Christchurch, butcher.'* The adjacent building was owned by Sir George Henry Rose, and the property described as having belonged to John Stevens, then Meshach Pike and subsequently Edmund Domone. The term was for 28 years at an annual rental of £18. Though it is not conclusive, it seems likely that Edmund Domone took over an existing butchery business and, like the Pikes, used the pastures he rented to keep his cattle.

We know from the Census of 1841 and the tithe map of 1844 that the town was growing both in size and population. It was also a time when far more attention was being paid to hygiene and other matters of public health - there was a cholera epidemic in 1848 that killed over 52,000 people in England and Wales. It was also a time when there was a growing belief that epidemics might well be spread by contaminated water. It is therefore not surprising to find an indenture dated 25th July 1849 concerning drainage in Castle Street. The indenture is between Admiral Sir George Elliott Meyrick Tapps Gervis, of Hinton Admiral of the first part, the Mayor and burgesses and Edmund Domone of the second part, and Sir George Henry Rose, a Privy Councillor, of Sandhills, James Kemp Welch, surgeon, John North of Devizes, Excise Officer, and John Newman, Gent, of Richmond, Surrey of the third part.

The burden of the document concerned the Castle Green owned by Sir George Gervis, and the adjoining houses in Castle Street, *'the provision for carrying off the drainage and waste water from the said houses etc. is very inadequate and the said drainage etc. has been suffered to run upon the land of the said Sir George Gervis and hereto accumulate and become a nuisance'.* It is likely that these conditions had existed since time immemorial and it was only the new-found interest in public health and the growing knowledge of how diseases might be spread that caused the following action to be taken. However, it should be noted that the parties made no mention of any possible medical reasons for the new drain! *'It is agreed between the parties thereto that a drain be constructed from the House No. 2* [which was adjacent to the Town Hall in its original position at the junction of Castle Street and Church Street] *to the street drain in Castle Street and that the drain shall be the joint property of the parties thereto. That Sir George Gervis shall pay towards the expenses £5 and the parties of the 3rd part for every 20/- of the residue of the expense above £5 shall pay the sums set opposite his name and house in the Schedule. Repairs to be paid for in the same proportion. The construction of the drain to be under the superintendence of James Kemp Welch and Henry Pain, agent of Sir George Gervis, and of James Druitt, agent of Sir George Rose, and of the Mayor and Burgesses and the superintendence of repairs by some person or persons to be appointed when necessary by the contributors of the greater part of the expense of such repairs'.* The owners of the ten properties and their respective contributions to the cost of the drain are given as Nos. 1 & 2, John Newman (of Richmond) - 2/3d & 1/8d; Nos. 3 & 4, John North (Excise Officer of Devizes) - 1/10d & 1/8d; No. 5, James Kemp Welch - 3/10d; Nos. 6, 7, 8, & 9, Sir George Rose - 2/-, 2/4d, 3/-, & 1/5d. No. 10, the property owned by the Mayor and burgesses and leased to the Domone family, made no contribution to the cost of the drain. Presumably the drains were set below the road's surface and formed an early part of the 19th century drainage system for the town.

Christchurch was in fact somewhat ahead of its time, since it was only in 1865, during another cholera outbreak, that the Sanitary Act was passed, which greatly reduced the spread of such diseases. It is also interesting to note that of the ten occupants of these houses in 1849, who are also listed beside the owners in the schedule, only two, namely Sarah Newman at No. 6 and Edmund Domone at No. 10, had also lived there in 1841 at the time of the Census. The population of the town was apparently becoming more mobile by the end of the 1840's. Edmund Domone appears to have had a brother, named Joseph, both of whom are listed as being aged 35. However they were probably not twins, since the 1841 Census gave the ages of all adults to the nearest 5 years. There is also Harriett aged 30, but it is not stated if she was a wife or sister.

The Domone family continued in the same business of butchery for some time, for on 24th October 1854, *'George Ferrey, mayor of Christchurch and the burgesses of Christchurch leased to Joseph*

Domone, butcher, for a term of 14 years at an annual rental of £18' the same property and lands. It seems safe to assume that Joseph was Edmund's son. This lease not only mentions the liability to pay rent, rates and taxes and keep the property in good repair, but also for the first time includes a covenant *'to keep the property insured against fire in the sum of £300 at least and to produce when required the Policy and premium receipts'*. It is interesting to note how modern conditions on leases gradually came to be added.

The property seems to have continued as butcher's shop for some time. On 16th September 1872, the premises were described as *'formerly in the tenure of Joseph Domone then of William Arnold, afterwards of Benjamin Candy and then of the said William Scott, butcher'*. The lease was for a period of 7 years at an annual rental of £19. Once again, the small back parlour, mentioned in the 1812 lease, was to be available for local election purposes, and in addition there had to be *'free right of entry for the said Mayor and Burgesses their Town Clerk, agent and surveyor to view the condition of the premises'*. No doubt this was to ensure that they were in a fit state to be used for elections.

Ten years later, on 16th September 1882, *'James Kemp Welch, mayor of Christchurch and the burgesses of Christchurch, leased the same pastures and property to William Scott of Christchurch, butcher'*. The term was again seven years and the rental similarly £19 per annum, for there was little if any inflation at that time.

So far as can be ascertained, the Scott family seemed to have continued to lease the property and use it as a butcher's shop. There is a record of a Miss Henrietta Mabel Scott taking a lease for use as a pork butcher's, in 1926.

A change of use took place in June 1937, when the Sandy family leased the property as a modern and antiquarian bookseller, philatelist, stationer and dealer in fancy goods and bric-a-brac. The family also owned a perfumery business in the High Street and on 24th June 1944, less than three weeks after 'D Day', this was relocated in the Castle Street property.

Finally, in 1988, the present tenants, Bob and Heather FitzGibbon, took over the premises and continue the perfumery business there to this day, still making perfumes on the premises. In 1996, they converted what had been living accommodation on the ground floor into an 'old-style Tea Rooms', serving home made food, though its earlier use as a butcher's can be seen from the meat hooks still in the ceiling.

So this property in Castle Street has gone through many changes over the centuries. However it seems that for much of its history, the trades carried out there have often been connected in some way with animals, either their flesh, from butchery, or their hide for leatherwork. We are fortunate indeed to be able to trace the history of the property and its occupants over such a long period. Fortunate too that the mayors and burgesses of the town have taken such care of their trust for almost six centuries. We can only speculate as to how many of those who visit 'The Old Perfumery' are aware of its long, fascinating and varied history. To step through its door is to step back in time.

The old house in Castle Street.

For those who are interested in such things, there are other properties in the town that would probably reveal a history almost as long and interesting. The story is only waiting in the archives to be discovered. Many names seem to recur in documents referring to different properties. It is clear that certain families have, in the past, played an important part in the life of the town over the centuries. Of such is the history of Christchurch.

Chapter 9.

The Leper Hospital of St Mary Magdalen.

If you were to ask almost any inhabitant of Christchurch to direct you to the Leper Hospital of St Mary Magdalen, you would probably be greeted with surprised shock and horror, to be followed by a surreptitious moving away by the person you were addressing. The ancient fear that leprosy is a highly contagious and deadly disease is still widely held, even though modern medicine can control and cure the disease and it is now almost unknown in this country. There are, however, still a few who suffer from the disease in England, and a national charity exists that does all it can to care for lepers and break down the prejudices against the ailment.

Having overcome their initial shock and surprise, the more thoughtful inhabitants might direct your steps towards the Red House Museum, thinking that perhaps you were remembering its previous use as the old Workhouse. Others, particularly those who live in the St Catherine's Hill area, might think you were referring to the old Isolation Hospital that stood in the heath-land of Dudmoor, down a near deserted track, though this hospital has long since closed and been converted into ordinary dwellings. Others would probably send you to the site of Christchurch Hospital, telling you that probably the buildings had now been replaced by some of the new houses that now occupy much of that re-developed site; or perhaps suggest that it was on the site of the present wonderful Macmillan Unit. All of them would be wrong.

After much thought, a few people might suggest that, since there is a road called 'Magdalen Lane' adjacent to the Barrack Road recreation ground opposite the police station, that might perhaps be where the Leper Hospital used to stand. But they would add that the houses there have been in existence for about 150 years. These few would have come nearest to the truth, for indeed it was in that area that the ancient Leper Hospital once stood.

When exactly the hospital was founded is not known for certain and much of the history of the place is shrouded in mystery. Taylor Dyson, in his excellent *'History of Christchurch'* published in 1954 produced much valuable information about it. Since then there has been further examination of original documents and more detail has come to light. It is worth noting that in the Middle Ages, when medical knowledge was rudimentary, leprosy was the generic term used to describe all skin eruptions, so that the Leper Hospital may have always housed others besides true lepers. In addition, Mary Magdalen was the Patron Saint of Prostitutes - for obvious reasons.

It is known that the Leper Hospital stood on part of what used to be the Portfield, a large area outside the Bar Gate, stretching westwards on either side of what is now Barrack Road but mainly down towards the River Stour. The earliest certain record is a grant by John de Wareham of an acre of land to the hospital, dated Wednesday the feast of St Lawrence in the 10th year of Edward II's reign, (i.e. 1317). Unfortunately it appears that this document has for the moment been lost, though presumably it was examined in 1954. The deed poll apparently stated that *'John de Wareham the elder granted to the master of the Lazar House at Christchurch Twynham and the lepers and other sick therein, one acre of arable land in the Portfield between the land of Alicia de Godlye on the east and the land of John Duferes on the west and extending in length towards the south to the land of Luce Joye and towards the north to the house of the said Lazar House to be held in frankalmoign for the souls of the grantor and his parents'*. The grant was apparently confirmed that same day by Walter de Wareham, but we do not know if he was older or younger than John. However the family seems to have been quite large and prosperous since they are also mentioned in the Ralph Kene lease of about the same date, referred to in the previous chapter. In it, Roger de Wareham, a third member of the family, is stated as owning a messuage in Castle Street.

From this document, it is clear that the Leper Hospital was already of long standing and fairly prosperous, since it states that it was at that date, 1317, caring for those who suffered from other serious ailments other than leprosy. In all probability the hospital was originally founded shortly after the first Crusade ended, about the year 1100, and when those who had taken part in it had returned home. Leprosy had been a well-known disease in the Middle East for many centuries, though it was also active in Lombardy in A.D. 643, when King Rothar issued a decree expelling all lepers from his city and declaring them all effectively dead. Whenever the disease was mentioned, it was always with dread. Perhaps the most famous account of leprosy is in the Bible, 2 Kings chapter 5. There, Elisha refuses to visit Naaman, the Commander of the Syrian King's forces, who has leprosy, but nevertheless cures him from a distance. But Elisha's servant who does visit Naaman, succumbs to the disease, and leaves his presence 'a leper as white as snow'. Many crusaders, including some of their leaders, contracted the disease and returned home with it to the horror of their relatives and companions. The almost inevitable consequence was that lepers became outcasts and had to live out their lives in isolation, slowly rotting away. As with all-important national issues of the time, the Church took a leading role.

A leper.

The procedure for dealing with lepers was formalised by the Third Lateran Council in 1179. Suspect lepers were to be examined by a priest or magistrate and if they were found to be suffering from the disease, they were to be cast out from the community and considered 'dead' in a ritual act of symbolic burial. It was awesome ceremony. The leper stood in an open grave with a black cloth over his head. The priest cried aloud *'Be dead to the world, be reborn in God'* to which the leper replied, *'Jesus my redeemer, may I be reborn in Thee'*. This was followed by the priest intoning, *'I forbid you to enter church, monastery, fair, market place or tavern ..... I forbid you ever to leave your house without your leper's costume, or to walk barefoot. ..... I forbid you to wash or drink in the stream or fountain. ..... I forbid you to live with any woman other than your own. If you meet and talk with some person on the road, I forbid you to answer before you have moved down wind. ..... I forbid you to touch a well or well cord, without your gloves. I forbid you ever to touch children, or to give them anything. ..... I forbid you eating or drinking except with lepers.'* After this terrible proscription, the leper was led in procession to the place of exile. Such was the fear of leprosy. However, they were allowed to wander more or less at will, provided they were clothed in a long robe and hooded to hide their deformities and carried a bell to warn others of their approach. Their relatives could still speak to them - from a distance. To house a leper hospital on the Portfield, just outside the town wall, would not therefore be considered dangerous but rather considerate, in that they could keep some contact with their family.

Nor should it be supposed that it was only the poor who suffered the disease. Both a crusading King of Jerusalem, Baldwin IV, and Hugh d'Orivalle, Bishop of London who died in 1085, were victims.

As always, the Church came to their rescue and provided what succour they could. Though they had no knowledge of how to cure or even arrest the disease, we can only marvel at the courage of those priests who were prepared to risk their lives for the sake of their often horribly deformed patients. Consequently, leper hospitals were established in various parts of the country. Since many crusaders had sailed from the southern ports of England, of which Southampton was one of the more important, it was logical that a leper hospital should be established in Twynham, where there was an increasingly prosperous religious community based round a new and growing convent church.

It is almost certain that the secular monks at Twynham, shortly to become Augustinian Canons Regular, already owned land on the Portfield. The second Saxon Charter in the Cartulary, dated A.D. 985, states that King Ethelred had given to Sulfric the Priest[1] various lands including some at 'Cnolla' which is commonly believed to be the Portfield site. On Sulfric's death, this land would most likely have reverted to the church community at Twynham to which he belonged. What more logical place for the Church to establish a small leper hospital than a parcel of land that they already owned and which stood in isolation outside the burgh walls, but yet near enough for the monks to minister to the occupants. From these humble beginnings may well have sprung the Leper Hospital of St Mary Magdalen, to which John de Wareham in his turn gave his endowment. To this was added, in the same year, the grant of a house outside the Bar Gate, adjoining the road to Wimborne. Six years later, there is recorded the grant of the workshop of Robert Lumbard (or should it be Lombard, since there were many Italians then trading in England) a tailor in Church Street. The `former could well have housed some of the patients, and the latter provided a income for their support.

A further interesting grant occurred in 1329. On '*the feast of St John the Baptist in 2 Edward III*' (1329), there is a deed poll being '*a release from Richard Chyke to Richard Wade, master of the house of lepers at Christchurch Twynham of all his claims to a cottage with a curtilage in the village of Holdenhurst abutting on his land in the west*'. This is the earliest document which gives the name of the hospital master. Perhaps of greater importance is the fact that there

---

[1] See chapter 2

was then at Holdenhurst a small leper hospice. The site is still occupied by a medieval house, though it is now in private ownership, but it is likely that this was the cottage originally granted to the leper hospital. Since by then leprosy was declining in England, it may well have been that most of those still suffering from the disease were moved out to the more isolated area of Holdenhurst, while the hospital on the Portfield concentrated more on those suffering from other more common infectious diseases. Perhaps at the same time the hospital also began to take in those who had been maimed in the constant wars with the continent. Certainly there would have been no shortage of applicants for its beds.

The Leper Hospital's hospice at Holdenhurst.

Four other grants to the hospital during the years 1349 and 1350 need explaining. The first, in January 1349, was *'a grant from Walter son of William Williames for the good of the souls of his father, mother, brother, sister, ancestors and heirs, to the master of the Lazar House and his companions of two acres of land in Portfield which his father purchased of John Drynckhard and lying between the land of Richard Chaffeyn in the north and of Richard Pennard in the south'.* The second, in April 1349, was *'On the Saturday before the feast of St Mark the Evangelist. A deed poll, being a grant from John, son and heir of Richard le Blake for the good of his soul and the souls of his father and ancestors to the master of the leper house of Christchurch Twynham and the lepers and other such persons therein abiding, of the moiety* [a half] *of a messuage and curtilage adjoining, in the borough of Christchurch Twynham between the tenement of John Brown in the south and the tenement of William Wychwolf in the north*

- *without the Bar Gate'.* The third, also in 1349, was *'On the Wednesday after the feast of St Thomas, Archbishop and Martyr. A Power of Attorney from Andrew Elys to William Rogers to deliver seizin of two acres of land in Portfield to the master of the Lazar House'.* The fourth grant was in November 1350, *'On the Monday after the feast of All Saints, being a grant from John Feron of Poole to the master of the Lazar House and the lepers and other sick therein of two acres of arable land situated together in Holdenhurst in frankalmoign for the souls of himself and his parents'.*

Though the Leper Hospital received various other grants over the centuries, this seems to be the only occasion when there were four within the space of less than two years. The reason was almost certainly the arrival of the Black Death that reached Christchurch towards the end of 1348 and had run its course by the end of 1349. There seems to be a strong likelihood that these four grants were made, not only in memory of those who had died, but also as a thanksgiving by those who survived. The full effects of the plague on Christchurch are discussed in a later chapter. Unfortunately, the whereabouts of these four documents, examined in the 1950's is not known. If we add to this list, other grants that were made in the following years, it is clear that in the 14th century, the leper hospital was providing a very valuable service to the community. It is also clear from the wording of the deeds that the hospital was caring for other terminally ill people besides lepers, no doubt due to the decrease in the number of lepers.

It seems, therefore, that by 1498 if not before, the need for the Leper Hospice at Holdenhurst had ceased. In that year, *'On the eve of the nativity of the Blessed Virgin Mary in 14 Henry VII* [i.e 7th September 1498], *Nicholas Guylbert, chaplain, custodian of the Hospital of St Mary Magdalen and the brothers and sisters of the Hospital of St Mary Magdalen, leased to John Cotell of Holdenhurst and Michael* [sic, but perhaps Michelle] *his wife, a cottage at Holdenhurst for a term of 24 years at an annual rental of one silver penny.* The implication is that the cottage was no longer required for use as a hospice and could therefore be let out. The rental is certainly very low, perhaps because few were willing to take on a property that had housed lepers for so long. There may also have been a consideration paid in addition, of which we have no details. Certainly, half a century later, leprosy had greatly declined throughout Europe, only to be replaced by syphilis, whose sufferers probably then occupied the beds in the hospital vacated by the lepers.

About this time, there seems to have been a change in the supervision of the Leper Hospital. From its foundation until the suppression of the Priory in 1539 and the scattering of its canons, the overall control of the hospital would have been under the Prior, since it was apparently built on Priory land. Though most abbeys and priories would have supplied the majority of the medical care that existed in the country, it was nearly always Augustinian houses that provided the leper hospitals, usually named after St Mary Magdalen. The hospital master would normally be one of the canons and would have had day-to-day control. With the departure of Prior Draper and the canons, and the surrender of the Priory's lands, the oversight of the hospital that stood on Priory land, would presumably have passed to the new Lord of the Manor. This initially meant Henry VIII and later Edward VI. Kings would obviously have had little interest in the day-to-day running of their estates, provided an income continued to flow from them into the royal coffers. Those caring for the hospital inmates would have continued to be local people. With the departure of the Augustinian canons, this care would have fallen onto the Mayor and burgesses, possibly assisted by the Vicar, John Smith, who was probably the person who knew most about the poor and sick of his parish. This becomes clear from the records, where from 1550 onwards, the signatories to the leases are always the Mayor and burgesses.

Clearly the wider use of the hospital for invalids other than lepers had the support of the mayor and burgesses. There was an application by them in 1590 to Sir Christopher Hatton, the Lord Chancellor. In it they outlined the detailed needs of the hospital. There were at that time '20 poor lame, maimed and impotent and diseased persons not able to live but by charity'. There was neither sufficient land nor funds to support them, so they were requesting a licence to allow Robert Phillips, the Proctor of the hospital, to collect alms. Four years later, Thomas Saddlier, who was the Guider, or Master, of the hospital, received a warrant to allow him or his deputy to collect alms and two years later, John Phillips, now the Guider and presumably a relative of Robert, appointed Henry Saddlier to collect alms. These two local families seem to have been running the hospital between them.

It would appear that the work of the hospital prospered and became widely known. Quite when the appointment of the hospital Master became shared between the Sovereign, the Lord of the Manor, and the Mayor and burgesses of Christchurch, is not known, but it was possibly during the reign of Mary Tudor. There is a document in the hospital archives with a red wax seal showing a Tudor rose, and 'M' 'R'. She gave the Manor to Catherine Pole, granddaughter of the executed Lady Margaret Pole, Countess of Salisbury. Certainly in 1597, Julius Caesar (sic) writing on behalf of Queen Elizabeth, appointed Evan Jones of Southwark in Surrey to be Master of the hospital, and 'that he shall faithfully order and govern the poor people

69

inhabiting the hospital, providing such food, drink and clothing as shall be necessary and ensuring the repair and upkeep of the building. And that he shall be of good behaviour and peaceable and fair in his dealings with the inhabitants of the hospital'.

It seems therefore that by the beginning of the 17th century, there were three separate interests in the hospital; King, Lord of the Manor and Mayor. Records show that they often worked in concert. In 1594, Elizabeth I *'advised by the Mayor and Burgesses'* appointed Thomas Sabley, the Governor of the hospital, to collect alms in Gloucestershire and Warwickshire for the relief of the poor, maimed and impotent people in the hospital.

By 1601, the Lordship of the Manor had been bought by Thomas Arundel, Lord Wardour, who took a considerable interest in the hospital. One document in the hospital archives not only has the signature of Thomas Arundel, but has also been sealed with his signet ring. This depicts the three Sussex Martlets (birds with no feet) of his crest. One can imagine him first appending his signature to the parchment and then drawing off his gold signet ring from his little finger and impressing it onto the soft wax before handing the now legal document to his clerk. It is also apparent that monarchs continued to take an interest in the hospital.

A problem arose in April 1609, when the mastership fell vacant. On the instructions of James I, Henry, Earl of Northampton wrote to Sir John Jeffreys and also the Mayor of Christchurch, telling them that *'the King has bestowed the place of guider of the hospital on Nicholas Compton, a poor maimed soldier in consideration of his hurts received in the Wars of Elizabeth I. He is much moved by the man's plight, but is concerned that the post may not be the best means of helping him. He has therefore stopped the grant at the privy seal until he is informed by some gentleman of worth residing at Christchurch as to the state of the Hospital and of what quality the guider should be, and what uses of charity are limited by the foundation. He therefore asks Sir John or the Mayor to send him the information as quickly as possible that he may give satisfaction to the poor man'.*

This is the first instance, but not the last, of the hospital master himself being chosen for being a person deserving charity rather than for his ability as an administrator. It produced an instant reaction in the form of a letter, dated 24th April 1609, that is in the archives.

'Right honorable: as it appeareth by your letters diverted unto Sir John Jeffreys and to the mayor of Christchurch, it seemeth your honour would be informed as well of the value of the hospital of St Mary Magdalen at Christchurch as also of the state thereof because the king's majesty should bestow 'feasance' upon one Nicholas Compton in recompence of his service. May it please your honour: to

be advised, that the value is not above 20 nobles [£6.13s.4d] a year. The gift thereof now remaineth in the deposition of the right honorable Thomas Lord Arundel Baron of Warder [Wardour] who hath bestowed the same upon one John Agar as Guider or Governor thereof, during his life, if he behave himself as well as he might, towards the poor people there remaining. And after his decease the next nomination is in the mayor and burgesses of Christchurch for the like term of life, unto whomsoever they shall bestow the same, and then again in the gift of the king's majesty even as has always been bestowed successively: viz first the king to give to whom it pleaseth his majesty during the life of whom it pleaseth his majesty appointeth and secondly whom my Lord of Warder shall appoint and last of all whom the mayor and burgesses of Christchurch shall appoint: until which time expired the disposition thereof of right is not the king's majesty all which I thought good to certify your honour for the future with my prayer to god for the health and prosperity long to continue. Christchurch xxxiiij th April 1609. Your honour's to command.'

Unfortunately, the letter is unsigned, though it is likely to have come from Sir John Jeffreys. One can well understand his unwillingness to append his signature to the letter that contained such a strong rebuke to his sovereign. So far as can be made out, John Agar, appointed by Thomas Arundel, continued as hospital Master until at least 1633.

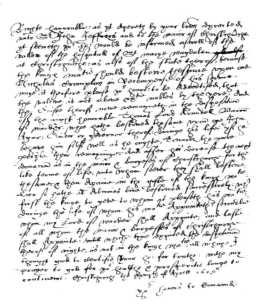

Letter to the Earl of Northampton.

71

In 1646, the post of hospital Master itself was again made by charitable considerations. Richard Flurry, who may well have succeeded John Agar, was appointed, this time by the Mayor and burgesses, for life, *'taking into consideration the poverty of the said Richard Flurry having a wife and many small children for his and their better sustenation and livelihood and for the good causes and considerations ....provided that he should out of the profits of the said hospital and premises repair the same and also in fit and customary manner succour and relieve such and so many poor alms people as the mayor and burgesses shall from time to time place and appoint there and that he should be ordered ruled and guided by the said Mayor and burgesses in all things concerning the said hospital with the land and appurtenances thereto belonging to the mastership and government thereof.* Like so many charities of the period, the master was allowed to make what he could out of his appointment. Unfortunately this was often at the expense of the inmates, though it is to be hoped that, because the Mayor and burgesses were keeping a close eye on the master, things may not have been too bad at Christchurch.

Richard Flurrey was probably the last person to be appointed Master with the instruction to keep the building in good repair. At some time between 1646 and 1699, when Richard Holloway was appointed Master in succession to Samuel Carter who had died, the hospital building probably fell into decay and was pulled down.

This may have come about as a result of a change in the administration of the hospital that probably occurred about this time. With the execution of Charles I and the imposition of the Commonwealth, there was no longer a king to take an interest in, or control over, the hospital. The Lord of the Manor after Lord Arundel was the Earl of Clarendon, who fell from power and was impeached in 1667 and fled the country. He therefore would have then been unable to take any further interest in the hospital. The sole control of the hospital presumably then fell, perhaps by default, on the Mayor and burgesses. Certainly from 1699, the Masters of the hospital were being appointed only by the Mayor and burgesses. It is possible that the hospital building may have been damaged during the Civil War, either during one of the attacks on the town, or perhaps because it was used as a barracks for the Parliamentary troops garrisoned in the town. Unfortunately there are nor records to prove this either way.

By the end of the century, conditions in the country seem to have so improved that the charter of the hospital needed to be widened. Even the Plague of 1665 that devastated London, may not have affected Christchurch too severely, since the burgesses had ordered *'a watch of two men by day and four by night to prevent the introduction of the plague and pestilence; no man known to be infected shall be allowed to enter the town for 20 days'.* It is not therefore surprising to find that the hospital's Minute Book for 1699 records, *'By the mercy of God the leprosy for the relief and cure of which the small revenue of the said lazar house was appropriated and directed to be applied was so far ceased that there was not nor had been for many years past any leper who had resorted to the said hospital for relief and the Mayor and burgesses being desirous that the said revenue and all the profits belonging to the said hospital should be laid out and expended in and for good and charitable purposes as herinafter is mentioned and agreed upon'.* unanimously elected Richard Holloway to be Master of the hospital. He was to render accounts annually within 14 days after Michaelmas and hand over all monies less 20 shillings which he was allowed to keep as payment for the work involved. The new constitution directed that all sums received *'shall be disposed of for the relief of lazars and lepers (if any should desire relief of them) and if there be no lazar or leper who shall desire relief of them then for other good or charitable uses in the said town and not for any benefit or advantage of the said Mayor and burgesses or any other private use whatsoever'.* The Master had full discretion as to which poor persons of the Borough were to be *'the fittest objects of charity'.*

The deed also stated that the Master could not grant any leases of the hospital's many properties without the consent of the Mayor and burgesses. Where leases had been granted in previous centuries, there had often been a covenant that a tenement should be built on the land. This would often account for the low annual rental, since at the end of the lease, the tenement would revert to the hospital. A very satisfactory arrangement, particularly if at the time there was little need for a large income. Two examples of this are a 99 year lease in 1715 of some land adjoining the hospital for an annual rental of one penny with the condition that a cottage be erected upon it, and a 65 year lease in 1829 of a quarter acre site for a cottage and garden for an annual rent of 25 shillings, with a covenant to build a large property costing £250.

By 1825, it would appear that the Charity was in decline and perhaps not particularly well run. It appears that Robert Reeks, who had been appointed as a burgess as a minor in 1746 and appointed Master of the hospital in 1812, resigned in 1824. By then he must have been in his 90's. As a consequence, the next year the Charity Commissioners were constrained to order a survey of its possessions and income. This was assessed at only £41.6s.0d. Fortunately Benjamin Ferrey was appointed Master the same year and he took matters in hand. There were understandable difficulties in collecting rents since he found that two properties were uninhabited and in ruins and the sites had to be cleared. Four others were such wretched hovels that their annual rents had to be reduced from 40 shillings to 5 shillings, which as he reported to the Commissioners, reduced the total rental to £31.10s.0d. Most of this income was at that time used to buy bread to distribute to the poor. In 1835 this amounted to 556 gallons of bread, at a cost of £30.7s.8½d. This would have provided at least 21 poor families with a regular supply of two large 2 pound loaves of good bread each week; a not inconsiderable addition to an otherwise meagre diet. In a town the size of Christchurch, this probably had a major effect in relieving the poverty in the town. It was also at this time, between 1804 and 1846, that the Corn Laws that kept the price of wheat unnaturally high resulted in greatly aggravated poverty. By 1850, when food prices had stabilised, bread distribution in Christchurch had been replaced by small quarterly payments, which naturally gave some freedom of choice to the recipients as to its use. However, bread and clothes were still distributed amongst the poor of the town by Brown's Charity that had been established in Christchurch in 1667.

The accounts of the period show that almost the whole of the small income from the charity was distributed to the poor, often in sums of 2/6d that even in those days did not go very far. Nor was there much left for the maintenance or repair of the estate, which was very largely only agricultural land.

It is evident that over the years the number of poor people in the borough steadily increased, partly due to the depressed state of agriculture at the end of the 18th and beginning of the 19th centuries. The Tolpuddle Martyrs, whose wages were below starvation level, were deported to Australia in 1834 and the inhabitants of Christchurch would have known all about them and would themselves have been suffering a similar decline in wages.

By 1837, it seems that it was finally decided that there was no further need for the old hospital building at Holdenhurst, that had probably originally been used as a hospice for the terminally sick. The property was therefore finally let at a modest rental. That same year it was noted that 17 pieces of land on the Portfield were put down to crops; 2 with rye, 3 with potatoes, 2 with hay, 7 with wheat and 3 with barley. It is probable that they were still being farmed under the medieval strip farming system, which can still today be seen at Laxton. If so, they may have measured 22 yards, or a chain wide, and 220 yards, which is ten chains or a furrow (or furlong), in length. The total area being a rectangle one acre in size. It is worth remembering that the acre, though a square measure consisting of ten square chains, is hard to make into a perfect square area, and was never intended to be such.

In 1847, George Ferrey, who was Mayor in 1852, '54, '60 and '69, and presumably had his own substantial house, was appointed hospital Master in succession to his father, Benjamin. It is probably under his leadership that the first move was made to improve the estate and build on parts of it to increase the income. He and the burgesses granted a 99 year lease to John Edward Holloway of a parcel of land *'being the site of the hospital',* with the condition that a house, originally called 'Fairlight' but later 'Vancouver', be built on the site at a cost of £300. There was a rider that £75 was to be repaid by the hospital master on completion of the dwelling, which indeed happened the same year. It seems likely that the site of the original hospital had been derelict for a considerable time. Another plot of land was also leased for 99 years at £9 a year for a house to built at a cost of £700. The long-term benefit of these leases was to have a marked effect on the Charity.

As a result of the Enclosure Act of 1878, nearly 300 acres of the Portfield that had been effectively common land, was conveyed to the hospital for use as building land. This led to the income of the Charity rising to £120 in 1879, and grants to the poor rising to 40/-. Ten years later the income had risen to £265 with grants of up to 60/- being made, and there were 'new trustees'. In the years that followed, more houses were built and leased, particularly in what is now Magdalen Lane and along Barrack Road. The old leper hospice building at Holdenhurst that had become very dilapidated, was sold in 1889 to Edward Cooper-Dean for £700.

In its early days, the inhabitants of the St Mary Magdalen Hospital and the recipients of other forms of charity had been largely chosen by the hospital Master, though with guidance from above. In its early years, as has been explained, he would have been guided by the Prior, and after the suppression of the Priory, he would have been guided by the town's Mayor and burgesses. One of the reasons for the town asking Queen Victoria in 1885 for a Charter of Incorporation was to rid themselves of this responsibility, particularly as the hospital building had by then been pulled down long before. In consequence, the charter of 1886 handed over the running of the St Mary Magdalen Hospital Charity to the Charity Commissioners, who were quick to appoint local Trustees. They took over from the last Master, John Edward Holloway, who became one of the Trustees, and continued to administer the Trust for the benefit of the poor of the Borough. Because of the nature of the leases, the rental income continued for many years to be quite small, though the capital of the Trust increased for the benefit of future generations.

During this time, those responsible for running the Charity acted on many occasions for the great benefit of the town at large. Land was sold in 1865 and again in 1889 to allow the railway to be built. This was not without its difficulties and had ultimately to be settled by arbitration. In 1899, a water main was laid to supply the houses in Magdalen Lane and three years later, main sewers began to be laid to the properties on the Charity's land and the rest of the town. In 1923, land in Barrack Road was sold to Hampshire County Council on which the Primary School was built. And in 1931, permission was given for an electric cable to be laid over the Charity's land to what is now Twynham School, so that they no longer had to read and work by gaslight.

With the more active management of the hospital's funds, it was possible to raise the payments to the poor even in 1942 during wartime conditions, to £5 each for 40 people. There have been further increases over the years and the payments are £80 each per quarter at the present time.

Changes in the law under a succession of Leasehold Reform Acts, culminating in the Act of 1967 enabled people who had long leases to buy their freeholds. Since many of the properties owned by the Hospital Trust were let in this manner, a great number had to be sold to the tenants at quite low figures. Though this was in many ways of great benefit to large numbers of people, it had a major effect on such charities as the Mary Magdalen Hospital Charity, since it effectively converted much of the capital from property into cash over a short period of time. The proceeds of the sales were judiciously invested with the effect that the annual income of the Charity rose steadily.

Other problems now arose. The Charity was limited to helping only those who were resident in the Ancient Borough of Christchurch. This consisted of the area within the ancient walls of the burgh and also the older parts of the Portfield and the Bargates area. The number of people living within this area was quite limited and excluded much of what had long become Christchurch. In order to spend the income, the Trustees raised the level of payments to alms-people, but even this was limited in its effect because the amount a person could receive at that time was low before state benefits were reduced pound for pound, making further payments pointless.

Consequently, in 1979, the Trustees resolved to apply to the Charity Commissioners to increase the area of benefit to include Purewell as a means of resolving the problem. However, in 1980 the problem was exacerbated by the sale of a large area of land for housing development at the bottom of Magdalen Lane. This resulted in a further significant increase in the Charity's income. Further discussions were held with the Charity Commissioners and various solutions proposed over the next few years. In February 1984, agreement was reached with the Charity Commissioners to establish a

New Scheme for the hospital. This established first, five independent Trustees and second, extended the care of benefit to cover the whole of the modern Borough of Christchurch. At last the Charity was able to reach such areas as Somerford and Highcliffe, which had previously been outside its jurisdiction.

On 28th February 1986, the New Scheme was established. From that date, the Mary Magdalen Leper Hospital Trust changed out of all recognition. The Clerk of 35 years standing, John Williams, retired, having steered the Charity through the various changes. A new Clerk, the present incumbent, Alastair Hoare, was appointed. Douglas Preston, a Trustee since 1967, was elected Chairman of the Trustees and further Trustees were appointed to bring the number up to five. Caring organisations were contacted throughout the Borough and by mid 1986, the number of meetings had to be increased from one to four to cope with the applications. In June, two meetings were held to cope with the extra requests for help. By 1987, a close working relationship had been established with the Social Services Department and the scope of the help was increased from simple quarterly payments, to payments for particular crises. In this way, the Charity was able to assist families to overcome serious difficulties, whether financial or physical, perhaps by adapting a property or providing mobility assistance such as an electric wheelchair for example.

The number of people helped per year varies, but it is about 60 at the present time, in addition to the individual regular payments that continue to be made in suitable cases. Also, increasing amounts of money are paid to organisations such as the Citizens Advice Bureau, schools, and charities for disabled people in Christchurch, as a way of reaching the greatest number of people. In this way, the ancient Mary Magdalen Leper Hospital, arguably one of the oldest charities in England, has been able to adapt once more to the needs of the present. It thus continues to play a major role in the charitable affairs of the town, as it has done over the past centuries, helping many who find themselves in financial difficulty, perhaps through no fault of their own.

Thus the charitable gifts of our ancestors that stretch over no less a period than 700 years, continue to play an important part in making Christchurch a place for some, who without it, would not be able to say that it is a town 'Where Life is Pleasant'.

Chapter 10.

An Indulgence from Simon Meopham
Archbishop of Canterbury, 1331.

Since time immemorial, Crime and Punishment have gone hand in hand, the first leading inexorably to the second. However, there has always also been the need for reparation. The Old Testament "eye for an eye" was all very well, in that it naturally tended to restrain men's anger and aggressive tendencies, because of the fear of a like fate falling upon the perpetrator in the event of discovery. One of the problems with such a code of justice was that it frequently led to a vendetta rather than the resolution of the injustice. Very early on it became clear that justice could sometimes be better done if reparation were to be made to the injured party. In this way, not only could justice seen to be done in the eyes of the community, but also the originator of the misconduct was shamed before his fellows. Quite early, it had become the established custom in the Christian Church, for priests to hear confession and grant absolution to those who were truly penitent, in return for some suitable penance. For those in the higher strata of society, it became possible to commute their penance, either by a cash payment to the Church, or more often by building or adding to the glory of a church or monastery. Both men and women also frequently adopted the practice of building a chantry and establishing a priest in it, to pray for their souls and those of their family. From this developed the custom, first for the Pope, and later for bishops, to grant remission of sins in return for a suitable gift to the Church. The system was also adopted very early in civil justice through the use of the fine. Men, hailed before the Lord of the Manor's court, were said to be 'at the mercy of the court'. The court records showed that both justice and mercy occurred, and the offender was 'amerced' or fined. The Court Rolls of the Christchurch Hundred for the years 1542-5, translated by David Stagg, show that by then the system was already well established. The records give details of numerous offences and the fines imposed. These are listed as 'mercy 3d' or 'mercy 1 shilling' for example, for various minor offences usually connected with trade, such as illegal brewing or excessive profit on the sale of goods. Even the Priory did not escape the mercy of the court. Earlier, in 1519, there are several entries where the prior was fined 3s.4d. and 6s.8d. because "he had not yet made his hedges towards the meadow of the Lady Margaret Countess of Salisbury, (who was the Lord of the Manor) called 'Portrevesmede' (probably Portfield).

The Indulgence

The custom was therefore long established. that reparation should be made to right a wrong.

As has been said. the Church had already adopted a similar system for its own benefit as well as for the salvation of the souls of its people. This developed into the system of "Indulgences". Men were encouraged to show their repentance in a tangible way. by performing some act for the benefit of the community at large. Certainly by the 14th century. senior clerics were prepared to grant indulgences in general terms. At a later date. when St Peter's Church was being built in Rome. there was widespread abuse of the system. when with papal authority. wandering friars sold indulgences wholesale as a ready way of raising the huge funds needed to pay for the magnificent church that was under construction.

Christchurch is fortunate enough to have in its archives three original parchment Indulgences. They are beautifully written in the shortened Latin of the day. but unfortunately none of the seals that originally hung from them have survived. though their parchment seal tags are still present. These parchments are dated 1331, 1367 and 1373. and were issued respectively by Simon Meopham, Archbishop of Canterbury. Gervase de Castro, Bishop of Bangor. and Geoffrey. Archbishop of Damascus. All three documents are couched in almost identical terms. so that one is left with the impression that the later two are in effect a reiteration of the earliest one. Simon Meopham's Indulgence reads in translation:-

To all the sons of Holy mother Church to whose notice this writing shall come. Symon, by divine dispensation Archbishop of Canterbury. Primate of all England, sends greeting in him through whom there shall be remission of sins. In order that we might rouse the souls of the faithful to works of piety through encouraging rewards of indulgences. trusting in the grace of Almighty God and in his unbounded mercy and also most piously in his merits and the prayers and good offices of the blessed Thomas the glorious martyr and of all the saints. we mercifully grant indulgence of 45 days pardon to all Christians settled everywhere throughout our province of Canterbury. who. truly penitent and shriven of their sins. shall have bestowed to the fabric or repair of the bridge at Christchurch Twynham in the diocese of Winchester. anything from their goods. conferred on them by God. or shall have sent grants of charity. Ratifying and confirming. as far as we are able by right. all and each separate. indulgence granted and thenceforward to be granted rightly on account of this matter. In witness of which we have made to append our seal to these presents. Given at Donhead the fourth of the Nones of July in the year of our lord 1331 and in the fourth year of our consecration. [Friday 28th June 1331].

The main difference between this Indulgence and the later two, is that they only grant indulgence for 40 days penance rather than 45 days. It may be argued that '40 days' is a generic rather than specific period. as in the biblical '40 days and 40 nights' that Christ was in the wilderness before the Temptations. It would also tie in with the normal 'quarantine' period (derived from the Latin word for 40) used in medieval times. Ships coming particularly from the Middle East at the time of the Crusades. were required to tie up at a safe distance from a port for a period sufficiently long to be certain that the crew were not suffering from any malignant disease, such as leprosy or the Plague. This was normally considered to be 40 days, or about six weeks.

There are other minor differences in the three Indulgences, mainly to do with the saints to which each refers. Simon Meopham refers to *the blessed Thomas the glorious martyr*. This is his predecessor at Canterbury, Thomas à Becket, murdered in his cathedral in 1170, to whose tomb the faithful and others still at that time made pilgrimage. Gervase de Castro refers to the Virgin Mary and *the blessed Daniel bishop and Confessor, our patron*, Bishop of Bangor in A.D. 584. He had founded the abbey at Bangor and many of the Welsh churches. Gervase was probably a suffragan bishop of Winchester *in partibus infidelium* or in heathen parts. Geoffrey, likewise held a title *in partibus infidelium* as a suffragan of Winchester. He refers to the Virgin Mary and also the apostles Peter and Paul, since they were his patron saints in Damascus. It was the custom at that time for suffragan bishops to be given titles of extinct bishoprics, many of which were by then, as in the case of Damascus, in the hands of the 'Infidels' – in that case the Mohammedans. The See of Bangor had also ceased to exist at that time, so that the title could be used for a suffragan. These suffragans were essential to the administration of the episcopal sees, since many of the diocesan bishops, and particularly the Bishop of Winchester, were amongst the King's closest advisers and as such were frequently away from their sees. The suffragans relied on fees they could charge for their work, such as ordaining priests, consecrating and re-consecrating desecrated churches and church-yards, confirming the faithful, anointing virgins besides issuing indulgences.

The important questions to ask are why the Archbishop of Canterbury rather than the Bishop of Winchester or his suffragan granted the Indulgence in 1331, and why was it granted at Donhead, which is a small village in Wiltshire. John de Stratford had been

Bishop of Winchester for 18 years and was one of Edward III's principle advisers and was to become Archbishop of Canterbury in 1333. However, in 1331 he was sent to France on various important and secret missions for the King, which may explain his absence from his see at the relevant time. Secondly, the Lord of the Manor of Twynham at that time was William de Montacute, who also acted for Edward III on several secret missions to France. It is quite likely that he accompanied John de Stratford. William de Montacute owned lands in Donhead, as did the Prior of Twynham, if the first Saxon charter is to be believed. It is also known that Simon Meopham was making a tour of his province of Canterbury in 1331, which would explain his presence at Donhead.

It is necessary to refer to the two earliest charters in the Christchurch Cartulary[1] to create the link between Donhead and the bridge at Christchurch. The lands given to Sulfric in both Donhead and Twynham were *free of secular dues save those of military service, fortress work and bridging*. The responsibility for the maintenance of the town's ancient bridges would fall upon the lord of the manor in particular and also other major landowners. It would be a constant drain on their resources and it was not unusual for tolls for their use to be levied at the riverbank, though the right to do this may have been questionable. The importance of bridges as a means of keeping open transport routes was obvious to all, and is even mentioned in Magna Carta. *'No village or individual shall be compelled to make bridges at river banks, except those who from of old were legally bound to do so'.* From the Saxon charters it is clear that there was an ancient legal obligation for the bridges at Twynham to be maintained in good condition, which had later been legally established in Magna Carta. These bridges, over the two arms of the River Avon as well as the smaller one over the millstream would have been constructed of timber. The main balks to form the uprights would probably not have come from oak trees in the nearby New Forest, since that was a royal hunting ground. Suitable oak trees would have had to be found elsewhere and the lighter timbers would perhaps have been of less durable wood, cut nearer at hand. This would have presented an opportunity for local people either to supply the timber necessary for repairs, or provide the labour, some of which would be skilled, that was necessary to carry out the work. The provision of labour would have placed considerable strain on the individual, since in the case of men tied to the land, the work would have to be done after all work due to their landlord had been completed. There was also a community benefit, since those doing the work would be seen by their

---

[1] See chapter 2

fellows and their penitence duly acknowledged. Though no doubt many of those involved resented what they could regard as a public humiliation, in either case there would have been a deterrent effect on possible future offenders. It is interesting that modern Justice has adopted a similar practice in the Community Service penalty now increasingly used in the lower courts. Both then and now, the philosophy of encouraging people to do something positive and constructive for the community that they have harmed, has obvious benefits.

The town's bridges would have been in frequent need of repair as a result of the regular wear and tear that they would have suffered from the constant flow of foot and horse traffic. The heavily laden carts that would daily pass in and out of the town, often with goods brought in by ship to the town quay near the Priory Church, would have taken their toll. The main timber supports suffered occasionally from the effects of the river when in flood. It was not unusual for bridges to be carried away when struck by an accumulation of debris including uprooted trees at times of severe flooding, of which there are numerous recorded examples.

William de Montacute would have had plenty to occupy his mind without having to concern himself with the bridge over the river at the entrance to one small estate amongst his many larger land holdings. It seems likely therefore, that, knowing that he was about to be absent from his estates for some time, he looked for an opportunity to off-load the maintenance of the Twynham bridges onto the shoulders of the sinners of the town itself. If he was indeed at Donhead in June 1331, what better chance had he of achieving such an opportunity, and obtaining the same result for this and other responsibilities he had elsewhere in his large land holdings, probably by obtaining similar indulgences. It is also recorded that Simon Meopham was by no means popular. He had successfully angered many of the greatest in the land and on one occasion his actions had led to a near riot in the West Country. He would therefore have been more than willing to curry favour with one of the King's chief advisers by granting him a small favour with a few indulgences. William de Montacute would have been equally happy to be free of a troublesome, if small, burden.

There are probably two reasons for the later decline in the use of the indulgence system to keep the bridges in good repair. In the first place, the wholesale abuse of indulgences at the time of the building of St. Peter's, Rome, would have brought the system into disrepute. Secondly, shortly afterwards, the wooden bridges of Christchurch-Twynham were replaced by more sturdy stone structures such as we have today. Though initially more costly, once in place, there would have been little need for maintenance other than the occasional resurfacing. It also became more acceptable to charge tolls for the use of a stone bridge that was wider than the previous wooden structure and as such more serviceable. Being a more sturdy structure the populace would be happy to stand on it in their idle hours and peacefully watch the flow of water and the fish beneath. This certainly happens today. A wooden bridge that inevitably vibrated somewhat with the force of the water would not produce the same tranquillity of spirit.

Although some of this must be speculation, it was certainly what was happening up and down the country. Church and State had to work together in most things, even though there was constant competition between the two for supremacy, of which the quarrel between Henry II and Thomas à Becket is but one famous example. What is certain however, is that the bridges at Twynham continued to be properly maintained, so that trade could continue to flourish by land as well as by sea. In addition, the town remained easily accessible to the ever growing number of pilgrims that continued to flock to see and worship the many holy relics, including what were supposed to be bones of saints, that were displayed at the several altars in the great Priory Church.

What may have been a chance meeting between two senior representatives of Church and State, resulting in a mutually convenient accommodation, seems to have had an important and lasting effect on the life of the town. As so often happens, our simplest actions sometimes have continuing effects that at the time no-one could envisage.

Chapter 11

The Black Death 1348 - 1349.

There can be little doubt that one of the most traumatic events that took place in Christchurch-Twynham was the arrival of the Black Death. What we now know to have been Bubonic Plague, first reached the English shore probably in one of two small ships that came into the little harbour of Melcombe, a small hamlet adjacent to Weymouth. The exact date is not certain, but the general consensus seems to indicate that it was sometime during the last week in June 1348. The event is recorded in a 14th century chronicle from the Grey Friars at Lynn, which makes it effectively a contemporary account and as such may be accepted as being accurate. *'In this year 1348, in Melcombe, in the county of Dorset, a little before the Feast of St John the Baptist, two ships, one of them from Bristol, came alongside. One of the sailors had brought with him from Gascony the seeds of the terrible pestilence and, through him, the men of that town of Melcombe were the first in England to be infected'.* If one of the ships came from Bristol, it may be that the doubtful honour of bringing the plague to England should be granted to that city. Much would depend on whether the sailor went ashore there or not. There is also some doubt that the ship came from Gascony to Melcombe, since little trade took place between the two. More likely is that the other ship came from the Channel Islands with which there was regular trade, and where the plague was already rampant. Other chroniclers maintain that the first outbreak was at Southampton. In either case, it could not be long before it reached Christchurch.

The terrible disease seems to have taken two different forms, though the results of each were equally fatal. One version produced tumours particularly in the armpits and groin that might grow to the size of a small apple, finally erupting as a stinking boil. The other version brought internal injury that led first to a high fever, quickly followed by spitting blood. Both versions also brought the patient out in black and livid spots that erupted and led to death. In the case of the bubonic version which brought them out in tumours, death usually occurred within five days, whereas those who contacted the pneumonic version and spat blood usually succumbed within a matter of hours, though they might linger in agony for up to a couple of days.

1348 was by no means the first known occurrence of the plague. As far back as A.D. 543, it is recorded that no less than 200,000 people died in the eastern Roman Empire, centred round Constantinople, whence the plague had arrived from central Asia. Even the

Emperor Justinian succumbed, though he was lucky enough to survive – why we cannot know, though it may have been because he was better fed and lived in cleaner conditions than many of his subjects. Tales of the devastation to the population were naturally brought to these shores, both in A.D. 543 and in later centuries when the plague struck the Middle East. Unfortunately, those living in England either then or during the first few centuries of the second millennium, took little notice, since it was all happening in distant lands. Those living particularly on the south coast of England, failed to realise that they lay at the crossroads of the trade routes from Scandinavia, the Atlantic and Mediterranean coasts of Europe and North Africa and the main continental rivers that flow into the North Sea and English Channel. Along these routes, the Black Death could flow unchecked and into English ports far more easily than it could travel by land across the Alps or other continental land routes. The watery defence behind which the English thought they were sheltered would prove instead to be an efficient route by which the dreaded plague could enter.

The Plague was seen as a punishment from God.

The inhabitants of Christchurch-Twynham would once again have heard plenty of gruesome tales of this horrifying scourge that was gradually sweeping across Europe. The first vague tales reached them sometime around 1346, probably brought by sailors who had travelled to the eastern end of the Mediterranean. Such tales would have found fascinated listeners in the taverns, particularly if the teller used his imagination to enlarge on the horrific effects of the disease. But it would have been of little immediate concern to the listeners, since it was all happening far away in the distant and no doubt magical lands of the Orient. Not until the middle of 1348 did the plague reach Bordeaux and Paris and so come to the immediate notice of the crews of the ships bringing wine and other goods from the Atlantic coasts of Spain, Portugal and France. Rumour had it that the Pope had encouraged men to pray harder and process to their holy shrines to confess their sins and lead better lives. But as everyone knew, those living on the continent of Europe were an aggressive bunch who were constantly trying to recapture land which more properly belonged to England. The plague was therefore God's just revenge on their evil ways and greed. It certainly would not touch England. Did it not spread through the evil mists in the air? And any way, England was an island and surely secure from such pestilence – or so they imagined.

The last week in June 1348 brought a rude awakening to the inhabitants of Melcombe. A sailor died in agonies within a day or two of his arrival. The ship would have immediately been driven from the harbour taking with it its grizzly cargo, which the rest of the crew promptly heaved overboard, probably to be washed up on land somewhere along the coast.

With the regular trade between the Atlantic ports, the Channel Islands, and England, there can be little doubt that within a matter of days, or a week or two at most, a ship similarly affected with the plague would have reached ports along the South Coast. Christchurch-Twynham, and no doubt Wareham and Southampton would almost certainly have suffered the shock of finding themselves likewise afflicted by the terrible scourge that was now known to be decimating the rest of Continental Europe. Exactly when the first case appeared in Christchurch is not known, but clearly it must have been by the middle of July, brought either by one of the rats that all ships carried, or else on the body of one of the crew. Modern medicine has discovered that the disease was carried by a flea, often found on black rats, but it was also carried by man in his clothing.

The effect on the population was devastating. Though it cannot be exactly estimated how much of the population died, and this naturally differed from place to place, it is generally accepted that about one third of the population of the country died. There is no reason to assume that Christchurch would have escaped more lightly that other places. Indeed, because of the amount of cross-channel trade entering the harbour, it seems likely that the town would have been harder hit than some of the more isolated inland towns and villages. One mitigating factor may have been the presence of the great royal forest to the east and the barren heathland to the west, which to some extent would have cut off Christchurch from the neighbouring ports of Southampton and Poole. The plague would therefore have entered the town from a ship, rather than travelling over land from a neighbouring community. It is also possible that, because the water supply for the town was probably purer than in many places and because the dwellings may well have been less crowded together than in other more prosperous towns, there may have been less fertile breeding grounds for the disease. We know from contemporary records that the population of England had not been increasing for some time and in some places had actually decreased, so that there may well have been empty properties in the town and little if any overcrowding within the dwellings themselves. All these factors would have helped to prevent the spread of the disease, though once it had taken hold there was little to prevent a complete household from being afflicted. Why some members of a household died and others survived, we do not know. Perhaps some had a greater immunity than others. Perhaps the fleas that lived on the black rats, which were the main carriers, did not bite some people and so infect them, because their skin repelled them. Perhaps the rats did not enter some homes. There is certainly evidence that rats seemed to keep clear of buildings used for tanning, of which there were probably several in Christchurch. Whatever the reason, many families did escape either completely or in part.

The effect on households must have been shattering. A man would get up in the morning healthy and sit down to break his fast. By lunchtime his flesh was erupting in blackening boils and he was uttering his last gasp. Within a few days there might well be few if any members of the household left alive and yet their neighbours might be unaffected. Certainly each household kept very much to itself and well away from their neighbours for fear of catching the disease, since it was thought that the plague spread through mists and foul air, though rumour and panic spread all kinds of unlikely suggestions.

Men naturally turned to the Church for help and salvation in their hour of need. However neither the pope, bishops nor senior clergy could offer much guidance other than to suggest that men should go in procession to Mass, confess their sins, and submit to all kinds of penance, including flagellation and starvation. This tended to whip up penitential fervour and mass hysteria and bring crowds together rather than disperse them, which almost certainly helped to spread rather than control the disease.

Bodies of Plague victims deposited in large communal graves.

The clerics themselves tended to divide into two groups. Those like the bishops and other senior clergy who had isolated manors or well-protected dwellings, to which they could retire, frequently did so, in attempt to cut themselves off from all contact with the plague. One bishop wrote complaining about the lack of priests willing to take on new parishes or visit the sick 'perhaps for fear of contagion or infection' – and who could blame them. The wealthy discovered to their cost that stout walls or even moats were no protection against the rats and their infected fleas. Others, particularly parish priests and members of the monastic Orders, especially when a lead was given by the Abbot or Prior, felt it their Christian duty to be amongst their afflicted flocks and suffer with them if necessary and by their presence, try to ease the burdens and anxieties of the humbler folk.

It seems likely that the Prior at Christchurch may well have been one such. Records show that priors tended to hold their office for a considerable length of time, presumably from the date of their appointment until their death. The 1793 list of priors provided by Richard Warner who was a pupil in St Michael's Loft School and ultimately was elected a Fellow of the Royal Society, provides some interesting information. Though Warner's list differs from other authorities, his has the merit of more precise detail, and often gives both the day and month as well as the year of a prior's installation.

89

According to Warner, when Richard de Leigh, prior from 21st August 1340, died, his successor, Henry Eyre, was appointed in March 1347 and was himself succeeded by William Tyrwachus on 18th March 1349. He continued in office till succeeded by John Wodenham on 21st July 1377, a period of 28 years. Unless he died a very old man, it seems likely that he was appointed as a fairly young man, perhaps because in 1349 there were few senior and experienced clerics still alive to take on the heavy burden of running a priory the size of Christchurch. Since Henry Eyre only held office for 2 years, it seems quite likely that he, like so many of his brother priests succumbed to the plague. Such was the disruption caused by the Black Death, that it is likely that many priors and abbots did not receive the usual official seal of appointment at the time but had to wait until life had returned more to normal conditions.

We do not know how many of the 24 Canons Regular, who comprised the establishment at Christchurch, fell victims of the plague, for there are no extant records. Assuming that Christchurch fared no better or worse that the average town in Dorset, it is probable that about 30% of the population of the town died and perhaps as many as 50% of the canons. This higher figure could be explained by the fact that the canons would have put themselves in greater danger by ministering to the sick and dying. On the other hand, the canons probably lived in cleaner surroundings than the ordinary folk, and would therefore be less likely to come into contact with the black rats carrying the disease. However, it is known for example that nearly 48% of the beneficed clergy in the neighbouring diocese of Bath and Wells died of the Black Death. Since there were many trading ports along the coast of the Winchester diocese, it is unlikely that the percentage of clergy deaths would have been lower here. It is also recorded that no less than 100 Dorset benefices required new incumbents in the 7 months from October 1348 to April 1349, the period when the plague was at its most severe in this area. Though there are no records that priests, other than the prior, were appointed at Christchurch during the period, Shaftesbury had to appoint no less than 4 vicars between the end of November 1348 and mid May 1349. Wareham also lost the head of its priory in October 1348 and two vicars had to be appointed in December that year, and two others in May and June the following year.

The dearth of priests undermined the position of the church in several ways. It was customary for the dying to confess their sins and receive Extreme Unction on their deathbed, and thus secure their way to Heaven. This now frequently became impossible, and one bishop told his priests that *The Sacrament of the Eucharist, when no priest is available, may be administered by a deacon. If, however, there is no priest to administer the Sacrament of Extreme Unction, then, as in other matters, faith must suffice'*. It was also ordained that where no priest was available, a man might confess to his neighbour rather than die unshriven. Whether such a desperate situation existed in Christchurch may be doubtful, since, with an original complement of 24 canons, some must surely have survived.

Because Christchurch was an important trading port with the Channel Islands and Bordeaux and the Normandy ports, it seems inevitable that the loss of life during the short period from mid 1348 to mid 1349 would have been devastating. At least one third of the population would have died, leaving perhaps the same number of properties empty. Indeed the number of empty properties may well have been higher, since it was common for whole families to decamp to what they hoped would be safer and more isolated areas as soon as the plague struck. Many would never have returned, since they would have settled in already empty hovels in other parts of the county and taken over previously abandoned land. This they would have been encouraged to do by their new landlord, who would be only too pleased to have someone to till his fields and pay even a small rental for their few acres. Such a system was already growing with the increase of sheep farming which needed less labour. However, with fewer crops being grown, prices began to rise and with them wages but not rents, so that landlords found themselves worse off. Thus it seems likely that, like other places, the economy of the town would have suffered considerably. Not only would this have affected the agriculture, but also the fishing industry. It is known, for example, that Edward III had to write to the Governor of Jersey to tell him that *'By reason of the mortality among the people and fishing folk of these islands, which here as elsewhere has been so great, our rent for the fishing which has been yearly paid us, cannot be now obtained without the impoverishing and excessive oppression of those fishermen still left.'* What was true of Jersey would have been equally true of Christchurch.

By December 1349 it seems that the plague in Dorset had run its course, and life was beginning to return to something near normality. Services of thanksgiving were taking place, attended by all those who had survived. The Priory Church at Christchurch might perhaps have been half filled by those who had survived, though as they looked round at the empty spaces where their friends whom they had helped to bury once stood, they must have wondered if life could ever be the same.

It is difficult to know how the survivors would have felt. Philip Ziegler, in his excellent book on the Black Death likens the effects of the plague to the way people reacted to the continuous wartime bombing of London or other major cities. First there was anger directed against the 'enemy' coupled with vows of vengeance and stoical pride in the courage and solidarity with the victims. Why else would men have been prepared to risk their own lives to succour their afflicted neighbours? There would also have been panic at times and a brief breakdown in morale. The capacity to remain disciplined or produce rational responses to the terrible events that seemed to be overwhelming them would have been strained to the limits. Ultimately there would follow apathy and indifference and later still a grudging acceptance of events and an adaptation of life to the needs of the new situation. Where the Church could not help and what Man could not cure and when the rich were as likely to die as the poor were, the common folk would have to endure. Consequently, when the plague had done its worst, killing off a man's friends and relations, those who were left returned to till their fields and cultivate what they could. The medieval Englishman of all classes, like his World War II successor, obstinately decided to carry on as he had before so far as he could. Things were far from being normal, but both landlord and peasant did their best to make them so. Where tenants had died, so far as was possible, their successors still paid oxen or cattle as 'heriots' so that they could inherit the land of their dead kinsmen. However the manorial system which was already breaking down, continued its more rapid decline. Life in Christchurch was never to be the same again.

By the end of 1350, a visitor to Christchurch would probably have noticed a marked difference in the town to what he had known say three years previously. As he approached the town bridges he would have seen many uncultivated fields. The bridge he crossed to enter the town would be in need of repair and he could see that many of the houses were empty and showing signs of decay. Roofs would be leaking, and doors and windows missing, while the gardens round the dwellings would be weed-filled and neglected. The market would be unnaturally quiet, with little either for sale or being bought. There is unfortunately no record of how many of the burgesses suffered, or if the mayors survived, since there are no records of who was mayor between the years 1320 and 1397, but inevitably some would have succumbed. Those burgesses who did survive no doubt did their best with the prior and remaining canons to rally the spirits of the remaining citizens. As in every other town and village throughout the country, there would probably have been an air of despondency, but also signs of resurgent activity. Being a robust race, the English peasant would find a means of rising above adversity, turning it to his advantage wherever possible.

There would appear to be documentary evidence to suggest that some of the survivors seem to have realised their good fortune, and given thanks in a positive way. No doubt they were encouraged to do so by the new prior and remaining burgesses. The records of the Leper Hospital of St Mary Magdalen situated on the Portfield, show that on 10th January 1349 *'A grant from Walter son of William Williames for the good of the souls of his father, mother, brother, sister, ancestors and heirs to the master of the Lazar House and his companions of two acres of land in Portfield which his father purchased from John Drynckhard and lying between the land of Richard Chaffeyn in the north and Richard Pennard in the south'*. Since so many of his family seem to have died, it appears likely that they may have succumbed to the plague. A little later, *'on Saturday before the feast of St Mark'*, that is shortly before 25th April 1349, there was gifted by *'John, son and heir of Richard le Blake for the good of his soul and the souls of his father and ancestors to the master of the leper house of Christchurch Twynham and the lepers and other such persons therein abiding, of a moiety of a messuage and curtilage adjoining, in the borough of Christchurch Twynham between the tenement of John Brown in the south and the tenement of William Wychwolf in the north - without the Bargate'*. This seems to imply that sick people other than lepers were housed there at that time. *'The souls of his father and ancestors'* could imply that several of the family had died recently, perhaps of the plague, though there is no definite proof of this. Likewise on the *'Wednesday after the feast of St Thomas, Archbishop and Martyr. Power of attorney from Andrew Elys to William Rogers to deliver seizin of '2 acres of land in the Portfield to the master of the Lazar House'*. Next year, 1350 in November, in a deed made on the Monday after All Saints, *'John Feron of Poole granted to the master of the Lazar House and the lepers and other sick therein two acres of arable land situated together in Courtie Croft at Holdenhurst in frankalmoign for the souls of himself and his parents'*. This was the area where the hospice of the Leper Hospital was situated. Could it be that these various citizens, having survived the plague, gave thanks for their survival by giving the Leper Hospital a property or some land? According to the hospital records, the last gift before the plague was 23 years before, in 1325, and the next gift after the plague was 13 years later in 1367. There appear to have been no similar gifts to the Priory. Nor do the town's documents now contain any charters between the years 1331 and 1385, though such a lack does not prove that none originally existed. That the hospital rather than the Priory received these four gifts, may be because those who were struck down by the plague were taken to the hospital just outside the town walls, rather than the Priory's infirmary. There are two reasons for this. First, the treatment at the leper hospital and its isolation from the rest of the community may well have been more effective than what was on offer in the Priory infirmary. Second, by common consent, people would have wished those infected to be isolated as soon as possible. The leper hospital would have satisfied this desire. If this is true, and since the Church had proved to be ineffective in controlling the spread of the plague, then benefactors may well have preferred to make their gifts to the hospital rather than the Priory.

Christchurch, like every other city, town and village in the country, would have been shattered by the Black Death. It is fair to assume that the number of deaths would have been no less than the country's average of about 30 to 35% of its inhabitants. The presence of a thriving monastic community within the town probably provided greater support for the inhabitants than in towns where no such community existed. Likewise, the existence of the leper hospital just outside its walls, to which those stricken down could be quickly removed, may have helped to provide some comfort to the survivors. They could feel that at least something was being done on their behalf.

There were however many permanent changes. Much of the 120 acres of the Portfield as well as much other land, was parcelled out amongst new tenants who henceforward farmed the acres for themselves, paying money rents rather than service to their landlord. Fishing, boat-building and water-borne trade probably began to play a greater part, particularly as a result of the increase of woollen exports. (The importance of this growing trade was appreciated by Edward III when in 1347 he instituted 'Poundage', a tax on every pound of wool exported.) In one sense, the plague did the country a service, since the country had been considerably over-populated, so that peasants seldom cultivated sufficient land to provide enough food to properly fill the bellies of their families. The plague certainly corrected that, though in an unpleasantly dramatic way and it was to be a century or more before the population began to regain anything like the figure it had attained before 1348

A new era was beginning, to which everyone would have to adapt if they were to survive. As usual, they did.

Chapter 12

The Manumission of Thomas Aylward, 1481

One of the more unusual documents to be found in the town's archives is a beautifully preserved parchment that turns out to be a 'Manumission'. Such documents had been in use at least since Roman times. Then they referred to the freeing of a slave. In the wealthier Roman households it was not uncommon to find highly educated slaves, who were often Greeks, acting as tutors to the children of the patricians. As such, they were respected members of the household, even though they were slaves. It became common practice, in the great days of the Roman Empire particularly, for such slaves to be given their freedom when their chief purpose of educating the children had been accomplished. They might well continue thereafter as members of the household, frequently becoming the confidants of the parents. Slavery therefore did not always mean outright oppression, though for many, particularly for those at the bottom of the social scale, it frequently was. As always, much depended on the nature and quality of the master of the household. Certainly in Roman times, freedom was highly valued, since only free men could claim justice under Roman Law. When St Paul uttered the famous phrase *'Civis Romanus sum'* – I am a Roman Citizen – he thus claimed his right to be tried in Rome where he could hope for a fair trial.

In medieval England, particularly until the time of the Black Death in 1348/9, a fair proportion of the population were bound to the land, and could be bought and sold like cattle as part of the stock on the landholding. Others were free in the sense that they worked the land that they rented from their overlord in return for a number of days' labour on the lord's demesne. This was usually divided into 'week-work' which meant doing so many days labour on the demesne each week, and 'boon-work' which entailed extra days working for the lord of the manor at harvest and ploughing time, the busiest periods in the agricultural year. There were also various extra tasks to be performed, such as carting loads for the manor, and payment in kind of such things as fowls and eggs. These several tasks tended to make a large proportion of the population not free in one way or another, since the lord of the manor depended on these people to cultivate his demesne. All these people were collectively known as 'villeins', though technically a villein was only one class amongst many different categories of the labour force. Nor was there any set pattern of servitude. There was a further complication, in that Roman law, on which English law is based, treated serfs as chattels with no rights, though in practice, unless they were actual slaves, most men were free to a lesser or greater degree.

With the passage of time, coinage began to replace barter, whether of goods or service, as the means of conducting trade. This led to the payment of money rents rather than service. The arrival of the Black Death, which swept away about one third of the population obviously hastened this change, partly because so many families decamped to what they hoped was an area free of the plague. Though technically illegal, few landlords were prepared to send such people back to their former village, being only too happy to have some labour to cultivate their land that otherwise would have lain derelict. There they were able to sell their labour for cash rather than service to their new lord and with the dearth of labour could often set their own price. The reverse also became increasingly common, with men paying the rent for their land in cash. In both cases, men felt increasingly free, as they became masters of their own time.

The result of all these changes was that there were increasingly fewer serfs. Enlightened landowners also found it more uncomfortable to 'own' men and tended to grant long serving servants their freedom. This was usually done in the time-honoured way used by the Romans. A man was 'Manumitted' by placing in his hands the document setting him free. (from the Latin 'Manu' = hand, 'Mitto' = to let go. i.e. to set at liberty.) Such a document was given to Thomas Aylward by the Abbot of Athelney, an abbey situated about four miles from Bridgwater in Somerset. It has come down to us, carefully written in the shortened Latin of the day, beautifully preserved having been carefully folded in four, so that it could be secreted in a man's scrip if need be. In translation it reads:-

'To all the believers in Christ to whom the present writing shall come, Robert by god's sufferance Abbot of the monastery of Athelney and the Convent of St. Benedict of the same place, sends greeting in the everlasting Lord. Be it known that we, the aforesaid Abbot Robert and the convent with one accord and will have manumitted and made free Thomas Aylward, son of Peter Aylward lately and for a long time in the county of Somerset our villein, with all his household, both those born and those yet to be born, with all the goods and chattels of the same Thomas. So that the same Thomas, as aforesaid, with all his household both those born and yet to be born with all the goods and chattels of the same Thomas, in this way shall be free as far as we and our successors are concerned, and discharged from the whole yoke of slavery serfdom and villeinage by these presents. In witness of which our seal is appended to the present agreement. Given at the aforesaid Athelney in our Chapter house the fourth day of the month of June, the

twenty first year of the reign of King Edward IV after the Conquest.
[Monday 4th June 1481].'

Though the abbot's seal is missing, we know what it looked like, since several examples still exist. The 15th century version was circular and about 2½ inches in diameter. It takes the form of three niches, containing the principle patrons of the abbey. Where earlier versions of the seal had shown St Athelwine of Athelney, the central figure now depicts Christ, His right hand raised in benediction, his left hand holding an orb with a long cross and flag. To his left is St Peter, identifiable as a pope, and to his right is St Paul holding a sword and a book. To the left of the niches is a shield with a horn and three crowns, and to the right three crowns quartered with a cross. Round the rim of the seal runs the Latin legend *'Sigillum Comune Abbitis et Conventus de Athelney'* (The seal of the abbey and convent of Athelney). Like most important seals, it is a beautiful piece of craftsmanship that required great skill to cast, making it almost impossible to copy. It is indeed a pity that the seal is now missing from this fascinating document.

What thoughts must have passed through the mind of Thomas Aylward as Abbot Robert placed this parchment in the hands of this newly freed man? No longer were he and his family serfs, but free men and women. Henceforth, Thomas could live and work where he liked. He had become one of the Yeomen of England, self-reliant and responsible and able to rise from fettered serfdom to make of his life what he would. No wonder he took the parchment carefully and placed it safely in his scrip. It was his passport to a new life for himself and his family. Thomas Aylward must have left the presence of the abbot and his chapter with head held high and a firm step as he returned to his home to show his family with great pride the evidence of his newly acquired freedom. It must have been an excited if apprehensive household that day, as they contemplated their free future.

We know that Athelney was a Benedictine House and the Abbot, Robert Hylle, or Hull, held that office from 1458, three years after the start of the War of the Roses, until 1485, the year of the Battle of Bosworth that ended the war between the Lancastrians and the Yorkists. His time as Abbot of Athelney was therefore one of confusion and discord, though how much he was directly affected by the fighting we do not know. Certainly life for him, as for the prior at Christchurch would have been difficult and he must have been an old and tired man when he decided to free Thomas Aylward, and perhaps others of his household. Athelney Abbey may have been in a state of decline at that period with the buildings in need of considerable repairs and even re-building. With civil war raging, it was not the time to attempt to raise the necessary funds for such major works. There is also evidence that the abbey may have backed the wrong side at some period during or shortly after the war, since in 1497, Robert Hylle's successor was fined 100 marks for supporting the pretender Perkin Warbeck. If things were not going well for the abbey in 1481, there would have been sound reasons for the abbot, nearing the end of his life, to try to make peace with his Maker by setting at liberty those of his household who had served him long and well. Certainly the practice was becoming increasingly common. In Thomas Aylward's case, it seems that he was a man of substance since he owned goods and may even have been renting land from the abbot. The Manumission specifically states that he had both goods and chattels. He was also clearly married with a family, all of whom were to be freed. It is not however clear how old he was, since the reference to his household 'both born and yet to be born' could refer to grandchildren rather than just his own offspring. In view of his possessions, it is probable that he was himself at least in mid-life.

An important question still remains to be answered. How did this document come to be in the Christchurch town archives? Athelney Abbey was a Benedictine House and situated over 100 miles from Twynham, whereas the convent here was under the rule of St Augustine, whose prior between 1477 and 1502 was the first John Draper. It may be that Thomas Aylward had decided that there was little prospect of advancement in the area of Bridgwater and that he felt that he and his family would have a better chance of prospering if he moved nearer to the centre of things. It is not known exactly when he and his family came to Twynham. Perhaps it was after the accession of Henry VII in 1485, in which year the King gave the Manor of Twynham to his mother, Margaret Countess of Richmond. Alternatively, it may have been before that date, since the previous Lord of the Manor of Twynham had been the de Montacute family, who also held estates in the vicinity of Bridgwater. That would be reason enough to choose Twynham.

At whatever date he came here, Thomas Aylward, presumably, would have visited the constable and presented his credentials as a free man. This would have been important, since without such knowledge, the constable would have been at liberty to arrest him and return him from whence he came. Having cleared his position with the civil authority, no doubt he would have gone to see the prior. Though under a different rule, the prior would have taken note of Robert Hylle's action in freeing Thomas Aylward. From it he could assume that here was an honest hard-working man who could be trusted and if a place could be found for him, would probably serve the Twynham

Priory as well as he had served the abbey at Athelney. If there were no place readily available on the Priory's estates, then the prior would have used his best endeavours, in Christian charity, to find him employment with someone else in the town. That could well have been with one of the burgesses, most of them were the more successful traders or larger farmers in the town.

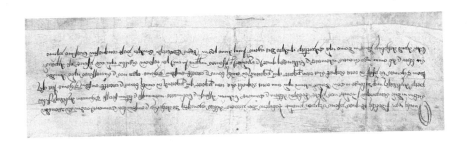

Thomas Aylward's Manumission.

It may be assumed that Thomas Aylward, having shown his freedom certificate to those authorities in the town who needed to see it, would have put the document away in some safe place, since it was of immense importance to him. It is possible that he may have lodged it either with the prior or the mayor for safekeeping, obtaining a receipt for it to show to any who might question his right to live and work as a free man in Twynham. If it were lodged with the mayor, then it would certainly explain how the document came to be in the town's archives. Since more and more men were acquiring their freedom, it is probable that there were other similar documents circulating amongst the inhabitants of Twynham. The pity of it is that we do not have any others.

Men like Thomas Aylward, who had the enterprise to move with their families to a completely new area, and set themselves up as free men to make their own way in life, would have a great deal to offer to the town where they finally settled. It was such men as him, the Yeomen of England, who by their self-reliance and ambition, helped in his generation as in later centuries, to bring prosperity to Twynham.

Chapter 13

John Draper - the Last Prior, 1520 - 1539.

It is not uncommon to find that people who lived in the Middle Ages and Tudor times, left behind them remarkably little information about their lives. John Draper, the last prior of the Augustinian convent at Christchurch, is one such person, particularly for his early years. Even such world-famous people as William Shakespeare leave us in doubt as to when exactly they were born, though, unlike him, we do at least know where John Draper is buried. He lies beneath his tomb slab that now rests outside his chantry at the eastern end of the South Quire Aisle of the Priory Church.

The early years of John Draper's life seem to be shrouded in mystery. Indeed, the earliest record we have of him is 1520, the date that he succeeded William Eyre as Prior at Twynham. It is unlikely that he would have been appointed to such an important post before he had proved himself as a wise and efficient priest, so it is probable that he would, by then, have been in the middle years of his life. This is further borne out by the fact that he lived for another 32 years until 1552. Assuming that he lived into his 70's, a not uncommon age even in those days, this would mean that he was appointed Prior at about the age of 40. He would then have been young enough to be able to hold office for 20 to 30 years as seems to have been the average, but old enough to have the necessary experience that would carry weight with the older canons in the convent.

It is however recorded that there was a previous John Draper who was elected Prior in 1477. He preceded William Eyre who was elected in 1502. The previous year, 1501, there had been a very thorough visitation of the Priory of which certain details exist. Thirteen of the 24 canons, including the prior, John Draper, are named and their offices are given, so that there are eleven unnamed. Had one of these been the second John Draper, then presumably he would have been named, even if he was only a novice or a junior member of the community, if only to differentiate him from the prior with the same name. It can be assumed therefore that he came to Christchurch sometime after 1502, when William Eyre was Prior. It must also be assumed that the second Draper was not a direct descendant of the first, since a prior, or any priest, could not marry. He might however have been a more distant relative; perhaps the son or more likely a grandson of the brother of the first John Draper, since the second was elected Prior 43 years after the first. Nepotism was rife as always, and it is not unreasonable to assume that the first John Draper may have assisted his younger relative to obtain a profitable and secure position in a neighbouring abbey or priory. He may well have put it to his sub prior, William Eyre, that if, in due course, a suitable vacancy were to occur at the Twynham Convent, the young John Draper should be offered it.

So far as can be ascertained, there is no record of where John Draper was educated. He probably attended the University of Oxford, or possibly Cambridge. It is also quite likely that if he was ambitious, he also attended one of the major continental universities as well, to broaden his knowledge and experience. Unless he had particularly influential friends at court and amongst the bishops, such wider experience would have been essential to enable him to climb the ecclesiastical ladder. This we know he did, since in about 1532, twelve years after he became Prior, he was appointed as a suffragan bishop of Winchester. At that time, this entailed a visit to Rome, in order to receive his episcopal authority from the Pope. He would have been one of the last English bishops to do so, since Henry put a stop to the practice soon after he had himself declared Head of the English Church. The title John Draper received was Bishop of Neapolis. This was probably the city on the eastern coast of Macedonia (now part of Greece), that was visited by St Paul on his third journey. In early Christian times, there had been a bishop there, but the see had long since ceased to exist, since the whole area had long been under the Muslim control. It was the custom for suffragan bishops, who had to be attached to a Christian see somewhere, to be given such titles *'in partibus infidelium'* - 'in heathen parts'. Unlike diocesan bishops, who usually held a variety of livings, besides frequently being great officers of state, with all the revenues that such positions would bring, suffragan bishops survived on the fees they could collect for the duties they performed. Their income was largely payment by results, with a modest £40 or £50 being the stipend attached to the appointment. Though such an amount would provide for a basic living, it was certainly insufficient to maintain a bishop's household. The duties they performed were mainly pastoral and particularly itinerant, such as confirmation of children, ordination of clergy, dedication and consecration of churches and churchyards, and their re-consecration when they had been desecrated, and anointing virgins for example. They also acted sometimes as visiting inspectors, to see that the local priests were performing their duties conscientiously. A suffragan's duties necessarily took him all over the diocese to which he was attached.. In those days the Diocese of Winchester stretched from the Parish of Twynham including Holdenhurst on the coast, north via the Cranborne Chase to Malmsbury and then east to Cricklade. The northern boundary was the River Thames as far as Southwark, where the Bishop of Winchester had his prison in Clink Street. The boundary then turned south as far as Lingfield, and then west to Bramshot, before turning south again to join the coast at Hayling Island. It also included the Isle of Wight, where the Priory of Twynham held various estates. John Draper would therefore have been acquainted with quite a large area of southern England, including some large abbeys and monasteries, and several convents, like Twynham, of the Augustinian order.

We know, also, that Henry VIII appointed John Draper to be one of his personal chaplains. Such an appointment must have implied that he was already well known at Court and indeed had the confidence of the King. The duties were fairly light, being mainly preaching before his Majesty on occasions and perhaps sometimes acting as a spiritual advisor to the royal children. He may occasionally have had to hear the King's confession if his usual confessor were not on hand. Certainly no king, and particularly Henry VIII, would have appointed anyone to a position where he could hear and absolve the Royal Sins unless he had absolute trust in him. It is safe to assume therefore, that John Draper had both the King's ear and his trust.

By the late 1530's, John Draper would have been well aware of Henry's intentions concerning the future, not only of the lax and inefficient chantries and abbeys, but also of the great and well-run houses, of which Twynham was certainly one. Having persuaded the bishops to appoint him Supreme Head of the Church in England - though they were canny enough to add the phrase "so far as the laws of God allow" - Henry proceeded to have collated a complete register of all the Church's land holdings, known as the 'Valor Ecclesiasticus'. He would have remembered that his predecessor, William the Norman, had acted similarly when he had assembled the great Domesday Record of all the land in England in 1086. The Twynham Convent's lands were assessed as *'five hundred and twenty eight pounds six shillings and one farthing and one pound of pepper and one pound of cummin'*. This not only supported the prior and his 24 canons, but enabled them to perform their many charitable, medical and educational duties, in some comfort. In addition the vicarage had *'settled land known as the glebe land tithe the obligations and other casual payments as recorded in the notebooks of sixteen pounds'*. This provided the income for John Smith, the Vicar. The initial reason for Henry's enquiries were to discover the value of the tithe, or tenth part, of these assets which, as Head of the English Church, would now be paid to him rather than the Pope. So far as the Priory was concerned, this would have amounted to £31.4s.11d, since there were considerable expenses that could be offset against the gross income. The vicar would have had to pay £1.12s.0d. However it soon became clear that the King's ultimate purpose was to take over and suppress all religious houses - though not parish churches.

Being well aware of the King's intentions, John Draper wrote personally to Henry in 1538, pleading that the Twynham Convent should be spared. The letter survives and includes the following.

'... your place of Christchurch-Twynham, nigh to your New Forest, in your county of Southampton, ... is situate and set in a desolate place of your realm and in a very barren county out and far from all highways in an angle or a corner, having no woods nor commodious country about it, nor nigh no good town, but only the said poor town of Christchurch, which is a very poor town and slenderly inhabited, nor hath no commodius domaines, neither temporal nor lordships royal of temporal lands but only certain poor villages and granges and the most part with farms of parsonages and spiritual tithes, the church of which place is not only a church and a place for poor religious men but also is the parish church unto the said town of Christchurch and of the other hamlets thereabouts, parishioners to the same in the which parish is the number of 15 or 16 hundred house-lying people and above, and neither church, town nor parish of any substance where any honourable or honest man may have any succour or repose, on horseback or o n foot, nigh thereto by the space of eight or nine miles and someways by the space of 16 or 18 miles but only that poor place of Christchurch to the which both rich and poor doth repair and repose'.

Having thus painted as black a picture of the town as he felt able and knowing that Henry personally had never visited the town, John Draper then elaborated on the support given by the canons to the town of Twynham.

'Daily there relieved and sustained with bread and ale purposely baked and brewed for the weakly, to no little quantities, according to their foundation, and a house ordained purposely for them and their officers according duly given attendance to serve them to their great comfort and relief. Which charitable alms appeareth in your Majesty's books where it is your Majesty's goodness graciously allowed and your said orators and their predecessors have used continually hitherto to keep a master to teach grammar to children and scholars there and certain of them having meat, drink and clothes. And now according to your godly ordinance in your grace's visitation it is also kept continually a lecture of Divinity'.

This last point may have been made to imply to Henry that Christ-church supported his theological thesis which had earned for the King the title of *'Fidei Defensor'* (Defender of the Faith) from the Pope - a title English sovereigns have ever since been proud to proclaim. It is likely also that the reference to the provision of bread and ale for the poor was a deliberate reminder to Henry that exactly the same thing was happening daily at St Cross in Winchester, not a mile from his Court when he made his frequent visits to that town. This 'dole', probably the oldest in the country, is still available on request today.

John Draper then reminds Henry that *'if the said place there should be suppressed and lack then should not only the said town and parish but also the country thereabout decay and be right bare and desolate to the great ruin and desolation of that part of a little corner of your realm to a great pity'.*

Somerford Grange.

Unfortunately John Draper's pleas seem to have fallen on deaf ears, at least at first and the convent at Christchurch was suppressed along with every other religious house in the land. As with many other abbeys and monasteries, though the lands were taken and sold to the King's friends, not all the buildings were destroyed. The full details of what was taken, what was left and the pensions that were paid to the canons, are all known and are recorded, amongst other places, in my book 'John Draper's Treasure - a tale of Christchurch'. It is clear from

104

the size of the pension awarded to John Draper - £133.6s.8d a year and the Manor of Somerford to live in for the rest of his life - that he was regarded highly. This was indeed one of the largest pensions paid to any dispossessed prior or abbot. The comparison with even the elderly sub prior's pension of £10 is stark while the other canons received either £6.13s.4d. or a bare £6. However we may be sure that John Draper was able to find positions for at least some of these either in vacant benefices elsewhere in the diocese or as clerks or secretaries to some of the new owners of the confiscated estates. Their help would have been invaluable to the new landowners, since they at least could read and write and keep the accounts, while some may even have had personal knowledge of some of the estates. There is, however, no mention of John Smith, the Vicar of the parish, who was almost certainly one of the canons, receiving a pension. This was presumably deliberate, since he was supposed to continue to have the 'cure' of the souls of the parishioners - even if he did not have a church in which to celebrate Mass.

From the surrender document, which valued the Priory's assets as totalling £519.3s.6¼d, it seems that there was from the beginning some confusion. In the first place, Henry never suppressed or destroyed a parish church. Secondly, the surrender document specifically states that only two of the Priory's seven bells were to be removed, the other five being assigned to the parish. This would reduce the church from cathedral status to that of an ordinary parish church. The confusion lies in the fact that the surrender document specifically states that the church was deemed superfluous and the lead that was to be stripped from the church roof was also valued. Where, then were the people of Christchurch and the surrounding villages now supposed to worship?

It is probable that John Draper was able to exert some influence on the commissioners, in particular Robert Southwell, the head of the local commission and Richard Poulet, who was charged with receiving the property, treasures and goods during their time in Christchurch. There is evidence of this in Southwell's letter to Henry in which he lists particularly important items of gold and jewelled treasures that the Priory then owned, all of which had been gifts from wealthy pilgrims and other devout visitors. Of particular interest are *'two goodly basins double gilt having the king's arms well enamelled'*. Which king had given these to the Priory is not known, but the purpose of mentioning them may well have been to point out to Henry that at least one of his predecessors had had an unusually high opinion of the place, which he could do well to remember. Two matters mentioned in Southwell's letter are interesting. He states first that *'we found the prior a very honest comfortable person and the house well furnished with jewels and plate* ... and later on he says *'The surveying of the demesnes of this house which be large and barren and some parts thereof twenty miles from the monastery...'* Could there have been some collusion between Robert Southwell and John Draper? Provided Henry received plenty in the form of gold and silver plate and jewels, he might not have been too concerned about the value of the lands which were said to be scattered and barren and would in any case be sold off cheaply to his friends. Certainly Southwell seems to imply that John Draper was very co-operative over the seizure of his house and assets, a fact that was perhaps recognised in the size of the pension he was granted.

It is also worth remembering that, although Henry was eager to acquire the vast wealth of the religious houses, he had no intention of destroying the parish churches of the Church of which he was now head. This goes some way towards explaining why in 1540 Henry was persuaded to return the whole church building intact, something that happened at only one other place, Tewkesbury Abbey. The argument put forward was probably that though Henry could certainly suppress the Convent and destroy its buildings and the monastic part of the church, namely the Great Quire and the chantry chapels beside it, he should leave intact the crypt chapel beneath it that was used by the parish. He should also leave the West Tower, and the nave, with its parish altar, the North and South Transepts with their chapels and crypt chapels beneath, and also the Lady Chapel to the east of the monastic Quire, since all these parts were for the use of the parish-ioners as opposed to the Augustinian Canons. Such partial destruction would have created almost impossible structural complications for the surviving parish church. Certainly the mayor and burgesses played an important part in petitioning Henry with these arguments for the return of the church, though it is probable that John Draper gave them the benefit of his advice. This would be based on his personal knowledge of the King and how best to frame their arguments so that they would carry most weight with the King, as well as using the tacit support suggested in Southwell's letter. Whether they did this in person or by letter is not known, but it was probably the former. The end result was certainly very satisfactory for the town.

On 23rd October 1540, having previously agreed verbally to what was then put into the Charter, Henry wrote, *'Know ye that we, at the humble supplication of Edward Lewyn and Robert Westbury gentlemen, and Thomas Hancocke and James Trym, yeomen, Wardens of the parish Church of Christchurch Twynham, in our county of Southampton, and the Inhabitants of our town of Christchurch Twynham aforesaid, of our special grace, certain knowledge and mere motion, have given and granted, and by these presents do give and*

*grant, that the aforesaid Wardens and inhabitants of our town
aforesaid, shall be one body and have perpetual succession and be
persons able and capable in law; and that the same Wardens and
Inhabitants of the Town aforesaid, under the name of Wardens and
Inhabitants of the Town aforesaid, of out gift may be able to receive,
have and enjoy, the site, foundation, ambit, circuit, and precinct of the
Church of the late Monastery or Priory of Christchurch Twynham, in
the county aforesaid and the entire Church aforesaid, that is to say, as
well as the choir, belfry, stones, timber, iron, glass, and lead of the
roof and gutters of the aforesaid Church, as everything whereof the
Church is erected, built and covered; and the Churchyard of the same
Church, lying and being on the north part of the church aforesaid;
together with the seven bells now hanging in the belfry aforesaid to
them and their successors for ever. ... ...All and singular which
premises came into our hands by reason or pretence of a certain Deed
of Gift, Grant and Confirmation thereof made to Us, our heirs and
successors by the late Prior and Convent of the said Monastery. To
have and to hold the said Church of the late Prior and Monastery or
Priory, and all and singular the premises, to the aforesaid Wardens
and Inhabitants and their successors for ever in as ample a manner
and form as the late Prior and Convent, ...To the intent that the
aforesaid Wardens and Inhabitants and their successors for the future,
shall have and enjoy, and use the said Church of the late Priory or
Monastery of Christchurch aforesaid as the Parish Church of all the
parishioners of the Town and Parish of Christchurch Twynham
aforesaid. ... ...'.* This charter Henry himself sealed.

As has been said, this singular success must surely be attributed in
large measure to John Draper. It is also interesting that the King
specifically stated that seven bells were to be returned to the town.
The implication must be that the church was still to be regarded as
being almost of cathedral status, which its size certainly warranted.
However the two bells that had already been removed, were never
returned, for the very good reason that they had almost certainly by
then been melted down and re-cast into cannons for the King's ships,
at the royal dockyard of Chatham. A further matter of interest is that
John Smith, the Vicar of the parish, was never given the freehold of
his church, - this remaining in the hands of the Wardens and
townsfolk, - a state of affairs that exists perhaps uniquely today.

Having been largely instrumental in obtaining the return of the
church to the town, we may assume that John Draper, even though he
now had no official position in the town, would have continued to
assist the vicar in every way possible. He was after all still a suffragan
bishop and as such could visit his late Priory Church whenever
invited. The details of his published will, which is quoted in full in

'John Draper's Treasure', seems to imply that, even though he had by then been appointed a canon of Winchester Cathedral, he continued to take a great interest in the affairs of Christchurch and its inhabitants. There are certain specific gifts to named people in Christchurch, besides a more general bequest for the benefit of the poor of the town.

There is one other matter in which John Draper almost certainly had a hand. As a result of Henry's gift of the church to the 'Wardens and Inhabitants of Christchurch' and the King having established them as a 'lawful body', it became necessary for a group of men to be appointed with proper powers to oversee the maintenance and running of the church and churchyard. With his legal knowledge and wide practical experience of running the Priory through its chapter, John Draper would have been able to advise on how best to set up such a body and outline the powers they should have and their jurisdiction. No doubt if John Beverey, the elderly sub-prior and also William Clerk who, as Precentor, was responsible for the fabric, had remained in the area in retirement, they too would have been of great assistance, though it is doubtful if they would have been members of the new body. There are no contemporary records of its exact composition, nor the exact date when it was established, but there are a series of minute books in the Priory's archives referring to a body called 'The Sixteene'. The earliest known record seems to be in a minute book that has since been lost. The entry refers to Thomas Kerby of Bure tithing being elected a churchwarden "At the Assemblie of the Sixteene held the 13th of Marche 1631". Such an entry clearly implies that by that date, the body had been operating for some time. It is not unreasonable to suppose that this would have been the body set up to administer the Priory Church and its churchyard that were from 1540 onwards the responsibility of the town. This body later became known as 'The Vestry'. It seems likely that it consisted of the mayor and burgesses, who probably at that date numbered 12 in total, the vicar, his two wardens and the sexton, who, amongst other duties, was responsible for looking after the churchyard and digging the graves. This would mean ¾ of the 'Sixteene' representing the town, to whom the church and churchyard now belonged, with responsibility for maintaining the fabric, and ¼ representing Mother Church, with responsibility for the proper conduct of services and other ecclesiastical duties. A similar division of representation existed for many years on County Police Authorities, where $^2/_3$ of the members were county councillors, responsible amongst other things for paying the bills, and $^1/_3$ were magistrates whose greater concern was to oversee the proper functioning of the Police Service.

The earliest surviving Minute Book of the 'Sixteene' dates from 1640, and is in very poor condition. The entry reads *'March 13th 1640.*

The last Churchwardens' (George Toomer and Henry Preston) accounts delivered. The Parish in debt so a double rate ordered to be collected by the new Churchwardens'. An entry for 1643 notes that one of the new churchwardens was William Pawson. His family appears in the list of mayors for over 100 years, starting in 1588. There are entries for 1640 in the 'Sixteene's' Minute Books listing a fine of 3s.4d for fouling the churchyard and a fine of 5s.4d *'if any hoggs or piggs shall happen to come within the precinct of the church'.* In 1643, the churchwardens had to buy two new surplices and in 1646 Thomas Boorne rented the churchyard for his stock, which he had to fence in. In 1652, the 'Sixteene' made a free gift to *'maimed soldiers'* of £1.6s.8d. And in March 1663, Martayne Stokes, churchwarden, held £24.12s.2d of 'Bell Money', while in October that year, *'it was ordered that a single rate be added to the two former rates which the whole makes three single rates for the present year'.* In February 1664, it was *'ordered that same day the Sexton shall give in the names of idle boys that abuseth the church to the churchwardens and they to the Sixteene.'*

From these entries is seems clear that the 'Sixteene's' authority was wide. Since Church and Town had been closely linked, not only before the Dissolution of the Monasteries in 1539, a policy that John Draper no had doubt sought to foster during his time as Prior, but even more so after the Priory was given to the town's inhabitants, it was logical that the bodies controlling both should include many of the same people. This would help to ensure that the policies adopted for the benefit of the one did not contradict those pursued for the benefit of the other.

The last prior surely used all his skills and connections at Court and elsewhere to make sure that the magnificent building that until then had been the centre of the life of the town, should continue to stand and remain the central focus in Christchurch after his departure. Establishing one body, many of whose members had the care of both, would greatly assist this and his legacy continued for centuries afterwards. Only in the 19th century did the functions become separated into the Borough Council and Parochial Church Council that we know today. However, John Draper would surely have been pleased to know that the Mayor still has his chaplain who always leads the Council in prayer before its deliberations, and that Civic Services remain an important event in the mayoral calendar.

Chapter 14.

Margaret, Countess of Salisbury: 1473 - 1541.

One of the most tragic figures in the history of Christchurch must surely be Margaret, Countess of Salisbury, who for 28 years was Lord of the Manor of Christchurch. She was the daughter of George, Duke of Clarence who led a somewhat turbulent political life that ended in 1487. He was attainted by Parliament, imprisoned in the Tower of London, and condemned to death, as a result of which all his lands, including the Manor of Christchurch, were escheated to the Crown. Whether he was secretly executed, or as rumour has it, drowned in a butt of Malmsey wine, has never been resolved. He was, however a direct descendant of the Plantagenet kings, which was later to cause a significant problem for his daughter, Margaret.

The Montacute family, who became Earls of Salisbury in 1337, had acquired the Lordship of the Christchurch Manor in 1377 and held it until the Duke of Clarence's death. They served their kings well, both on the field of battle and as diplomats and politicians. William, the 1st Earl, was not only one of Edward III's most trusted advisors but also Marshal of England. He conquered the Isle of Man and was thereafter crowned its King. What other town can lay claim to having one king as lord of its manor while at the same time owing allegiance to its national sovereign? William, the 2nd Earl, was one of the original Knights of the Garter in 1350, while the 4th Earl, the most famous soldier of his day, fought with great distinction beside Henry V at Agincourt, but was later killed during the Siege of Orleans in 1428. Since he had some years earlier suffered the tragedy of killing his only son in a joust, the title passed through the female line, ultimately to the Plantagenet Duke of Clarence. This was the royal ancestry of Margaret, his daughter.

Henry VII married Margaret off at the age of 18, to Buckinghamshire knight, Sir Richard Pole, later appointing him as a Knight of the Garter. In 1513, Henry VIII returned to Margaret most of the lands of the Earls of Salisbury, including the Manor of Christchurch. One particular house she owned in the town was in Castle Street, next door to the oldest existing property in the town[1]. The return of the Salisbury lands was partly to make amends for the execution of her brother, Edward, which Henry had ordered since, as a male Plantagenet, he was a possible contender for the Throne. Margaret's possible claim seems to have been discounted however for she found favour at Court.

---

[1] See chapter 8

She was, throughout her life, a staunch Catholic and at one stage, dismissed Gervase Tyndall from her household 'because he belonged to the New Learning'. Henry VIII himself described her as 'a saintly woman'. Consequently he not only chose her to be godmother to the young Princess Mary, his eldest child and daughter of the ill-starred Catherine of Aragon, but also appointed her to be her governess. Her son, Reginald Pole, two years after he was granted his B.A. degree at Oxford, was appointed Dean of Wimborne Minster in 1517, even though he was a layman and only 17 years of age. This post he held for 20 years, though much of the time he was either in Padua or Rome.

Very little is known about where the Countess Margaret lived. We know that she appointed Sir Thomas Englefield to be steward of all her castles and manors, for which he was paid 40 shillings out of her Manor of Ringwood. It is known that she lived in Warblington Manor, between Chichester and Southampton in 1526, and was probably at Newhall near Chelmsford with the Princess Mary during the period 1527 - 31. She may also have been with her at Richmond Palace in 1431 and Hatfield in 1534, in her capacity as governess and close companion. Certainly the Princess Mary was herself staunchly Catholic, as many Protestants discovered to their cost when she became Queen, and it is not unreasonable to conclude that Margaret may have strengthened her belief in the faith. If these dates can be relied upon, then it seems that there were very few occasions when Margaret could have lived in Christchurch. Nor was there any suitable house in which she could have accommodated her entourage, even if she only had her own household with her. Christchurch's castle would have been far too uncomfortable and the Constable's House would have been too small for anything other than a passing visit, during which many of her attendants would have had to find lodging elsewhere in the town. That she had a strong attachment to the town will become clear later, and may be in part due to her son's position as Dean of Wimborne - even if he hardly visited the town. Probably her chief knowledge of Christchurch came from the occasions when she was with the Court at Winchester, or perhaps from her acquaintance with Prior John Draper in his capacity of Chaplain to Henry VIII.

Unfortunately, the Countess Margaret fell from grace for several reasons connected with Henry's divorce from Catherine. First, the Princess Mary, to whom she was governess, was declared a bastard, an event that must have been deeply shocking to Margaret, as a good Catholic. Secondly, and possibly as a result, she refused to give up Mary's jewels to Anne Boleyn on her marriage to Henry. And thirdly because her son, Reginald, had refused Henry's bribe of the offer of the Archbishopric of York if he would approve the divorce. Indeed Reginald Pole went further and though he was genuinely fond of his

King, in 1536 he wrote an extremely critical treatise on Henry's proposed divorce and his intention to over-ride the Pope's supremacy. Whereupon Pope Paul III made him a cardinal. Being unable to reach Cardinal Pole, who wisely stayed in Italy, Henry took his revenge on the rest of the family on the somewhat flimsy grounds that they were all involved in a plot to overthrow him. As a consequence, all three were attainted on the grounds of high treason. Both Countess Margaret's other sons were arrested, the elder, Lord Montague being executed and the second, Geoffrey, though condemned, was pardoned and exiled. In 1539, their mother, the Countess, by then aged 67, was likewise arrested and confined to the Tower, where she languished for the next two years.

There was a further reason for Henry's hatred and mistrust of the Countess. With her two eldest sons executed and banished, and the youngest a priest, there was no surviving male Plantagenet left who could threaten Henry's throne. He could discount Reginald Pole, who, now that he was a priest could not marry and produce a legitimate heir. Prince Edward, had been born in 1537 and though a sickly child, Henry felt that he now had a male heir to succeed him, and might surely have another in due course as a back-up should Edward succumb. To rid himself of the Countess would mean that the last remaining Plantagenet would be out of the way and his throne would be secure from any usurper.

The Countess Margaret probably lived in reasonable comfort during her two years in the Tower, since she would have been able to buy the necessities of life and even have a lady-in-waiting to attend her. She was however closely confined and disgraced and as an elderly lady who had been used to all the pleasures and comforts of the royal court, or even the lesser though still comfortable household of Princess Mary, life must have been grim. She was however a lady of deep religious conviction and strong spirit. Henry would have been infuriated by the reports he certainly received of the dignified way in which the royally connected Countess conducted herself in her confined quarters in the Tower. Finally, in 1541, frustrated by her continued conduct and perhaps fearing that because of her unjust imprisonment she might become the centre of a conspiracy to over-throw him, Henry ordered her execution.

The Countess still had a final card to play that would cause embarrassment to the King. She insisted, as was her right in view of her station in life, that the headsman should not use an axe upon her, as if she were a common traitor, but should behead her with a sword. This caused some delay, while a suitable person was brought over from France, since it appeared that there was no-one in England willing or able to perform the act. On the appointed day, she was led out from her cell in the Tower to the place of execution to face the block. There, according to an early if not contemporary account, she stood, grey headed and dignified. *'She refused to lay her head on the block, saying "So should Traitors die, and I am none". Neither did it serve that the Executioner told her it was the fashion. So turning here grey head every way, she bade him, if he would, to get it as he could. So that he was constrained to fetch it off slovenly. And thus ended the last of the right line of the Plantagenets (with a sounder title to the crown than any Tudor').* Indeed, that was almost certainly the true reason for Henry's action.

Margaret, Countess of Salisbury being beheaded.

Some years previously, in 1529, The Countess had built for herself and her son Reginald a magnificent chantry in the Priory. It was designed, and perhaps built by the great Florentine sculptor Pietro Torrigiano, whom Henry VIII himself had commissioned to build the magnificent chapel in Westminster Abbey for his parents, Henry VII and Elizabeth of York. Though she used the same sculptor as the King, which many would regard as a compliment to her sovereign, Henry was far more likely to be irritated, lest some should think that her chantry might be finer than his. One may also wonder why, since Margaret seems hardly ever to have visited Christchurch, she chose the town as her final resting place. The reason was probably that the Priory was by far the largest and most important church on any of her manors. However, to build it where she did, into the monastic part of the Priory and beside the high altar, would have required the consent of John Draper. She would surely have known him well, not only in his capacity as Prior of the convent in her manor, but also as a suffragan bishop of Winchester and one of Henry's personal chaplains. Nor was John Draper likely to object to having such a distinguished personage so magnificently buried in his Priory, to which she would have added lustre. In 1529, he was not to know the fate that was to befall her.

The Salisbury Chantry.

The Salisbury Chantry is one of the jewels of the Priory and by far the finest of all its chantries, putting even John Draper's own chantry in the shade. The exterior carving depicts in many places the *planta genista* (the broom plant) that the Plantagenet kings had taken as their emblem. The ceiling within is intricately carved with fan-vaulting and three carved and painted bosses. The western of the three bosses contained the arms of her husband, Sir Richard Pole, K.G. The central boss depicted the Countess kneeling before the Trinity, in a reference to her staunch Catholic faith. It may also have been in recognition of the fact that the parish altar was dedicated to the Trinity. The eastern boss contained Margaret's own shield. This contained not only the arms of English Plantagenets and of France, from her royal ancestry, but also her connections with the Neville, Beauchamp, Warwick, Montacute, Mouthermer, Clare and Despenser families. Few people could claim such a wide connection with the leading families in the country, a matter of which Henry did not wish to be reminded. It is not surprising therefore that at the time that Henry took over the Priory, he ordered these achievements to be defaced, so that only a few traces of the Countess's lineage are still visible. Thus they have remained to this day, perhaps as a reminder of Henry's bitter rage. Neither the Countess Margaret, nor her son, Cardinal Reginald, was buried in her chantry. She was buried in the graveyard of St Peter ad Vincula by the Tower. He, appointed later by Queen Mary to be Archbishop of Canterbury, and the last to be so appointed by the Pope, was buried in Canterbury Cathedral.

Public opinion, certainly in the South of England, does not seem to have supported Henry over Margaret, Countess of Salisbury. The steps leading up into the Salisbury Chantry have been so deeply worn away by the countless numbers of pilgrims that have visited it and prayed there, that it is now scarcely possible to ascend them in safety. The people of Christchurch were no doubt devastated by her death, not only because she had been the Lord of the Manor for so long, but also because she had enriched their Priory with one of its most magnificent features. In all probability she has also bestowed other gifts on the Priory. One may wonder whether the *'two goodly basins double gilt having the king's arms well enamelled'* that were specifically mentioned by Robert Southwell in his letter to Henry at the time of the suppression of the Priory, had come down to her from her Plantagenet ancestors and that it was she who had then given them to the Priory.

It is probably safe to say that the people of Christchurch would have become even less enamoured with their King as a result of the loss of their Lord of the Manor so soon after the loss of the many benefits that the Priory had provided. To combat the double loss, no doubt they encouraged pilgrims to visit her chantry, even if it was empty of her body. This would have been made easier after she was beatified by Pope Gregory XIII in 1583 - an event that was ratified later in 1886 by Pope Leo XIII. The townsfolk would certainly have missed the support that the noble lady had given the town and would have drawn comfort from her beatification. It is also likely that the good people of Christchurch, on a more practical level, would have made the most of their opportunities to smuggle wool out and wine in, and thus deprive Henry of the Tonnage and Poundage, one of his chief sources of revenue. Certainly today our sympathy is with the Countess Margaret, who was so cruelly struck down. It must also help to explain why countless thousands still come on pilgrimage to her magnificent shrine.

Chapter 15.

The Burgesses' Disputes over Commoners Rights, 1566 - 1600.

It was only to be expected that as a result of the suppression of the Priory, the disposal of all its lands in 1539 and the forfeiture of the Manor of Christchurch to the Crown on the execution of the Lord of the Manor, Lady Margaret of Salisbury in 1541, that there would be considerable confusion as to who had what rights over much of the land surrounding the town. It is not therefore surprising to find that there were several disputes arising in the succeeding years. Some of these were quickly and probably amicably settled. Others were more serious and tended to drag on for some years and involved some of the chief men of the town at the time, particularly when the land involved was Common Land. On much of this, many of the citizens of the town could claim grazing and other rights for which the borough had to pay an annual rent to the lord of the manor. The importance of these rights is clear from the extent of the land at issue. In total it comprised an area of about 600 acres, all of which was controlled directly or indirectly by the burgesses.

There were about 100 acres of Town Common on St Catherine's Hill, over which the inhabitants of the borough had the right to roam, cut turf, heath and furze, dig sand, gravel and clay for use on their own property, and pasture their animals at certain times of the year. On the 70 acres of Cowards (cowherds) Marsh, those living in the borough could graze their horses and cattle for a small fee. Between 21st May and 11th July each year, the land was closed off so that a hay crop could be taken from it. This, together with any gorse cut, was used for the benefit of the poor of the town. Next to it stood Ogber, a large meadow of some 66 acres, that was open to the citizens to graze their stock, between 12th August (Candlemas Day) and 14th February (Lammas Day), once the first hay crop had been gathered - the "aftermath". A small five-acre meadow, known as the Quomps, lay beside the Stour, between Wick Ferry and Town Quay. This was originally freely available to the town for grazing, though later each animal was charged a small rent. Its use deteriorated over the centuries as the land became progressively more liable to flooding. Beside the Avon, stood the 14 acres of Millhams Meadow that could be grazed for the same period as Ogber. On the opposite bank of the Avon stood Barlins, a meadow of 23 acres that could be similarly grazed, but only by the inhabitants of the Street Tithing. The largest area of land was the Portfield that extended over almost 300 acres. Though much of this land was cultivated, the area nearest to the Stour was available to all the town's citizens to graze their cattle between Lammas Day and Candlemas Day. Thus, by using Ogber and Millhams on the one hand, and the grazing part of the Portfield on the other, the citizens of Christchurch had grazing for their cattle all the year round. This arrangement meant that all the meadows had a time to recover from being grazed. It also meant that they were well manured and kept in good heart. There were other meadows where the inhabitants had various limited grazing rights such as "after pasture". These were Convent Meadows, Stocker's Mead, Campes Mead, Barnard's Mead and Bure Mead. Some of these were limited to certain groups of inhabitants. These pastures taken together were of great value to the inhabitants, and without them, some would have been hard put to it to graze their stock upon which they relied to make ends meet.

In the turmoil that followed the suppression of the Priory, when land often changed hands several times in quick succession as each owner made a quick profit, some of the pastures may have been little used by the local inhabitants. By 1566, it seems that several of the burgesses had taken to using the pastures for their own stock to the exclusion of other inhabitants. Since there appeared to be a danger that the custom might become established, several of the more upright citizens who were not burgesses, feared that the commoners rights were in danger of being lost. To prevent this happening, they seem to have thought it prudent to bring the matter to the notice of the Crown. Seven of them 'laid an Information' before John Gwynne, who was the Queen's Surveyor of Hampshire. The burden of their case was that Henry Pawson, Thomas Hancock, Alban White, Richard Colgill, Richard Inwood, William Meryett and John Frayle, all of whom either had been or were later to be mayors, and Vincent Clerk who, like them, was probably also a burgess, had *'forcibly usurped the common pasture of Bure, Barnard's, Ogber, Millham's, Stocker's, Campes Meads and Coward's Marsh, all of which had previously been the property of the Priory, to their own use'*. They claimed that these men had been using the meadows for their own stock only, *'which has prevented the Queen's tenants from exercising their lawful rights'*. In this they were probably partly incorrect, since in 1554, Queen Mary had given the Manor to Catherine Pole, the granddaughter of the executed Countess of Salisbury. However, in 1566 they were all subjects, if not direct tenants, of Queen Elizabeth.

The charitable interpretation of the affair may be that the situation had grown up over a number of years. The burgesses were probably more wealthy than many of the other citizens, and as such owned more livestock. Initially they may have found that at least some of the meadows were effectively seldom used by the general community.

Perhaps also the fences had not been kept in good repair. They may have decided between them to fence the meadows properly, and since no one else seemed to be using the land, to put it to full use for their own stock. Initially their intentions may have been intended to be for the long-term benefit of the whole community, with they themselves recouping their outlay from the stock they grazed. As the years passed others probably thought that they were acquiring "squatters rights" and so decided to take action to put a stop to it. Alternatively, the burgesses may have always intended to feather their own nests. We do not know. Whatever their intentions, the result of the case was that the rights of Common Pasture were re-established for all those who were entitled to them. This was to become important some years later and remains so today.

In 1591 the Mayor and burgesses had occasion themselves to claim that one William Osborne, who lived at Fordingbridge, was laying claim to part of Stocker's Mead. This land, they claimed had been given to the town by Baldwin de Redvers in his charter of 1150. The case was tried at Andover, where it seems that the burgesses were poorly represented, for Osborne won and was awarded £21 in damages and costs. Osborne subsequently took a hay crop from the land, but because he had not fenced it properly, cattle from the neighbouring common strayed onto the land and ate the hay. It appears that Osborne was of a somewhat fiery disposition. When he discovered the stray cattle, he drew his sword and killed one of the cows that unfortunately belonged to Robert Carter who had been Mayor two years before. He also injured another cow and a bullock so badly that they had to be destroyed. Two of the owners settled their claim with Osborne, but the third took the matter to the Sheriff's Court at Andover, where Osborne, surprisingly, was awarded £16.8s.4d presumably as damages and costs. The burgesses however maintained that the Andover jury had been *'influenced by bad men's oaths'.*

It seems to have been an extraordinary affair. In the first place, one has to wonder why Osborne found it necessary to travel about always apparently armed with a sword. The Armada had been defeated three years previously, and although Catholics were still being persecuted to some extent and households were supposedly being examined weekly concerning their church attendance and beliefs, there was no threat of civil unrest. Taxation had increased considerably and harvests were generally below average, but none of that was likely to mean that a man needed to be constantly armed. One is led to the conclusion that Osborne had personal reasons to carry a sword, perhaps because he knew he had many enemies. Certainly his conduct towards the inhabitants of Christchurch gives strength to that view. Nor does he seem to have been a good farmer. Though the care of animals had not reached its present level, no responsible husbandman or stock-breeder would surely deliberately slaughter a straying cow or so injure two other beasts and leave them maimed in the field so that they had to be destroyed. Osborne's interests seem to have been entirely financial.

Matters did not end there, because Osborne then asked the burgesses for a lease of the after-pasture of Stocker's Mead for 21 years. This the burgesses refused because of his *'shameless practices and his cruelty in law and subtlety therein'*. Despite this, Osborne seems to have claimed the land and locked the gate into it, which the burgesses had to break open on several occasions. Osborne refused to let matters rest, and apparently harassed the widow of John Nutkins, who had been Mayor that year and had just died, and several other people. It was even claimed that one Richard Markendale died as a result of Osborne's treatment. Ultimately, in 1592, the matter came before the Earl of Huntingdon, who by then had inherited the Lordship of the Manor. In an effort to resolve the dispute that was becoming increasingly acrimonious, he ruled that Osborne should be allowed to lease the land from the burgesses for 21 years. Though at first sight this may have seemed to be a just solution, since there was no legal reason to deny Osborne the lease, it probably prolonged the dispute. Had he been denied the lease, he would have had no reason to keep coming to Christchurch. As it was, he kept making trouble and it seems refused to let the dispute rest.

A Burgess.

Osborne then had Thomas Hancock arrested by the Bailiff of the Ringwood Hundred on various charges that appear to have been trumped up. Three other burgesses, who were all later to become mayors, were accused by Osborne. All four, Hancock, Pawson, Colgill and Frayle, petitioned Sir Edmund Anderson, Lord Chief Justice of Assize for Southampton (i.e. Hampshire), to have Osborne restrained. Despite being bound over to keep the peace, Osborne had shot and wounded William Pope *'who was going about his husbandry. He threatens devilish disorder to the citizens of the borough and their wives and children'* and sought *'protection from his continuous vexatious practices'.*

The whole affair was further complicated by the fact that John Hopkins was being sued by Osborne for damages in the sum of £16.13s.4d, while Hopkins was counter suing the borough for £1.19s.11d in connection with a lease that he maintained he had taken on Stocker's Mead. It seems that Osborne had a prior claim to a lease, since the borough had to pay Hopkins £20 first and £8 some time later. There also seems to have been some evidence that the burgesses were at least in part at fault, since they agreed to pay Hopkins' costs of 21 shillings. However they failed to pay up.

Whatever the rights and wrongs of this long drawn out and acrimonious case, it would appear that tempers ran extremely high on both sides. It does however seem that William Osborne was the main cause of the trouble, in that he seems to have refused to let the matter rest once he had got his teeth into it. By all accounts, he appears to have been unnecessarily aggressive. There also seems to be some evidence that juries could be influenced, threatened, or perhaps even bribed, by a man who gave the appearance of being powerful. One wonders why Osborne had his case tried at Andover and why he had to use the Ringwood Bailiff for matters that occurred in Christchurch, unless he knew that he could influence matters in those towns. The burgesses, for their part, may perhaps have been slipshod in the way they had granted leases, even to the extent of granting both Osborne and Hopkins a lease on the same piece of land but it is doubtful if they were dishonest. The problem would appear to have been that Osborne was a very forceful character and may have used extremely sharp lawyers. The burgesses for their part may have been a little naïve and certainly seem to have lacked either the resources or the contacts to hire sufficiently competent lawyers to defend themselves effectively.

Trying to deal with the various claims for use of the town's pastures was not an easy task then, and has continued to raise problems ever since. There were further cases in 1600 and 1633 of cattle being detained that were probably grazing unlawfully on the common lands. There are a quantity of documents concerning all these cases in the borough archives, that often give great detail and present a clear picture of legal procedures in the reign of Elizabeth I. They also highlight the problems that the mayors and burgesses had to resolve in the 16th and 17th centuries. Happily, they are the exception, since for most of the time common sense prevailed and problems were usually resolved sensibly.

Over the last four centuries, the need for the commons and the uses to which they have been put have changed considerably. Few people now either can or wish to exercise their rights of grazing stock on the commons. Some commoners voluntarily surrendered their rights in times past in return for other benefits attached to their properties. In other cases conditions led to other uses of the lands being of greater benefit to the wider community. Changes were then brought about by legislation. Some areas, such as Ogber, Cowards Marsh, Millhams and Barlins are still grazed. Others, like Town Common, remain pleasantly wild but are managed in order to preserve their natural beauty. Other areas, such as Quomps, Bernard's Mead and parts of Portfield have been improved to make greater use of them for recreational purposes and as open spaces. Other areas have been added, sometimes by purchase and sometimes by generous gifts from local inhabitants. A large part of Stanpit Marsh and 2 Riversmeet have been raised from their previous marshy levels, and now form important areas for recreational and sporting use. Many of the common lands and other open spaces in and around the town are of such importance and have been so successfully managed that they have been declared Sites of Special Scientific Interest (S.S.S.I.) or given some other protected status. These include Ogber, Cowards Marsh, Town Common and parts of Stanpit Marsh. Over the centuries, the control and management of the common lands and other open areas has sometimes changed. Today, some are administered by Dorset County Council, others, along with many other open spaces in and around the town, are managed by the Borough Council, and others come under the Lord of the Manor. In every case, however, the primary object is that they should be properly managed for the benefit of the community at large. As a result, the town is blessed with a comprehensive variety of open spaces. They range in size from the small Tutton's Well site near Purewell, to the wide expanse of St Catherine's Hill, and are enjoyed in many different ways by the citizens of Christchurch and the countless visitors to the town. As in the past, these areas provided the inhabitants with areas where they could improve their livelihood, so today they play a major part in making Christchurch a place "Where Time is Pleasant."

Chapter 16.

A Justices Dinner, 1617.

Amongst the many documents in the archives of the Borough of Christchurch is a single sheet of paper that looks at first sight like a grocer's bill of little importance. Turn it over, and there is another bill, shorter than the first, for work done and a few purchases. How it came to be amongst the town's papers, we shall never know. In all probability it had been lying on someone's desk and was swept up in a pile of other papers of importance and filed away, to be lost from view for almost 400 years. It is however a surprisingly informative document when examined more closely. It also seems that, though the writing dates from about the same period, the two sides have probably been written by different people. This may well have been the case, since paper was valuable and the second writer was merely being economical in using the blank side of the first bill. This was the normal custom, particularly in churches, and is the reason why so many early church records have disappeared. The local priest would use the back of old registers to write new records of births for example or even perhaps notes for his forthcoming sermon. These would then probably be thrown away, so that many of the older entries were lost forever. To find this sheet of paper in the town's archives is therefore important. As written, and with its original spelling, it reads as follows:-

For the Justices Dinner the eighth of May 1617 at the firming of the boundyes.

Item	*for bread and beer*	*11 sh.*
Item	*for 3 peces of boyled beff* [beef]	*4 sh.*
Item	*for 2 ledges* [legs] *of Motton*	*3 sh. 4d.*
Item	*for 3 quarters of lam* [lamb]	*5 sh.*
Item	*for 4 joynte of veall & bacon*	*7 sh.*
Item	*for 2 capons*	*3 sh. 4d.*
Item	*for a Gammon*	*18 sh.*
Item	*for boyling the gammon*	*2 sh.*
Item	*for Mylottes* [mullet ?]	*4 sh.*
Item	*for a great Carpe*	*3 sh. 4d.*
Item	*for a trought* [trout]	*1 sh.*
Item	*for 3 pare of polles (chickens)*	*2 sh.*
Item	*for a pick* [pike] *and flat fishe* [turbot ?]	*2 sh.*
Item	*for 20 Lapprews* [lampreys] *& 6 crabes*	*8 sh.*
Item	*for 5 hundred of prawns*	*2 sh.*

Item	for 6 pounds of butter	2 sh.
Item	for 6 quarts of port	6 sh.
Item	for 10 quarts of Clarrett	5 sh.
Item	housework at 3d.	3 sh.

Comd. Totall is £4. 11 sh.

For the some of this bill by Mr. Mayor. Mr. Rogers and Mr. Burgess Pawson this xxth (20th) of May I pay £4. 11 sh.

By me   John Templeman.

The town records show that John Templeman was Mayor four times between 1617 and 1630. Henry Rogers was Mayor eight times between 1615 and 1639. and Thomas Pawson also appears as Mayor eight times between 1592 and 1622. Add to these three William Colgill who was Mayor nine times between 1593 and 1632. and we find that four families rotated the mayoralty between them. except for four years. during the period 1612 to 1635 and effectively controlled the town for 31 years out of 47 at this time.

Hidden in this sheet of paper is a great deal of information about life in the town during the middle years of the reign of James I.

In the first place. because the bill is somewhat scrappily written. with no great detail as to the occasion. we can assume that it was not the first time such a dinner had been held. This would be particularly likely if the other men named on the bill had held similar dinners during the previous years when they had themselves been Mayor. This surely means that the Justices of the Peace had been sitting in the town for some considerable time. It had for long been customary for the mayor to be a Justice of the Peace. They had been established as a regular part of the judicial system in England by Edward III in 1363 and ordered to hold sessions four times a year. for which reason the sittings were called 'Quarter Sessions'. They tended to deal with the more serious cases. leaving the local Manor Courts to deal with the lesser offences. such as matters to do with trade. like underweight bread and illegal brewing. road and hedge repairs. straying animals. trespass and unpaid debts. These Manor Courts usually sat every three weeks. so that justice was not only seen to be done. but also was swift. Indeed. local justice was often swifter in the early 17th century than it is in the late 20th century. in spite of all the technology available today. About the only fortunate result of the execution of Margaret Countess of Salisbury was that the Lordship of the Manor of Christchurch reverted to the Crown. and the Manor Court Rolls for the two years after her death have survived amongst the royal archives. These have been carefully translated, edited and published by David Stagg. Besides the criminal matters that the justices would have dealt with, their jurisdiction also extended during the 16th century to such matters as Poor Relief and boundary disputes. It is in connection with this function that the justices seem to have been exercising their authority in May 1617.

It had long been the custom to perambulate the bounds of the manor and parish, stopping at each boundary stone or post, not only to make sure that it was clearly visible, but also that the inhabitants were aware of its location. The traditional time for this was a Rogation Day, one of which in 1617 fell early in May. The custom had grown up that the town's dignitaries would be accompanied by children from the town when they perambulated the bounds. At each marker point, one of the children would be upended and lowered head first onto the marker post or stone to physically impress upon him its location. On other occasions, the boys would be beaten - usually symbolically - with hazel or birch twigs, to further impress upon their persons where the boundaries were. Though this was originally a manorial matter, it sometimes widened into a parochial matter. Since the Parish of Christchurch at that time stretched from Bashley in the east to Hinton, Walkford, Burton, Hurn, and Iford, continuing west to include Throop, Holdenhurst and Muscliffe, which covers much of modern Bournemouth, the perambulation must have been a lengthy operation. It is likely that only part of the boundary was covered each year, but the importance of 'Beating of the Bounds' as it was called, was recognised. It made sure that everyone on the town and parish knew exactly where the boundaries were, so that disputes could be more easily settled and there was less likelihood of someone pleading ignorance, which was in any case no defence. The custom still continues in various parts of the country to this day, but not, regrettably, in Christchurch. Today, the mayor is usually accompanied by the local vicar with his choirboys whose heads are physically impressed on the boundary stones. Something similar would often have happened in Stuart times, and in view of the close link between the Priory and the town, it would almost certainly have been the practice in Christchurch in those days.

Those involved in the perambulation would therefore have been, the mayor, many of his burgesses, the vicar, his two wardens and probably the sexton. It is worth remembering that since the time of Edward III, the churchwardens had also had a particular duty to supervise all males between the ages of 16 and 60 at the archery butts after Mass on Sundays, so their presence in the ceremony would be readily accepted. We know that most of these men would have comprised the 'Sixteene' that has already been described in an earlier chapter. It is also likely that the reeve. constable and bailiff. who would have been present at the Hundred Court. would also have been in the party. However. some of these men may have held more than one office. Consequently it would appear that those sitting down to dinner would probably not have exceeded eighteen in number. The assumption must be that any children or choirboys would have eaten separately in another room and probably from a different menu.

It is worth considering the menu in detail. The eleven shillings spent on the first item of bread. probably made from wheat flour. and beer seems excessive when compared with the other items of food. This is probably because it was mainly for the use of the twelve servants and cooks. who were paid 3d each. and the children. Though plates were by then in common use. bread often made from the coarser grains was still used by the poor as a trencher and by most people to sop up the gravy. though the more affluent would have used wheaten bread for this. Beer came in three strengths: strong ale. which would have been on the dinner table. beer. which would have been for the servants and small beer for the children. Home-made small beer was also used for scrubbing down the kitchen tables in the larger households.

The cost of the gammon appears expensive in relation to the other items If. however. it cost two shillings to boil. it means that it was probably a whole large sow. This too may have been mainly for the servants and children. Though several types of fish are listed. there is no mention of salmon. which. when caught in Christchurch. is now considered a particular delicacy. It had always been part of the staple diet locally. Witness the Norman charters which expressly state that the first salmon caught each year. and a tithe of those caught thereafter. were to be given to the Priory. However in Tudor and Stuart times salmon was so common that the indentures of apprentices frequently stated that they were not to be given salmon more than three times a week. There was good reason therefore not to include salmon in the menu. Nor are vegetables included on the bill. Their cost would have been minimal and as yet Sir Walter Raleigh's discovery of the potato had had little effect on the normal diet. Vegetables would probably have been provided free from the mayor's own garden. such things not usually being recorded in the household accounts. The vegetables that would have accompanied the various dishes would have been onions. leeks. cabbage and various pulses such as peas and beans. There is likewise no mention of any dessert. This too would probably have come from the mayor's own kitchen at minimal cost. though they would have taken some time to prepare. It is also possible that the charges for the meats and fish were sufficient to cover any additional cost of the raw materials for the dessert.

ffor the Justices Dinner the xxte
of may 1617 at the huing of the Coudgeb

for bread & bere ——————————— xij d —
for iij peces of boyled beffe ——— iiij s
for ij ledges of motton ——————— iij s — iiij d
for iij quarters of lam ————— ij s
for iiij joyntes of voall & baron — ij s iiij d
for ij Capons ————————————— iij s — iiij d
for a Gammon ——————————— xvj d
for boyling the Gammon ————————— ij d
for ij my Cotes ——————————— iiij s
for a great bapfe ——————————— iiij s — iiij d
for a Congett ———————————— ij d
for iij paer of sollet ——————— ij d
for a pint of heat fyfge ————— ij d
for ere Capftens & ij Crabes —— iiij s
for j gundred of pranes ————— ij s
for ij poundes of butter ————— ij s
for ij quartes of perke ————— ij s
for x quartes of Clarett ——— ij s
for gorsmrat 3t ——————————— iij s

Som Totall is iiij li — xij s

Ree the some of this Bill by me other
my Ryewes & my brother Thomson
this Debnt of xx — # Janu iij li xij s
me A'. Som & ... times

Document dated 1617 concerning the Justices Dinner.

There would certainly have been a dessert course consisting of a variety of 'puddings' and sweetmeats, though the ingredients would not have been particularly costly. One such could well have been made from a recipe that found its way into a cookery book published only 37 years after the dinner, in 1654, entitled *The ladies Companion, or A Table furnished with sundry sorts of Pies and Tarts, gracefull at a feast, ...'* that is now in Allestree Library in Christ Church, Oxford. The recipe is for 'Mrs. Medgates Hedge-hog Pudding'. It was a sort of bread-and-butter pudding, with cream, eggs, nutmeg and breadcrumbs, decorated with blanched almonds and raisins to look like a hedgehog. It contained beef suet, was boiled in beef broth, and served with melted butter sauce. Other desserts and tarts served at the dinner, such as macaroons and cheesecakes that are also mentioned in the book, may not have been so heavy, but 17th century appetites were certainly larger than ours today. However the Justices Dinner would not have risen to 'Marchpane'. Such a dish took about two days to prepare and would have been the centrepiece for royal banquets. The recipe reads: *'Steep two pounds of piked Almonds one day and two nights in fair water and blanch them out of it, then beat them well in a morter and bedew them with Rosewater, put to your Almonds so many pounds of Sugar, and beat your Sugar likewise with your Almonds, that done make wonderfull fine crust either of Paste or Wafers and bedew it with Rosewter and Sugar, and spread the stuff on it and bake it at a very soft fire always, bedewing it with Damask water, Civit, and Sugar, and lastly, with a gut of Dates gilt, or long Comfets gilt, or with Cinomon sticks gilt, or the Kernels of the pine-apple, so serve it forth'.* It would have been glorious to behold but sickly to eat.

Some idea of the quantity of meat that was provided may be calculated by estimating the weight of animals at that time. The edible weight of animal carcasses in the late Middle Ages is recorded as follows, but this should be increased slightly to take account of such improvements in breeding techniques that had been made by Stuart times. Cattle, between 113 and 204 Kg., pigs, between 32 and 41 Kg., sheep, 14 Kg., poultry, ½ to 1 Kg., and capons, which were large fattened cockerels, probably at least double. Fish would have weighed much the same as today. The six quarts of port and ten quarts of claret that were provided, would have meant that each adult dining would probably have had a quart of quite strong wine to drink, in addition to any strong ale he might consume.

Having had to walk for a considerable distance, it was not surprising therefore that in 1617 the justices, and those who accompanied them, reckoned that when the task of Beating the Bounds was completed, they had worked up a considerable appetite and felt that

127

they were entitled to a pleasant dinner. From the list of food and drink, it would indeed have been a merry party and it may be doubted how much work the mayor, burgesses and other officials did the next day. The children probably knew better than to make too much noise in school the day after such a dinner.

The items listed on the reverse of this paper are also interesting. It reads as follows:-

For my charges and repreves with gifts	*30 sh.*
For gorse lyme	*10d.*
For pots of iron unto Mr. Netherston	*20 sh.*
Bywden [bywarden (or churchwarden) Mr Cray]	
For conveyinge Propte [property]	*2 sh. 6d.*
In expenses in holding the Aussise [Assize]	*£1 3 sh.*

This again appears to be an account submitted by the Mayor. It seems that he had to make gifts to certain people for services rendered, though it is perhaps best not to enquire too closely what they were or why. No doubt they benefited the town in some way. The iron pots may well have been either for use in the Mary Magdalen Leper Hospital, or for making stews which would be distributed to the poor of the town. The gorse could well have been used as fuel for the communal bread ovens and the lime for whitewash or cleansing purposes. The final item of £1.3s.0d was presumably an item that would have occurred regularly every quarter when the Assizes were held. The mayor would have had to foot the bill initially, reimbursing himself from the town's coffers.

This single sheet of paper that seems to have found its way unintentionally into the archives of the Borough, provides a tantalising glimpse into some aspects of life in the town in Stuart times. There are other documents too, some dealing with squabbles between neighbours, others with irregular acts by leading men of the town. All go to make up the varied tapestry of a thriving community that has always been Christchurch. It only remains for someone to make a full and thorough examination of them. Life in Christchurch was certainly varied, full of surprises, and interesting.

Chapter 17.

The Civil War : 1642-1646.

Although Christchurch changed hands by conquest during the Civil War, the town suffered less than many others of similar size. Its position was in some ways unusual. Whereas Poole, Wareham and Southampton supported the Parliamentarians, Christchurch, like Corfe declared for the King. Both could be regarded as holding key positions, and yet both could be isolated and their inhabitants trapped and thus insulated from the main areas of conflict. Corfe held the strategic site controlling the Isle of Purbeck with access inland to the rest of Dorset and Wiltshire to the north. Christchurch guarded the river access up the Avon to Salisbury and the wide sheep rearing lands northwards to the Cotswolds. It is difficult to appreciate nowadays that the Avon was then still a useful navigable river. Indeed, two hundred years before, the citizens of Salisbury had built and manned a warship, *The Trout*, for Henry VI and sailed it down the Avon to Christchurch, where it was fitted out before sailing for service off the Kent coast. It was therefore a useful river for trade. However the main lines of communication from Southampton or Winchester towards the west bypassed Christchurch to the north, leaving it cut off by the New Forest. It is likely that Christchurch remained loyal to Charles, partly because the Lord of the Manor had for much of its history been the Sovereign. It is also possible that the town still held some residual gratitude to Henry VIII, who, though he had suppressed the town's great Priory 100 years previously, had returned the church to the townsfolk for use as their parish church.

Christchurch therefore, although near the front line between the Royalist and Parliamentarian forces, because of its somewhat sheltered position behind the New Forest, was initially left undisturbed. The town was also safe from attack by sea. Although a survey in 1574 had noted that the bay to the west of the town and to the east of Poole Harbour was considered to be *'a place very easy for the enemy to land there containing by estimation one quarter of a mile in length being devoid of all inhabiting'*, with Boscombe being *' an easy place for the enemy to land containing in length a flight shot'*, Christchurch itself presented a far more difficult problem. Any attempt to approach the town by water would present the defenders an easy target from both shores of the river to fire on the ships as they made their slow and winding way up to the town. However, any friendly vessel bringing provisions would be able to proceed at leisure into the harbour and up to Town Quay, where it would be received with general rejoicing. It is also worth noting a more recent account of the countryside round the town. In 1940 the military assessment in the face of a possible German invasion concluded that "the country is admirably suited to close fighting, in which battle courage, knowledge of the country and close quarter weapons will have every advantage over professional skill, armour and long range weapons". This assessment would have been equally valid in the 17th century.

Taking these two assessments together, it would seem that there were ample grounds for not attacking the town unless it appeared that it was a vital stronghold likely to prove a real thorn in the flesh to the enemy, or that it controlled a vital supply route. Since both Poole and Southampton were already held by Parliament, the second reason would seem not to apply. As regards the first, Christchurch was defended by only a small body of Royalists and could be easily bypassed and contained by an equally small force of Roundheads. The town's importance in the larger strategy of the war was therefore small. In addition, the defences of the town including the castle, which though it had a few cannon still in place, was in a poor state of repair. This was nothing unusual, for it was noted in 1628, only 14 years before the start of the war, that of the 27 brass cannon at Hurst Castle, only four or five were capable of being fired even if they had powder and shot, both of which were lacking. In fact, the general defences along the South Coast at this time were all in a poor state of repair or readiness.

It is important to understand the relationship between those who backed the Royalists and those who backed the Parliamentarians during the Civil War. Both considered themselves to be loyal Englishmen. However, it could be argued that the Parliamentarians, objecting to what the King was doing and to his claim of the Divine Right of Kings, were the initial aggressor, though with good reason. The Royalists found themselves torn between their loyalty to The Lord's Anointed, as they regarded the King, and disquiet at some of his actions and policies. The leaders of both sides were also frequently personal friends, and most made great personal sacrifices both in wealth and the hardships they were prepared to suffer. A good example of this can be found in the relationship between Sir William Waller, the Parliamentary General in this area, and Sir Ralph Hopton who commanded the Royalists defending the Cavalier strongholds in Hampshire and Dorset. Early in 1643, Waller wrote to Hotpon saying, *'My affections to you are so unchangeable that hostility itself cannot violate my friendship to your person, but I must be true to the cause wherein I serve. I should wait on you, according to your desire, but I look on you as engaged in that party without the possibility of retreat, and consequently incapable of being wrought upon by persuasion.*

That Great God, who is the searcher of all hearts, knows with what sad fear I go upon this service, and with what perfect hate I look upon war without an enemy. But I look upon it as 'Opus Domini' We are both on the stage and must act those parts that are assigned to us in this tragedy; but let us do it in the way of honour, and without personal animosity'. Waller was regarded as being kind to his own men and the Royalists similarly acknowledged his compassion to their followers. When the Royalist Earl of Hertford asked Waller if in future battles his men would give quarter, Waller replied that *'if any of his men should refuse to give quarter, so barbarously did he conceive of that action, that he would quarter him, and make him an example to others'.*

There were many other examples of friendship between the two sides. In 1643, Waller sent a present of wine to Lord Crawford, his Cavalier opponent at Alton, before the fight there, and afterwards asked for his personal surgeon to be returned in exchange for a suitable captive. Writing from Winchester on December 16th 1643, Hopton asked that Colonel Bolles be exchanged for a suitable captive or his body returned for burial. He also wished as many prisoners as possible to be exchanged as soon as possible, feeling no doubt that the common soldiers should not be made to suffer more than necessary as a result of the conflict that their superiors were waging. He concluded the letter, *'God give a sudden stop to this issue of English blood, which is the desire, Sir, of your faithful friend to serve you'.* It was this unwillingness of both sides to cause unnecessary harm to their fellow countrymen that characterised much of the Civil War. It also explains much of what happened in Christchurch.

The chief support for Christchurch came initially from Lord George Goring, who, as Governor of Portsmouth, supported the King. Until he was forced to surrender, he was able to keep Christchurch supplied by sea with such items as the inhabitants were unable to provide for themselves. Food they would have had from their surrounding farms, but military equipment and armaments were lacking. For the first two years of the war, very little happened in this locality to disturb the normal routine. Indeed, throughout the country, men went about their daily business unmolested except for the occasions when the troops of one side or the other tramped through their fields, ruining their crops, and taking such supplies as they needed. When bodies of troops from opposing sides came close, there would be a short skirmish resulting in a few deaths on each side and more wounds to be treated. The defeated side would then withdraw and the victors continued to advance, though probably with greater caution.

The first serious threat to Christchurch seems to have come in September 1643. About 300 troopers under the Cavalier Lord Crawford were attacked near Lymington. Seven of their number were killed and twenty four captured, while the remainder apparently made good their escape to Christchurch. Had they not done so, they would have had to surrender. The previous month, Corfe Castle had successfully withstood a Parliamentarian siege. Wimborne was also attacked. Christchurch folk would sleep less easily in their beds with fighting coming so close to their walls.

Parliamentarian at Christchurch

After the Battle of Cheriton early in 1644, a force of some 2,000 Roundhead cavalry under Waller began a determined push westwards with the intention of relieving Poole and Lyme Regis, that were in danger of falling to the Cavaliers. Sir John Mills, the Governor of Christchurch, had at the same time called a meeting of some Commissioners of Array to discuss recruiting men for Hopton's Royalist army. They had some success in enlisting men here, though they appear to have been somewhat slapdash as regards security. It seems that the Royalist troops and their new recruits were scattered in billets round the town and perhaps on the Portfield with no apparent defensive screen of outposts or pickets. They were consequently surprised by Waller's Parliamentarian troops, and taken without a fight. Though the recruits might have been willing to take up arms for their cause, they may not have had the weapons necessary to do so and certainly were not yet trained in the arts of war. Waller's attack was completely successful, though perhaps scarcely a great victory, since one may question how keen many of the new recruits would have been to fight. Waller's men rounded up 100 horse and 400 foot soldiers without resistance. It seems unlikely that so many men, enough to form a regiment, could surrender so easily unless there was some good reason, such as complete surprise and a probable lack of arms.

Amongst those taken were Colonel Sir John Mills, the town's Governor, Lieutenant Colonels Goddard and Paulet, Sergeant-Major (Major) Turney, Captains Gogill, Mill and Barrow, Captain-Lieutenant Sheiling, nine other lieutenants, four cornets (second lieutenants) four quartermasters, Mr Todd, who was probably the chaplain and ten gentlemen who were in the ranks of the ordinary soldiers. Several of those named would appear to have come from long-standing families in the town. The Vicar, Mr. Imber, was also *'plundered and imprisoned'*, probably because he was a High Churchman as opposed to the more puritanical Roundheads. It was fortunate for Christchurch, that on this occasion no damage was done to its buildings. One report that was sent announcing the event stated that *'Christchurch, a place of some importance near Poole'*, had been taken. The sender would have wished to make the most of his success, though the real importance was the capture without loss of what would today be a complete battalion with all its officers; no small victory.

What was the effect of this sudden and imposed change in allegiance on the townsfolk? Those who had been recruited through a sudden feeling of patriotism for the Royalist cause probably felt let down. The majority, however, who had enlisted for the pay that was offered rather than from patriotism, may have shrugged their shoulders, reckoning that it mattered little which side they were on - provided they were paid for their efforts. The chances of being killed or wounded were about equal on both sides and surrender was a far better option than either of the two alternatives. Since the Roundheads would have generally behaved decently towards their fellow Englishmen, life would have continued in the town much as before. It might even have become safer if Waller's men were to set about improving the defences of the town and set a proper watch against another surprise attack.

The main change would have been in the Priory. Whereas the Cavaliers would probably have garrisoned their horses within the bailey round the castle, or perhaps in their billets in the town, the Roundheads kept their horses secure in the church itself. This seems to have been their common practice. There is a record of an account in 1642 at Winchester Cathedral for *'2s.6d for cleansing the church against Christmas after the troopers had used it for a stable for their horses'*. Since the parliamentary forces would initially be considered to be 'enemies', it seems odd that they should have been prepared to antagonise the townsfolk by desecrating their magnificent church by using it as a stable. More especially so since many of Cromwell's New Model Army were devout Puritans who would normally have respected the sanctity of a church, even though they strongly disapproved of statues and other symbols of 'idolatry'. According to the evidence, the horses were stabled only in the Great Choir. It is commonly believed that the evidence of their presence can still be seen on the pew ends, which show signs of having been chewed by the horses during their time there. The Great Choir had been the monastic and Catholic - part of the building that had been suppressed by Henry VIII and surrendered to him with all the other monastic buildings a hundred years earlier. When he returned the church to the town for use as its parish church, it could be argued that the monastic Great Choir was in some way to be excluded. The argument could therefore be put to the townsfolk that Cromwell's cavalry were not desecrating the parish church as such. A thin argument no doubt, but one which at least showed some sensitivity for the feelings of the unhappy inhabitants.

Life in the town probably settled down fairly quickly again under the new commander and his men, with the traders making what they could out of them. If an account written in the 1860s is to be believed, the inhabitants bore the Parliamentarians little ill will and since they seem not to have been oppressive, were prepared to accept their presence. The story, which seems even then to have been of long standing, concerns a troop of Cromwellian cavalry returning from a scouting expedition by way of Mudeford.

'The day was hot, and the horses jaded. The commander of the troop noticed an old man standing without apprehension at the water's edge near the western end of the harbour where the land was muddy. On enquiring if the water beneath the mud was fit for cattle to drink, the old man replied, "No, 'tis brackish, but", he said pointing helpfully to what appeared to be a bog, "there is a strong spring here. I'll get a spade and dig a hole." This he did and the horses drank from it and so did the men, dipping into it with their hands. It is said that the old man's name was George Touting, from which it is suggested that the name became corrupted to Tutton's Well. The account continues, 'It is certainly a natural curiosity, for where else would you find beautiful sparkling spring water close to the sea water, covered every high tide without its being contaminated by its near vicinity, yet such it is on a level with the mud banks'.

It may also be that this tale is one reason for the belief, for which there is no real foundation, that Oliver Cromwell in person came to Christchurch. His men certainly did and some of his commanders, but there is no record that Cromwell ever came himself. Had he indeed been everywhere that claims his presence, it is reckoned that he would never have had time to sleep in a bed anywhere!

But in September 1644, Christchurch began to discover the cost of the occupation by their new masters. It was decided that anything over the £50 cost of keeping Hurst Castle, which was covered by the Committee of Revenue, should fall on the Hundred of Christchurch. This would have hit the townsfolk hard. Waller was also instructed by Oliver Cromwell to impress 500 horses for his cavalry and 600 for his artillery, with not more than two animals being taken from each team. Though they were paid for, the loss of those taken in Christchurch would have damaged the agriculture of the area seriously.

At the beginning of January 1645, Major Philip Lower, whom the Roundheads had installed as Governor of Christchurch, heard that a strong body of Cavalier cavalry under Lord Goring was only four miles from the town. As it was still effectively unfortified, Lower decided to evacuate his man towards Hurst Castle, sending all his ammunition there by sea in Christchurch boats. Though he was harassed by Goring's Cavaliers and suffered some loss, he managed to escape. Goring however was too far separated from the rest of the Royalist forces to be able to hold Christchurch himself, so had to withdraw, leaving the town open to be re-occupied by the Roundheads. Once more the town was spared destruction.

However, a few days later, on 15th January 1645, Lord Goring made a more determined attack with a larger force of some 1,000 men. Since his return from Hurst Castle, Major Lower, who now had 200 men, had made strenuous efforts to make the town's defences more secure and had pulled down many of the houses nearest to the castle, in order to increase the field of fire from it. But the town was still variously described as being 'meanly fortified' and 'a little unfortified fishing town'. There does seem to have been some element of surprise achieved by the attackers. They probably succeeded in crossing both the Avon and Mill Stream undetected and were apparently guided by a loyal Royalist townsman who led the attackers to an open space whereupon the town was quickly occupied. This Royalist unfortunately paid for his valour with his life, but the attackers were able to drive back the defenders from the outer defences into the castle itself. In addition, there was probably also a cavalry attack towards the Bar Gate, that may have been in part a diversion, since the cavalry would have known what to expect in the way of defences in the streets from chains and farm carts. After the first and successful assault, the situation settled down to a siege with the Parliamentary defenders holed up in the castle, the Priory itself - the two strongest stone buildings in the town - and the churchyard.

The plight of the defenders seemed sufficiently serious for them to light a beacon, either on the roof of the castle or more probably on the top of the Priory tower, being the highest building, as a signal to their comrades in Poole to come to their aid. None appears to have been sent, but a beacon was seen in the direction of Poole that was assumed to be a signal that help was on its way. Later it transpired that it was nothing of the sort. But the threat seems to have been sufficient to make the Royalist attackers fear an attack in their rear. They also came to the conclusion that the castle, with its few canon and still solid and high stone walls, was too strong to capture without larger calibre cannon than they possessed or siege engines which they lacked. News also came to them that Parliamentarian reinforcements sent from Yarmouth were likely to come from the direction of Lymington, either by land or sea. The Royalists therefore decided that having already suffered heavy losses, they would retire towards the New Forest, through which they were fortunate enough to make good their retreat, though not unscathed, and escape the much larger Parliamentary forces that then threatened them.

That the attack had been of some magnitude is clear from the number of cannon balls and shot from other weapons that have been found in the Mill Stream. The town had also suffered quite a lot of damage. Not only had many of the houses backing onto the old town ditch been deliberately pulled down in order to give the defenders in the castle a clear field of fire, but some of the other houses had either caught fire or been damaged in the fighting. The inhabitants were not unnaturally resentful and demanded compensation, which, as usual, was very slow in coming. As with the majority of the population in the country, the inhabitants of Christchurch regarded the quarrel between King and Parliament as not really their problem, and resented being caught up in it. Though they all supported one side or the other, and young men would always be prepared to go and fight, few families were prepared to take things to the extreme of having their houses destroyed for their beliefs.

Christchurch remained in the hands of the Parliamentary forces until the end of the war, though Major Lower, who had so successfully defended it against the determined Royalist attack was promoted to Lieutenant Colonel and made Governor of Winchester.

Though some effort was made to repair the damaged properties in the town, the main effort was expended on the castle and the other defences of the town. In 1646 the House of Lords voted that 30 tons of good oak should be sent to the town for their repair. Since by then the Civil War was over, it is to be hoped that much of the timber was used to repair the houses in the town rather than its defences, for which the mayor and burgesses probably thought there was by then little need.

Certainly this was the case four years later, when it was recorded that though the castle held some cannon, it had no garrison to use them. The fear was that this strong place could be seized by 'malignants', as Royalists were termed, and used against the Commonwealth by Royalist supporters. After discussion with officers in the army, the Governor of Southampton was instructed in November 1650 to solve the problem. This he did the next year by removing the cannon to Poole, which had always supported Parliament, and slighting the castle itself. It was obviously impossible to mine and blow up the walls, since that would have also destroyed much of the town. This had been possible at Corfe, where the castle was some distance from the houses. Instead, the north and south walls of the castle were eventually pulled down, leaving the building as we see it today. At the same time, the walls of the bailey were also probably destroyed. Those properties that had abutted the town ditch were rebuilt, with the rubble of the old buildings being used to fill in much of the ditch so that it can no longer be seen. There can be little doubt that their owners also took the opportunity to extend the gardens of their properties across the old ditch and up to the base of the castle mound. And who can blame them since they had suffered so much loss during the war.

Christchurch Castle.

During the 14 years that followed, what did William Pawson, Mayor in 1646, '54 and '58, and the others who held the chief office in the town, think of Oliver Cromwell, the victor of the war? What was their opinion of him who, for however good the reasons may have seemed at the time, overthrew and caused to be executed their anointed King? How did they rate the man who shunned democracy, suspended the House of Commons, abandoned rule by consent, and sacrificed civil liberties? What did they think of a person who said, "Government is for the people's good, not for what pleases them"? Certainly few in the town, except the most ardent Puritans, would have welcomed Cromwell's abolition of Christmas and maypole dancing. Having helped to smash the unconstitutional power of the monarchy, Cromwell tried to institute his own version of autocracy, in order to retain power in his own hands, just as the King whom he had supplanted had done. The chaos that ensued during the five months following Cromwell's death was only checked by the restoration of the dead King's son, as Charles II. We can assume that Thomas Crewe, Mayor in 1660 and his burgesses, led the general rejoicing that inevitably followed, with Christmas that year being an especially joyous celebration.

So ended a troublesome time for the town. Like the rest of the country, Christchurch folk were happy that peace had been restored. Trade and prosperity could once more be pursued. They would therefore have been more than a little alarmed when they heard, 35 years later, that the Duke of Monmouth had landed at Lyme Regis on June 11th 1685. Fearing that the invaders would naturally want to march on London, the citizens were probably relieved to hear that Monmouth was in fact marching west towards Bristol. Whatever their feelings about the rival claims of James II and the 'Protestant Duke' of Monmouth to the English throne as a result of the death of Charles II, none relished the thought of another Civil War. Some might even have recalled that it was in that same location that the terrible plague remembered as The Black Death had entered the country some 350 years before, with such devastating effect on the whole population. Most people in Christchurch would therefore be heartily thankful to learn the news of the Battle of Sedgemoor less than four weeks later on July 6th at which Lord Churchill had defeated Monmouth and thus prevented the possibility of a renewed conflict. Too many people were still alive in Christchurch who could remember the previous attacks on the town to want to risk a repetition of such an event. The citizens of Christchurch, led by their Mayor, John Blake, would have heaved a great sigh of relief and quietly celebrated their deliverance. It is interesting to note that John Blake continued as Mayor almost to the end of James II's reign, though whether the two events are in any way connected is doubtful. Certainly, if his continuing as Mayor for some years gave the town a greater sense of stability through continuity, then his four consecutive years as Mayor had merit. Then as now, Christchurch folk looked to live in a place 'Where Time is Pleasant'.

Chapter 18.

The School in the Church.

There is no record of exactly when the first school was established at Twynham. However it may reasonably be concluded that it was virtually as soon as the missionary priests sent by St Birinus had established their first little chapel, probably about A.D.700. Since their task was to preach and teach the Gospels with the object of converting the inhabitants to an understanding of and a belief in Christianity, they were in one sense running a school. By the time that Godric the priest was in charge of the church and chapels at Twynham when the great Domesday Record was being compiled in 1086, there would have been a more formal school established for the instruction of the children of the burgh. Some of the other priests attached to the Twynham church would probably also have been giving some basic instruction to other children in the outlying hamlets.

The first certain record of a school in the burgh occurs in Baldwin de Redvers' charter of about 1150. In it he not only confirmed to Dean Hilary the many lands and churches that were to be under the control of the newly established Augustinian Canons, but also refers to a school that was already in existance. The charter states '... ... *of which that church is seised and in perpetual alms all privileges as freely as ever, namely the school in the vill ... ...* '. There is no evidence of which building the school occupied, but it could have been either in the cloisters or the scriptorium or one of the rooms in the monastic buildings that was not needed for anything else. Most of the instruction would have centred around knowledge of the scriptures, though some reading, writing and calculation would have been taught as well. In an area so full of wild life and at a time when so much depended on agriculture in all its forms, one hopes that at least some time was spent on teaching the children something about their surroundings and how to make the best use of them. As so often in all education, much would depend on the particular interest of the priest who was in charge of the children. As any modern child knows, an inspiring teacher stimulates his pupils to take an interest in matters far outside the narrow curriculum. So it would sometimes have been in Norman times, just as much as it is today.

There was also soon established another 'school' at the Priory. This would have been particularly for the instruction of novices who wished to enter the priesthood. When the Lady Chapel had been completed in about 1400, there was also above it a large room available for these novices. This was the room known as St Michael's

Loft. It measures 56 feet long and is both light and airy, having windows on three sides. To the right of the three-bay eastern window, is a finely carved piscina and a large stone altar slab that the novices who were learning the various rituals of the services would have needed to use. Since one of the duties of the canons was to copy and illuminate manuscripts, this too may have been done either in the scriptorium or in St Michael's Loft, at least until Tudor times, by which time the art of printing began to supersede that of calligraphy. John Draper, in his letter to Henry VIII in 1538 refers to a schoolroom, stating, '... ... and your said orators [i.e. Draper] and their predecessors have used continually hitherto to keep a master to teach grammar to children and scholars there, and certain of them having meat drink and clothes.' Whether he was referring to St Michael's Loft is not certain, but he gives the impression of a flourishing free school.

St Michael's Loft.

It is possible that the St Michael's Loft may have been put to another use up to the time of the suppression of the monastery. Over the centuries, the church had acquired a large collection of 'holy relics' donated by the faithful and visiting pilgrims. It is doubtful if the provenance of many of them would today stand much scrutiny, but the more impressive were certainly on display in various places around the Priory. However perhaps the majority had to be stored somewhere and it is likely that this would have been St Michel's Loft. Most were discarded at the time of the Reformation, so that the Loft would once more have become an empty room.

However, after the canons had been dispersed in 1539, the room would no longer have been needed to train novices, since there were none. If the children of the town were not being taught there, then the room probably remained unused until after the church and its surrounding land were returned by Henry VIII to the town in 1540. At that time it may have been brought back into use as a schoolroom for the children though not perhaps on a permanent basis. Certainly, the room seems to have been in use as a school in 1617, and perhaps thereafter, because there is a record of St Michael's Loft windows being glazed at the expense of Sir George Hastings, a great-great-grandson of Margaret Countess of Salisbury, and six others. A later entry in the churchwardens' accounts of 1662 lists a payment of £4.8s. to Milliar Shurdelowe for glazing the school loft windows. There is also a note adding that *'the parish forever hereafter to be freed and discharged of glaseing any parts of the said school loft.'* This may have been as a result of some arrangement made between the mayor and burgesses, sitting as one body, and the Sixteene, who were largely the same people, sitting as another. If so, then it is likely that the Odber family played an important part.

The Odber family had taken a lease of Hurn Court in 1575 for a period of 99 years and had been both wealthy and influential in the area. They also had, and paid for, a pew in the Priory. Three of the family, were members of the Sixteene in 1664. The family therefore took a keen interest in the welfare of the town. With the Restoration of Charles II in 1660, there was a general feeling that things were returning to normal after the dull days of the Commonwealth. One improvement that year was that tea was first used as a drink in London and what an effect that was to have on the population of the whole country in the future!

Two years later, the Act of Uniformity required all clergy to consent to everything that was in the Book of Common Prayer of 1662. This not only led to the establishment of the Nonconformist Movement, but also to a greater emphasis on education being conducted on what were then considered to be proper Church of England lines. These included the use of James I Authorised Version of the Bible of 1611 as well as the 1662 Prayer Book. All schools under the supervision of the Church, would naturally have to conform. As a result, the newly enthroned Bishop George Morley of Winchester, granted a licence for a school previously held in Mr. Slade's private house, to be re-established in St Michael's Loft, for the proper instruction of the children of Christchurch. This was largely funded by Parkinson Odber who left £350 - a very considerable sum in those days - to be put to pious uses. The petition to the Bishop of Winchester reads: *'That ye sume of £350 was lately by ye last will of Parkinson Odber Esq deceased given for pious uses which was to be employed at ye discretion of John Newburgh Esq who thereupon about a year since with ye said money erected ye free-school in ye said Borough of Christchurch which through ye charity and benevolence of sundry neighbouring gentlemen and parishioners hath binn advanced and endowed with several sums of money, the better to maintain and establish ye same to ye advantage of those parts of ye Countrey, and encrease of good literature, and ye education of youth: that since one Mr. Slade an able and learned schoolmaster by Licence from your Lordship hath performed this Imployment to ye satisfaction of ye Petitioners and all others, by all which ye said school is much improved and increased. And no longer can continue in a private house, where it is now kept, neither is it for ye reputacon of a free school likely to be so well endowed to be kept any where but in some publique place. Now your Peticoners by ye unanimous approbacon of all concerned, have pitched upon (if your Lordship please licence ye same) a certaine great and spacious waste roome situate at ye east end of ye Church, called St Michael's Loft hertofore (as by tradicon we are informed) ye Chapter house for ye Prior and Convent of ye place for their private Affairs, into which Staires are to ascend out of ye Church yard (and is to have noe comunicacon at all with ye Church) repaired (being nowe much decayed) by ye Peticoners therefore most humbly pray your lordship's gracious Licence to erect and settle ye schoole in ye said St Michael's Loft.'* The petition was signed by Henry Hastings, as Mayor, who was probably a relative of Sir George who had paid for the glazing of the loft windows in 1617 and whose name is engraved on the old Borough Mace. John Newburgh as the trustee, and eight burgesses, one of whom was Edward Odber. It is possible that Mr. Slade was so successful with the school that he is the person who was elected a burgess in 1671. The reference to St Michael's Loft possibly being the old Chapter House is now considered to be without foundation.

The Records of the Sixteene contain a minute dated 7th March 1662 that reads: *'It is this day ordered that St Michael's loft shall forever hereafter and is hereby sett apart and appointed for a free Grammar Schooleroome to be fitted for that purpose as it is Articled and agreed on by John Newburgh Esq. in one paire of Indentures of the one parte sealed and Delivered and John Imber (etc) on the parts and behalf of the parish of the other parts sealed and delivered.'*

The following year, on November 5th 1663, the Mayor John Blake who succeeded Henry Hastings, John Imber the Vicar who had been a burgess in 1641 and was Mayor in 1679, and several others, signed a minute voting a disbursement by the mayor for the time being of a sum not less than £5 and not more than £10, out of the Common Treasury of the Borough towards a particular work of beautifying of the Free School. The money may have been used to plaster out the room, though this, in its turn, was removed in 1890 at the time that the roof was renovated.

There have been several occasions when the Lord of the Manor has taken a direct interest in the well being of the school. Baldwin de Redvers almost certainly was keen that the children in the burgh should receive such education as was then available and his successors would have been similarly supportive. One of the greatest bene-factions however, came from Henry, Earl of Clarendon, the son of Edward who had had such ambitions for opening up the Avon as a navigable route as far as Salisbury. In 1707, the year before he sold the Manor to Sir Peter Mews, Henry, Earl of Clarendon and two of his friends bought an annuity of £25 for 99 years at a cost of £387.10s.0d This was to be used to finance the running of the Free School in St Michael's Loft. In addition, a capital sum of £714.10s.0d was to be paid as directed by the governors of the school. The schoolmaster was to receive a salary of £17.5s.2d. a year, if the trustees thought fit - in other words if he did his job properly - otherwise the money should be put to good public use as directed by the Corporation of the Borough. Mr. Slade's successor would have been secure in his post. However it would seem that in 1748 there were arrears of payment of the salary amounting to 14 years, the reason for which is not clear. Certainly Edward Hooper of Lincoln's Inn was appointed to act as Trustee that year, probably to investigate what had been going wrong.

The school remained in St Michael's Loft for the next 200 years. During that time, it was not uncommon for the vicar either to be the schoolmaster or to take some part in the teaching, since he would be one of the few people who knew sufficient Latin to instruct his charges. Though in general the school flourished and had many dedicated masters, there was one master whose conduct appears to have fallen far below what was expected. The Borough archives hold much detail about the unfortunate Mr. Robert Barrett in 1773/4. He was accused of *cohabiting with another man's wife*, though he maintained that it was with the consent of her husband. There were also complaints that he was in the habit of visiting various alehouses during school hours and was frequently drunk during the day. His pupils seem to have been well aware of what was going on and one can imagine that they learnt very little of the usual curriculum, since Barrett was frequently absent from his class, or too drunk to teach, though they may have had their eyes opened to the ways of the world. The result was that Robert Barrett was sacked. It seems that he then locked the doors of St Michael's Loft and kept the key, so that the mayor had to force entry. However Barrett took the matter to court, claiming wrongful dismissal. This led to numerous affadavits from the boys themselves, their parents and other citizens outlining his many misdemeanours. His original referees who lived in Burford, claimed that they were unaware of the nature of his real character, or they would not have recommended him. However it appeared that one of them had later been hanged in effigy for stealing a bridle, so that his opinion might be considered suspect. A copy of Barrett's marriage certificate to Mary Whitnold, a widow, was also produced, to substantiate the immorality charge. The whole matter did the school little good and inevitably led to a great deal of gossip, much of it probably malicious. However it would certainly have enlivened the days for the schoolchildren.

As soon as Barrett was sacked, William Jackson, at that time the curate, was appointed to take over the school in October 1773. Upon him fell the difficult task of holding the school together and doing his best to focus the children's attention what they were supposed to be learning. According to Warner, who was a pupil at the time, *'unfortunately for the celebrity of our seminary, the gentleman who then filled the office of head-master of the free-school at Christchurch, though a worthy, amiable, and sensible man, and an excellent parish priest was no scholar. Few excelled him in the art of reading and the graces of elocution. Nature had gifted him with a voice deep, sonorous, flexible and of unequalled melody; with a fine manly person; a handsome intelligent countenance; and a great dignity of manner.'* The result was that his pupils excelled at public speaking. However, since Warner developed a great interest in the archaeology and geology of the region, it may be that his original interest was aroused by William Jackson who could easily have taken his charges along the Barton cliffs to study the now world famous fossils there. Fortunately also, the pupils had James Lockyer, the parish clerk, as their 'arithmetical usher'.

The town was however blessed with a fine preacher when Jackson was appointed Vicar to succeed James Talman in 1778, in which year he was also Mayor. We owe Jackson a further debt of gratitude, since it was his exertions that prevented part of the Constable's House being pulled down in 1792.

Conditions in St Michael's Loft must have been harsh for the pupils as well as their master. There was no fireplace, and the leaded lights of the windows could not guarantee to keep out the strong winds. The calls of nature also presented a problem. The nearest facility was the 'necessary' built beside the Mill Stream, much like the garderobe beside the Constable's House. To reach it, the boys had to run down the long spiral staircase that ended outside the church adjacent to the Chideoke Tomb. At least the boys would be warm on their return to the schoolroom after their long run and climb back up the stairs. This 'necessary' and also the schoolroom, were repaired in 1792, at a cost of £1.16s.1¼d.

In spite of the various donations that the school received, it sometimes struggled financially. Though Samuel Clapman was appointed Headmaster in January 1803 to succeed Jackson, the appointment was annulled in 1819 for lack of funds. Fortunately James Lockyer was prepared to teach five children to be chosen by the Parish Workhouse Committee, reading, writing and arithmetic at no charge, though the parish did agree to supply books, pens and slates for the pupils. This was a period when the country was going through a severe depression and local resources were being stretched to the limit.

Whatever the quality of the men who taught the boys in St Michael's Loft, when it was established as a free school in 1662, it is probable that many of them learnt as much from looking out of that room as from what they were taught in it. The 75 steps that had to be climbed to reach its position above the Lady Chapel and its many large windows, meant that the view over the surrounding countryside was impressive. To the immediate north stood the recently slighted remains of the ancient Norman castle keep. Further north lay first the town itself, whose busy streets could be observed often with familiar figures going about their business, beyond which lay St Catherine's Hill and the open countryside. Looking eastwards there were the open common meadows that rose towards the great forest. To the south lay the wide harbour with Hengistbury Head and the open seas beyond. Dull indeed would be the schoolboy who could not imagine the fierce clashes that had taken place around the castle, at first in living memory, during the Civil War. Which side would he choose to support, and what daring deeds would he himself have accomplished? Going back in time, he could imagine himself stealing the king's deer from his forest and getting away with it, much as he would himself poach rabbits. In later years, boys would have watched the smugglers bringing their loaded horses along Hengistbury Head, perhaps meeting the riding officers and cavalry from the local barracks, and having handed over a suitable toll, continuing on their way inland. From their high vantage point, they could also see ships out in the bay. Many boys would have known the names of each one and watched as they successfully outran the revenue cutters. What they witnessed with their eyes and imagined in their minds could have given them a far greater understanding of life as it really was than most of the dry lessons they were forced to endure. The best of their masters would certainly have drawn on these sights and fed the boys' imaginations. Such has always been the skill of the best teachers.

We have an accurate description of local education in the 1820's from James Druitt. Though he attended the school in Wimborne, it is likely that his experiences would have been similar to those of boys in Christchurch. Most of the pupils would have been day-boys, but some, like James Druitt, would have been boarded out with the masters running the school. The boys were roused by a church bell ringing at 5.45 a.m. School began at 6.15 a.m. and continued till 8 a.m. when there was breakfast. This usually consisted of bread and milk. Those who got into breakfast first would scrape the butter off the next boy's slice of bread and put it onto their own. Lessons continued from 9 a.m. until noon, when they went to lunch. This was a substantial meal of either roast or boiled good quality beef, mutton or veal. Sometimes for as change there would be a leg of pork and there were always potatoes and usually other vegetables. Once a week there would be a beefsteak pie that seems to have been a particular favourite. For desert there would often be fruit pies made from local apples, cranberries, or other garden fruits in season or that had been bottled for the winter. Lessons began again at 2 p.m. and continued until 5 o'clock, after which there was still up to an hour and a half of prep. This would be done by candlelight in the dark evenings. Supper was at 6 o'clock and consisted of bread and cheese, often accompanied by lettuce and other vegetables that boys had grown themselves in their gardens. At both lunch and supper there was home-brewed ale, served in mugs holding half a pint or more. If a boy broke his mug, he had to provide another. But this was no hardship, since he would make sure that it held more than half a pint. Sunday lunch inevitably was a bigger spread than on weekdays. It was usually roast fillet and shoulder of veal, followed by baked plum pudding - surely enough to satisfy even the largest appetite.

Team games had not at that time become part of the curriculum, nor were there any playing fields. There was however always a playground where the young could let off steam. Besides all the usual games of 'tag' and skipping, for example, one of the favourites among the older boys was fives. This was similar to squash, but was played against a wall using a ball as hard as a cricket ball but only about 3½ cm in diameter hitting it with either a bare hand or a glove that was lightly padded on the palm. At Christchurch it could well have been played against the north aisle wall with the north porch wall making one side wall and the first buttress making the other side. Since this was and is still unconsecrated ground, having originally been the archery ground since medieval times, it was ideally situated for use by boys let out from St Michael's Loft.

It seems that the school must have prospered despite the depressed conditions in the country and outgrew its location in St Michael's Loft. In 1828, Sir George Rose, who was Lord of the Manor of the Borough of Christchurch, gave a parcel of land that is now 15 High Street and

£100. so that a National School could be built. This cost £638.17s.10¾d.. and it was occupied in June 1829. Into the building moved the ten Free School boys. They had moved temporarily with their master Mr. G. Ballard. from St Michael's Loft to the Town Hall. that still at that time stood in the old Market Square at the junction of Castle Street Church Street and High Street. Conditions in St Michael's Loft were probably by then considered too harsh. and the room was in any case too large for the few boys using it.

There were. however insufficient funds to pay for the complete building. In 1832. John Spicer. who had been mayor was thanked. according to the council minutes. *'during the period of great popular Excitement and unprovoked aggression arising from the Protracted discussion and subsequent enactment of the Reform bill"* [as a result of which the town lost one of its two M.P.s] for *'his liberal donation of the sum of £29.1s.3d to be applied towards the liquidation of the Debt due for the erection of the National School Rooms'.*

Fortunately the mayors in 1836 and '37 had also been frugal and had saved £85.1s.6d that was then paid to the builders. The balance of the cost was found by the corporation by selling most of their holding of South Sea annuities. This was part of the capital endowment made to the Free School in 1707 by Henry. Earl of Clarendon and was surely a use of the funds of which he would have thoroughly approved.

Once more St Michael's Loft was left empty and remained so for a century and a half. Recently it was put to good use once more as a museum which displays items connected with its use as a school and the history of the Priory. It therefore still retains its educational use.

But the town was expanding rapidly in the more prosperous Victorian times and the building in the High Street was soon proving to be too small. The Corporation had for some time realised that the cost of the school was a constant drain on their resources. as the problem they had experienced in paying for the new building amply proved. They therefore applied to the Charity Commissioners in 1866 to transfer the trusteeship of the school that we know as the Priory School. to the vicar and churchwardens as the more proper body to take charge of the education of the young. In effect this was no more than reverting to the situation that had existed since 1662 and since Town and Church had been so indissolubly linked since 1540. it was a logical move. A new and larger site was found in Wick Lane and the present school was started in 1867. It cost about £2.000. which was raised partly by the gift of land from Sir William Rose and his brother. Lord Strathnairn. partly by subscription. partly by the exertions of Revd. Zachary Nash who was at that time the curate. and partly by the sale of the school building in the High Street.

Priory School and Wick Lane flooded c.1905

The present school is now a Church of England Voluntary Aided Primary School, of which the vicar is ex officio a member of the Board of Governors. Rightly, the school uses the Priory as its school chapel for major services and sometimes performs its plays there, much as Miracle Plays would have been performed in medieval times. Divinity is taught by one of the Priory's clergy so that the link with the parish church remains close, and its reputation remains high in the area. May it long remain so and continue to be the 'School in the Church'.

The Priory Church of England V.A. School 1998.
Courtesy of the Daily Echo, Bournemouth.

148

Chapter 19.

The Great Storm of 1703 and other Tempests.

Careful observation of the national and regional weather forecasts frequently seems to show a marked difference in conditions. In general, it seems that the regional forecast presents the prospect of far better weather than that offered nationally. This phenomenon seems to be even greater when it comes to considering the weather in the specific locality of Christchurch and its harbour. The micro-climate there seems usually to be more sunny than that found in much of the rest of the region, so that, whereas according to the forecast, it should be overcast and cool, in fact the town and harbour are bathed in warm sunshine. That is not to say that the locality never experiences severe weather. It does indeed, and the storms that occasionally hit Christchurch have sometimes been as severe as any experienced in other parts of the country.

The Anglo-Saxon Chronicle records that the years 1115 to 1118 produced the worst weather that had ever been known in England. Floods covered much low lying land, drowning untold numbers of animals and washing out many crops before they could be harvested or leaving them flat and rotting in the fields. Frosts were so severe that many were frozen to death in their beds; and the gales flattened vast areas of woodland. Twynham inevitably suffered greatly, particularly as it is so low-lying, though there is no accurate record of how great were the losses.

In the 19th century, there is a record of a severe gale during Matins on Sunday 11th February 1866. The Vicar, Revd. Zaccary Nash, was obliged to cut short the service after the lessons, when the force of the gale blew off several large stones from the north side of the nave roof. The *Christchurch Times* the following Saturday reported that *"the congregation dispersed (probably never before so rapidly! The falling bits of bits of plaster from the nave ceiling was an added incentive to flight) ... ...The premature conclusion of the service at the church caused anxious looks to be directed towards the church, from the roof of which the stones commenced to fall until a large hole 25 or 30 feet long and 10 to 12 feet wide had been made. About this time the wind obtained a lodgement under the roof just eastward of the tower, and a large portion of it was stripped at that place. A large portion of the tower (then covered with stone shingles) was also stripped... .....The gaps in the nave roof were temporarily filled with thatched hurdles".* There must also have been other damage in the town, but it was not sufficiently severe to cause additional comment. The good people of

Christchurch probably felt particularly aggrieved, as well as frightened, that the forces of nature should have seen fit to interrupt Divine Service.

During the 1880's, it would appear that Christchurch suffered at least two particularly severe winters. Photography was by then very much the vogue, and there are photos in the town's archives showing Castle Street in 1881, impassable under deep snow. A blizzard struck the town in January, almost cutting it off from the outside world. Even the rivers froze over that year, and the snow did not finally disappear until March. In 1885, the town was again submerged under snow, which, according to this photograph, seems to have been at least one foot deep in the High Street.

Christchurch High Street 1885.

It was during such hard winters that in London, when the Thames froze over, it was customary to roast an ox on the ice. Since the river had not at that time been narrowed by encroaching building on its banks, the flow of the stream was much slower and therefore could freeze over more easily.

In the severe winter of 1962/3 Christchurch Harbour also froze over. The effect on those involved in fishing was particularly cruel, since boats could not put to sea. However, Roy Stride, who had recently moved into the Watch House on the edge of the harbour in

Mudeford, refused to be idle. He constructed an ice-yacht in his boat yard out of scaffolding planks and ladders, fitted a rudder to it and rigged up a lug-sail and 'launched' himself onto the ice. Setting off across the harbour in a good breeze, he soon found Hengistbury Head fast approaching. Pushing the tiller hard away, he was delighted to discover that his 'boat' promptly went about as it would on the water. Thereafter, he and others had a great deal of unusual fun until the thaw finally came. He also records that his was one of the few houses that still had running water, so that he was able to help out his neighbours by running a hose to their properties to fill up their baths.

Roofless flats in Highcliffe 1987.
Courtesy of the Daily Echo, Bournemouth

In more recent times, the storm that hit much of southern England in 1987 will long be remembered by those still living there who witnessed its devastation. Woodlands and particularly in this area the

151

New Forest, suffered widespread damage to many of its ancient trees and others nearing maturity, with many roads blocked and vehicles crushed. There was particularly tragic loss of life, when two firemen were killed by a tree falling on the appliance in which they were hurrying to the assistance of others who had suffered in the storm. Severe flooding occurred in many places in and around the town and the defences against the sea and rivers were breached in many places. Tiles were scatted wholesale and complete roofs were ripped off properties and sent flying. Modern technology meant that the devastation was flashed round the world by television that showed pictures of roofless flats in Highcliffe. Once again the Priory Church suffered. One of the stone pinnacles on the top of the tower was caught in a whirlwind and twisted off and crashed down through the roof of the nave. There it lodged, its fall broken by one of the main roof timbers that prevented it from falling further. Had it done so, it would have fallen onto a group of dedicated workers who help to maintain the building with inevitable severe loss of life. It was several years before all traces of the damage were repaired. Such an event inevitably brought home to people the enormous power of nature that can be both benevolent and destructive. However, these occasional calamities have thankfully been more than offset by frequent hot summers, that local people and visitors alike have thoroughly enjoyed. Nor has the town suffered the droughts that have then often affected much of the rest of the country, since fortunately much of the town's water supply now comes from local rivers rather than reservoirs.

However it seems that nothing can compare with the devastating storm that struck the whole country during 26th and 27th November 1703. Both Daniel Defoe, best known as the author of *Robinson Crusoe*, and John Evelyn, of diary fame, recorded their own accounts of the event. From them it is clear that the loss of life and damage both on land and at sea was devastating. At sea, many ships were lost, and many more wrecked though later partly salvaged. As always, there were cases of apparently miraculous happenings. On one ship, a dozen men were washed overboard by a massive wave, only to have three of them washed back on board again by the next wave. On land, according to Defoe, the storm had been raging for at least a fortnight before it reached its peak on 26th and 27th. He recorded that the barometer had fallen like a stone. He continued, '... ... *nobody durst quit their tottering habitations; for whatever the danger was within doors, it was worse without. The bricks, tiles and stones, from the tops of the houses, flew with such a force, and so thick in the streets, that no one thought fit to venture out, though their houses were near demolished within. ... ... Unless they could have gone above 200 yards from any building, there was no security, for the force of the wind blew the tiles point blank. ... ...the author of this has seen tiles blown from a house above 30 or 40 yards and stuck from five to eight inches into the solid earth. Pieces of iron and sheets of lead have from the higher buildings been blown much further'.* According to Defoe, the direction of the wind was originally from the prevailing Southwest, but later veered to North-west, before backing once more to South. Immediately after the peak of the storm had passed, there were incredibly high tides, *'... ...that brought up the sea in such a raging manner, that in some parts of England it was incredible, the water rising six or eight feet higher than it was ever known to do in the memory of man; by which ships were fleeted up upon the firm land several rods off from the banks and an incredible number of cattle and people drowned'.*

John Evelyn's account records in some detail the damage done to the forests throughout the country. This was to have a marked effect on the shipbuilding industry, since many of the finest oak trees that would be needed to build the navy's men-of-war were destroyed. He records that one part only of the Forest of Dean lost no less than 3,000 mature oaks, and he himself lost 2,000 trees, torn up by the roots. In the New Forest, he records that 4,000 large oaks were destroyed, many of which were already earmarked for use by the Royal Navy. In addition, many areas of young trees were devastated.

There are other local records of the storm. At Hurst Spit, two salterns were almost ruined by the sea flooding over the beach. Lymington, perhaps because it was more sheltered, suffered less damage than elsewhere, though even there it was considerable. Ships were wrecked, roofs torn off and a new barn blown over.

The full extent of the damage done at Christchurch is not known, but there exists one contemporary letter from which a fair estimate of the damage can be assessed.

'Sir, In answer to yours, relating to the damages done by the late Great Storm in, and about our Town, is, that we had great part of the roof of our Church uncovered, which was covered with very large Purbeck-stone and the battlements of the Tower, and part of the Leads blown down, some Stones of a vast weight blown from the Tower, several of them being two or three hundred weight, were blown some Rods or Perches distance from the Church; and 12 Sheets of Lead rolled up together, that 20 men could not have done the like, to the great Amazement of those that saw them: and several Houses and Barnes blown down, with many hundreds of trees of all sorts; several Stacks of Chimneys being blown down, and particularly of one Thomas Spencer's of this Town who had his Top of a Brick Chimney taken off by the House and blown across a Cart Road, and lighting down upon a Barn of Richard Holloway's broke down the end of the said Barn, and fell upright upon one End, on a Mow of Corn in the

Barn; but the said Spencer and his Wife, although they were sitting by the Fire, knew nothing thereof until the Morning: And a Stack of Chimneys of one Mr. Imber's fell down upon a young Gentlewoman's Bed, she having but just got out of the same, and several Out-houses and Stables were blown down, some Cattle killed; and some Wheat-ricks entirely blown off their Stafolds; and lighted on their bottom without any damage; this is all the Relation I can give you that us Remarkable about us.

I remain your Friend and Servant, William Mitchell'.

This letter is interesting as much for what it says as what it omits. It appears that William Mitchell was a plumber and glazier by trade, though at the time that he wrote his letter he was probably managing his business rather than getting his hands dirty. There are many accounts of his firm working on the roof and windows of the Priory, where he seems to have been retained to keep the building in good repair. In 1721 he was one of the churchwardens. Both Thomas Spencer and Richard Holloway, damage to whose properties he mentions, were members of well-known and ancient local families. The impression given is that he was writing in answer to an official request for details of the damage suffered. As such, he may have felt that his reply should concentrate on damage suffered by important buildings and people, rather than comment on the sufferings of the general populace, or even the countryside, about which he probably knew little. Much of England was still living under a system of subsistence agriculture, where families grew what they could for their own needs, selling what little surplus they had to pay for what they could not provide for themselves. Most manufacture was local, since the Industrial Revolution was still 50 years in the future and 'Turnip' Townsend and Thomas Coke of Norfolk's agricultural improvements were still 80 years away. Thomas Mitchell may therefore have had little knowledge of anything outside his particular trade, and even that he would probably prefer not to allude to in too much detail, preferring to socialise with those into whose strata he had probably risen.

To estimate what damage this storm did to the locality, it is therefore necessary to take the few details he gives, and extrapolate them by reference to the details given in the accounts of storms in other parts of the country. We can assume that many of the fields would be flooded. However, since the storm took place in November, the damage to crops would be less than might have been expected since the harvest had long since been gathered. What damage there was would have been to unthreshed corn ricks, many of which were destroyed. The loss of livestock, drowned in the floods that followed the storm would have been severe, particularly since much of the grazing would have been on the low-lying water meadows. The many

154

smaller trees that were uprooted would have affected the ordinary cottagers. since they would have been in their orchards or gardens. Those involved in boat building would have felt the loss of the mature oaks that they would have had from the New Forest. Probably of more concern to Christchurch people would have been the loss of their boats. since many were involved either in offshore fishing. or coastal trading. Certainly the losses in Christchurch were severe. John Evelyn and others also provide useful records of the losses throughout the country. Bristol and the surrounding countryside suffered from the combined effects of wind and tide. driving the waters up the channel. The damage done to the riverbanks was estimated to be over £200.000. and in one low-lying area alone. 15.000 sheep were drowned. The first Eddystone Lighthouse was swept away and according to one report. *'Portsmouth. Plymouth. Weymouth and most of our seaport towns looked as if they had been bombarded. the damage of them is not easily computed'*. The Royal Navy lost a large number of ships and more than 1.500 sailors were drowned. The losses to merchant ships and other privately owned vessels were far greater. and Christchurch suffered its full share of losses. Twelve of those who lost their lives were buried in the Priory graveyard. For some years afterwards. there are entries in the parish accounts of payments made to distressed seamen. For the year 1704/5 there is also an entry in the parish accounts showing that 6 rates were collected amounting to £131.9s.2d.. all of which would have been needed for the repair of the church. One of the churchwardens was John Clingan.

Nor did the continent of Europe escape. Flanders suffered greatly. A quarter of Friesland. part of the present Netherlands. was flooded when the dykes burst. with considerable loss of life. The effects of the storm even reached Cologne. where. to add to the problems caused by the storm. they also suffered an earthquake.

The storm of 1703 was indeed a national disaster. As soon as the extent of the damage and terrible loss of both life and property was fully known. Queen Anne. who had ascended the throne only the year before. issued a proclamation calling on people to offer relief to the shipwrecked seamen and the widows of those who had been drowned. giving a lead herself. She also ordered a great number of new ships to be built to replace those that had been lost. The good people of Christchurch did their part in relieving the distress of those who had suffered and would certainly had obeyed the Queen's proclamation that January 19th 1704 should be a public Fast Day. with special prayers being said. Those who lived through the Great Storm. never forgot its terror. Christchurch people. because of their close connect-ion with the sea. would have commemorated it in sorrow for those lost and gratitude for their own deliverance. for many years afterwards.

Chapter 20.

John Clingan and his Charity.

So far as can be ascertained, John Clingan, who died in 1714, was a comparative newcomer to Christchurch, since there is no record of him or his family being here in the register that was compiled in 1673 for the Hearth Tax. It is however known that he was trading as a mercer, with his contacts on the continent, through Southampton as well as Christchurch. He would have had ample opportunity to build up a successful business dealing with silks, velvets and other high quality fabrics. These goods were being increasingly imported from the continent and the Far East to satisfy the demands of the wealthy merchants and landowners. Consequently John Clingan was able to become a very wealthy man.

John Clingan lived during an age of considerable change and prosperity. The Bank of England had been established in 1690. The Duke of Marlborough was fighting his successful battles on the continent, beginning with Blenheim in 1704, the same year that Gibraltar was captured, while three years later, the Act of Union brought England and Scotland together under one Parliament. It was "The Age of Elegance", and of such men as Dryden, Sir Isaac Newton, Wren and Hogarth. Two months before Queen Anne died in August 1714, John Clingan made his will. In that same month of June, the great Electress Sophia of Hanover, heiress to the throne of England, had died, thus ensuring that the next King of England would be her son George I, an event that was to usher in great changes for the government of England.

Little is known about John Clingan's early life, but at the time of the Great Storm in 1703, described in the last chapter, he was one of the churchwardens at the Priory. As such he was a member of the Sixteene, the body that was responsible for the administration, not only of the church, but also many of the affairs of the town. Duties such as the supervision of the Poor House, making sure that the parish doctor was not only paid but also carried out his ministrations within the limits of medical knowledge at that time, would both have come his way. A somewhat primitive fire service had been established early in the new century which again would have come within his responsibilities. He was therefore a man who was very much in touch with the needs of the town and in particular those who were either sick, poor or had suffered some calamity. It seems reasonable to suppose therefore that the suffering that he witnessed and had to help alleviate as a result of the storm at the end of 1703 may have made a lasting impression on him. Amongst other things, as churchwarden, he would have had a say in the burial of the twelve seamen who were lost locally in the 1703 storm, and who were interred in the Priory graveyard. He may in addition have provided some relief to the wives and families of some of those men in addition to the local families who had suffered loss and damage in the storm. If so, then he was doing no more than follow the excellent example set by Queen Anne. The hardship that he witnessed in Christchurch both in supervising the Poor House and also for those who put to sea, coupled with the perceived need for a proper training for apprentices that he would fully appreciate as a trader himself, would provide ample reason for the benefactions he made in his will.

The Poor Law papers for the Parish of Christchurch that form part of the Priory Church archives, shed considerable light on employment conditions in the town throughout the seventeenth and eighteenth centuries. John Clingan would have been familiar with these in his capacity as one of the overseers of the Poor House. From 1607, both boys and girls had been bound as apprentices to learn a variety of trades. The early records are not complete, since there is a gap between 1607 and 1653 and only 22 apprentices are listed during the next 37 years. However from 1690 to 1711 no less than 64 apprentices are listed and it may be that during much of those 21 years, John Clingan was taking an interest in the Poor House. Certainly the records give many interesting details. In 1667 there is the first record of an apprentice. Thomas Whittman, whose father had died, being bound to Robert Winsey, a seaman, in order to learn seamanship and the trade of a "Planter" in Newfoundland. There the term uniquely meant fishing on the Grand Banks and learning to cure the catch in the curing plants set up on land. This became a highly profitable trade, with boats from Poole and Christchurch leaving their home port in the spring to sail to Newfoundland and to return from there in the autumn, fully laden with cured fish, for which there was a ready market. The Poor Law records show that in 1698/9, two boys, Richard Morris and Isaac Southwell, both of whom appear to have lost their fathers, were apprenticed to fish planters in Newfoundland. The same year, Thomas Southwell, probably a brother or close relative of Isaac, was apprentised as a sailor. In 1705, John Clingan himself took Charity Collens as an apprentice, presumably as a domestic servant in his house. The records have frequent entries of girls being apprenticed to 'yeomen' or 'gents' which seems to imply that this was a common way of acquiring a domestic servant while at the same time discharging a social responsibility towards the less fortunate young people in the parish. Other sections of the Poor Law records list four "bonds" for keeping poor children between 1696 and 1701, and 25 "settlement certificates". sometimes for children and sometimes for whole families. in various towns in Dorset and Hampshire. From these records it seems clear that there was. as always. a continuing need to care for those. who for one reason or another had suffered misfortune. and were in need of assistance. In consequence. the charitable intentions of his will become easy to understand.

Made only seven months before he died. the will included much unnecessary detail. though its burden was comparatively simple. Its length was due to the practice of the time that lawyers were paid partly by the length of the documents they wrote. The result was often to cause unnecessary confusion in the interpretation of a document's meaning. which in turn created more work for the lawyers. This was a happy result for the lawyer if not the client. In this case it may well partly explain Samuel Hookey's lack of action as executor. and the reason for the matter going before the Lord Chancellor on 25th July 1730. Even then. the Decree for the administration of the Charity that Clingan wished to establish was not finally cleared by the Attorney General until 19th March 1736. 32 years after his death.

It is clear from his will that John Clingan was married. though. despite Katherine being *'his loving wife'*. he only left her £20 a year and *'my bed and bedstead with whatever furniture is in the room over that which was my shop. together with one iron pot one kettle one chamber pot one close stool and three good ordinary chairs and one silver spoon'*. He may have feared that she would contest his will. since she was to have such a small proportion of his estate. for he added that *'If in case she doth molest or disturb my Executor. hereinafter named in the enjoyment of my lands herein devised to him ... ... then I hereby require my Executor to pay her no more than Five Pounds per Annum'*. Clingan's married sister Marion and her three daughters were each left a capital sum of £50. and his daughter-in-law. Mary Belbin. £5 a year. He made other personal bequests; £100 to his faithful servant Robert Wilton. and to Charity and Sarah Dean. £50 each. Richard Hookey's son. Nicholas. was to receive £100 at the age of 21. and the son and two daughters of Nicholas Slade. deceased. were each left £10 when they reached a similar age. Miss Charity Collins. who may have been a ward of the elder Samuel Hookey. was left £10. *'in case she shall behave herself soberly and shall marry according to the liking of the said Mr. Hooke'*. Otherwise she was to receive ten shillings a year for the rest of her life. From this we may assume that he took care of those in whom he had a particularly close interest. John Clingan left a house and a clock to his executor and "well beloved friend" Samuel Hookey.

The rest of Clingan's considerable estate was to be devoted to charitable purposes. The simplest bequest was *'to the poor of the parish of Christchurch the sum of £50 to be distributed amongst them by my executor, in bread and meat, within nine months after my decease'.* We may assume that bequests were all faithfully carried out.

Clingan's House as 'Ferreys' during the coronation of Edward VII.

The major part of the estate that was to form the Charity consisted of three parts. First, what was then the largest house in the High Street. For many years this was leased by the Ferrey family to house their draper's shop, and later it became Smith's Furniture Showrooms. Today it houses Bookends Bookshop. Second, there were several land holdings: a farm at Iford, measuring 29 acres, 3 roods 28 poles; land at Roeshot, Somerford that measured 11 acres, 3 roods 39 poles; and a small plot of land at Pokesdown measuring 1 acre and 30 poles. (4 roods = 1 acre. 30¼ square yards = 1 square pole.) all of which was let out. In addition there were considerable investments and other goods. The will describes the whole as being *'all my houses, lands, goods, chattels household stuff, bills, bonds, credits'.* It was a valuable estate. Later, as a result of the 1802 Inclosure Act, when the desolate heath-land of the Liberty of Westover was enclosed, the Charity was awarded almost 17 acres of land in the area of what is now Pokesdown, bounded by Christchurch, Wolverton and Portman Roads, as compensation for loss of its commoning rights. The surplus cash funds in the Charity were already invested in South Sea Annuities and formed part of the National Debt. Although the South Sea Bubble had burst in 1720, the part that was guaranteed by the Government was safe enough and continued to pay good dividends.

Clingan's House as Bookends 1999.

After all debts and legacies had been discharged, John Clingan willed that Samuel Hookey was to use *'the overplus and interest from time to time to dispose amongst the poor of the said Parish for their use in such manner as he shall think fit. And that the Yearly Rents Issues and Profits be likewise distributed to such charitable uses ... ...'* giving Samuel Hookey wide discretion as to how the Charity was to be administered. It was however clear that the Charity was to be used to help particularly the adolescents of the town to establish themselves in the world by their own efforts. Self-help was regarded as a cardinal virtue that was to be encouraged and assisted where possible. It did, after all, personify the Yeomen of England.

The result of the High Court hearing in 1736 was that proper Trustees were appointed to administer the Charity. These were always to include the mayor, the vicar, and the steward of the Borough Court of Christchurch, which was a Court of Record. The original Board of Trustees included an additional 20 men, which gives some idea of the importance that was attached to the Charity by the Lord Chancellor of the day. Once again, it is clear that Church and Town were to work together for the good of the whole community. Today the Trustees number not less than 7 and not more than 9, including the Mayor and Vicar, ex officio. There was also to be a Receiver, who, in 1736, was *"to be allowed 12d in the Pound for his care and trouble in collecting the said Charity and keeping the said account"*. After the 264 years that the Charity has been operating, David Richardson, the 13th Receiver, was appointed in 1999. The previous Receivers were:-

1736	James Willis.
1755	John Willis.
1779	John Oake.
1786	Henry Oake.
1801	John Rickman.
1832	William Dibsdall.
1838	Henry Rowden.
1846	James Druitt.
1892	John Druitt.
1931	James Victor Druitt.
1944	Oscar Godfrey Vernon.
1973	Brian Pickering.

During the negotiations to set up the board of Trustees, it was laid down in 1735 that the Trustees were to meet at least once a year, usually in the Court House in Bridge Street, *'to elect and put out apprentice as many poor children of the said parish as the annual Interest or produce of the said Estate will bear and further to take such order and make such ordinances Bye-laws and elections of Trustees and Receivers for the due management and application of the said Charity as from time to time shall be necessary and expedient'*. The cost of binding each apprentice was not normally to exceed £5 and *'it is intended that a particular regard be had to Sea Service'*. The reason for this last condition may well be due not only to Christchurch's position as a seaport, but also to Clingan's memories of the storm of 1703.

The first order of the Trustees when they met in September 1736, was that *'Generally the ages of the children put out shall be between 11 and 15 as shall appear in the Parish Register, or otherwise to the satisfaction of the Trustees, and that if certificates of the ages of the children proposed, from the Parish Register or otherwise to the satisfaction of the Trustees were not produced, such children should not be put out'*. The purpose of this was to ensure not only that the apprentices were of the age that they purported to be, but also that they were locally born. The following year, at the second meeting of the Trustees, it was determined that *'The cost of the Indentures and the Duty should be paid out of the Charity Funds. On this footing children were apprenticed during a period'*. In 1763 it was further ordained that *'Apprentices should not be put to people residing in Christchurch Parish unless for Sea Service'*. In 1797 a further change was made. It was decided that *'£5 should in future be paid with children put out in the Parish of Christchurch and £7 to those put out in other parishes'*. Eleven years later, in 1808, a major change was agreed. *'Four Pound was ordered to be given with female apprentices on the mistresses undertaking to board and lodge the girls during their service and the same permissions was to be given with boys put out to the Sea Service'.*

Those that could be given financial assistance were to be living in the Parish of Christchurch, which at that time covered a much larger area than today. Along the coast, it stretched from the western boundary of Highcliffe to the chine where the small Bourne stream flows into the sea. Inland, it included Blackwater, then west to Hurn and Parley Green, before turning north to St Leonards and the edge of Ashley before turning south to Sopley Common. From there the boundary turned east to Dudmoor, then Bransgore and Thorney Hill before turning south-east to North Hinton, Beckley and Walkford. The land bounded in the west by Alum Chine and Muscliffe and stretching eastwards as far as the Stour, was all part of Holdenhurst Parish, that since Norman times had been attached to the Priory at Twynham and remained so until 1845. That year, St Peter's Church in the new town of Bournemouth was established. There is every reason to believe that some of those who benefited from the Charity of John Clingan lived Holdenhurst Parish, which certainly formed part of the Manor of Christchurch. However, until about 150 years ago much of the land was empty heath-land with only a few scattered hamlets and farms upon it. As such, the requests to the Charity for assistance from people living in those areas would at that time have been few. Today, however, young people living in what has become a large part of the modern Bournemouth are able to benefit from this ancient Christchurch Charity.

The records of the Charity are remarkably complete. There is a full record of the names of all the apprentices that were bound. With the exception of the first five indentures, issued in 1737, the documents themselves survive in the records.

The first apprentice whose indentures were paid for by the Charity, appears to have been Thomas Bound, who was apprenticed to James Shambler of Newfoundland to learn the trade of a "Planter". What more logical apprenticeship was there to satisfy John Clingan's wish that particular attention should be paid to those boys who wished to go to sea. However the other four apprentices that year were to a shoemaker in Winchester, and a hay-maker, butcher and tailor, all in Christchurch. In the succeeding years, both the number of apprentices and their trades varied. In 1738, they were apprenticed to a glover and shoemaker; 1739, weaver, tailor, cooper, hay-maker and tailor; 1740, wheelwright; 1742, barber; 1743, chain-maker, planter in New-foundland; 1744, tailor; 1745, carpenter, tailor; 1746, cordwainer (shoemaker); hay-maker, cooper; 1747, apothecary, shoemaker, tailor; 1748, cooper mercer, barber, mantua-maker (lace shawl); 1750, shoemaker mariner, mantua-maker; 1751, glover, two blacksmiths, wheelwright, shoemaker. Other trades that appear later are, bricklayer, milliner, yeoman, collar-maker, plumber and thatcher. However the most common trades appear for some years to have been those of cordwainer, wheelwright, mariner and blacksmith, all of which were essential trades in a coastal agricultural community.

Inevitably, not all the apprentices prospered as they should. There are entries which state *'complaints by the Master'*, *'apprentice left'*, *'apprentice absconded'*, *'Master absconded'*, *'boy dead'*, but these were rare.

The charity also tried to keep a close eye on the apprentices in an effort to ensure that they were not exploited, though those who went to Newfoundland were difficult to keep track of. There are several records of men, though not apprentices, fishing and working on the Grand Banks who contracted bigamous marriages, since it would be very difficult for one wife to hear of the other with the Atlantic Ocean between them. Where such information did get through, it came probably from another seaman who perhaps bore a grudge against the bigamist.

The terms and conditions of the apprenticeship were always specific as the Indenture of Joseph King in 1738, the second year of the Trust's operation, shows. The document reads:-

'THIS INDENTURE WITNESSETH that Joseph King son of Mary King of Christchurch Twynham in the County of Southton, widow, of the age of 11 years and upwards by the Approbation Choice and Direction of the Major Part of the Trustees appointed in and by a certain Decree or Decretal order made in the high Court of Chancery in a certain cause there depending wherein the Attorney General, at the relation of Robert Legrand Esquire, is plaintiff and Samuel Hookey Defendant, bearing the Date the nineteenth Day of March, in the ninth year of his present Majesty, for applying the charity under the Will of John Clingan late of Christchurch Twynham aforesaid deceased according to his said Will, Doth Put Himself Apprenticed to George Cram of Purrell [Purewell] in the said parish of Christchurch Twynham, Shoemaker, to learn his trade and with him after the manner of an apprentice to serve from the Day of the Date hereof until he shall arrive at the age of twenty one years during which term the said Apprentice, his said Master shall and will faithfully serve, his secrets keep, his lawfull commands everywhere gladly do. He shall do

no damage to his said Master nor see it or know it to be done by others but to his Power shall lett or forthwith give notice to his said Master of the same. The goods of his said Master he shall not waste nor lend unlawfully to any hurt to his said Master. He shall not do, cause or procure to be done he shall neither but nor sell without his said Master's leave. Taverns, Inns, or Alehouses he shall not haunt at Cards, Dice Tables, or any other unlawful Games he shall not play, nor from the Service of his said Master Day or Night absent himself, but in all things as an honest and faithfull Apprentice shall and will demean and behave himself towards his said Master and all his (family) during the said term. And the said George Cram, in consideration of the Sum of Five Pounds in Lawful Money of Great Britain to him in hand paid by James Willis of Ringwood in the county of Southton, Gentleman, one of the said Trustees and also the Receiver of the said Charity money by the direction and Appointment of the major part of the said Trustees, the receipt thereof is hereby acknowledged, the said apprentice in the Art Mystery or Occupation of a shoemaker which he now useth, shall teach and instruct or cause to be taught and instructed, in the best way and manner that he can, finding and allowing unto his said Apprentice sufficient wholesome Meat, Drink, Washing, Lodging, apparell and all other necessaries fit and convenient for him during the said term, and also at the end or other Expiration of the said Term, shall provide and give unto his said Apprentice one Good New Suit of Cloaths and all his old wearing apparell and for the true Performance of all and every the Covenants and Agreements aforesaid, either of the said Parties bindeth himself unto the other firmly by these presents. In Witness whereof the Parties abovesaid to these present Indentures interchangeably have sett their Hands and Seals, the Twenty First Day of October in the Twelfth Year of the Reign of our Sovereign Lord George the Second, by the Grace of God of Great Brittain France and Ireland King Defender of the Faith and so forth in the Year of our Lord 1738.'

Signed Sealed and Delivered   JOSEPH KING
In the presence of
    JAMES NOYES
    WILLIAM NOYCE
    JAS STEVENS.

The document is also stamped to show that the 8d. duty has been paid. It is interesting to note that King George II still regarded himself as King of France and the Royal Coat of Arms still displayed the French Fleur de Lys, even though England's last possessions in France had long since gone. He also claimed sovereignty over Ireland, though the Act of Union was still some 60 years in the future.

This Indenture Witnesseth That Joseph King son of Mary King of Christchurch Twynham in the County of Southton Widow of the Age of Eleven Years and Upward by the Approbation Choice & Direction of the Major Part of the Trustees appointed in & by a certain Decree or Decretall Order made in the High Court of Chancery in a certain Cause there Depending wherein the Attorney General at the Relation of Robert Fogard Esquire is Plaintiff and Samuel Hockey Defendant bearing Date the Nineteenth Day of March in the Ninth Year of this present Majesty for applying the charity under the will of John Clingan late of Christchurch — Twynsham aforesaid deceased according to his said Will Doth put himself Apprentice to George Cam of Burstom in the Parish of Christchurch Twynsham Shoemaker to learn his Trade and with him after the manner of an Apprentice to Serve from the Day of the Date hereof until the shall arrive at the Age of Twenty one Years during which Term the said Apprentice his said Master faithfully shall Serve his Secrets keep his lawfull commands every where gladly do He shall do no damage to his said Master nor see it or know it to be done by others but to his Power shall let or forthwith give Notice to his said Master of the same the Goods of his said Master he shall not waste nor them unlawfully to any hurt to his said Master he shall not do cause or procure to be done he shall neither buy nor sell without his said Masters Leave Taverns Inns or Alehouses he shall not Haunt at Cards Dice Tables or any other unlawfull Games he shall not play nor from the Service of his said Master Day or Night absent himself but in all things as a honest & faithful Apprentice shall and will Demean and behave himself towards his said Master & others during the said Term And the said George Cam in Consideration of the Sum of Five Pounds of Lawfull Money of Great Brittain to him in Hand Paid by James Stills of Ringwood in the County of Southton Gentleman one of the said Trustees & the Receiver of the said Charity Money by the direct & Appointment of the Major part of the said Trustees the Receipt whereof is hereby acknowledged the said Apprentice in the Art Mistery or Occupation of a Shoemaker which he now useth shall teach & instruct or cause to be taught and instructed in the best way & manner that he can finding & allowing unto his said Apprentice sufficient & wholesome Meat Drink washing Lodging Apparrell & all other necessaries fitt & convenient for him during the said Term & also at the End or other Expiration of the said Term shall provide and give unto his said Apprentice one Good New Sut of Cloaths & all his Olde wearing Apparrell & for the true Performance of all and every the covenants and Agreements aforesaid either of the said Parties bindeth himself unto the other firmly by these presents In Witness whereof the Parties abovesaid to these present Indentures Interchangeably have sett their Hands & Seals the Twentyfirst Day of October in the twelfth Year of the Reign of our Sovereign Lord G??? of the Second by the Grace of God of Great Brittain France & Ireland King Defender of the faith and so forth in the Year of our Lord 1738 f:

Signed Sealed and Delivered
in the presence of f:

Joseph King

Jar of Hoyes
William royce
Ja Stevens

The Indenture.

165

It is clear that the indenture bound both parties. The apprentice had to agree to work hard to learn his trade in return for being decently kept and properly trained by his master. There was also an acknowledgement of what are now termed Intellectual Property Rights, so that the apprentice could not reveal the secrets of the trade. Over the next two centuries, the form of indenture remained very much the same, though certainly by 1818 the documents were printed with suitable gaps left so that it could be personalised. By then, the form clearly allowed for both boy and girl apprentices and both male and female 'masters'. By the 20th century, when apprentices were seldom if ever living with their masters, the document made allowance for the apprentice to be paid a wage instead of board and lodging.

As employment conditions changed and the population increased, it was necessary to seek permission to amend the rules of the Charity. This happened in 1893, 1948, 1965 and most recently in 1996. By 1948, apprenticeships were becoming less common, so that it became necessary to widen the qualifications to include others who could be helped. The £5 limit of assistance for apprenticeships was varied several times. First it was raised to £11, then to £13 and later to *'such sum as the Trustees think fit'*. The regulations were also widened to allow assistance be given to those in the parish who were under 21 *'and are preparing for, entering upon or engaged in any trade, occupation or service, by outfits, payment of fees for instruction, payment of travelling expenses or such other means for their advancement in life or to enable them to earn their own living as the Trustees think fit'*. Progress by personal effort continued to be paramount.

In 1933, apprenticeships were usually for about five years from the age of 14 or 15, rather than until the age of 21. The premium for the apprentice had risen by then to £13 and the weekly wages for boys aged 14 or 15 tended to be 7s.6d. in the first year, rising to 10s., 15s., 17s.6d. and 25s. in succeeding years. Girls were still paid less and their training usually lasted only three years. Their weekly wages were in the region of 5s. in the first year rising to 7s.6d and 10s. in succeeding years. There were however still examples of girls living in with their mistress. One girl apprenticed to be a fancy draper aged 14 received respectively only 2s.6d., 5s. and 7s.6d. in addition to her board and lodging. However, provided she had a good mistress, this was probably a better deal for her than the usual higher girl's wage, since even in 1933 she would have had difficulty in feeding herself on 2s.6d. a week, or 4d. a day.

By 1946, the apprentice's premium was still usually £13, but their weekly wages had risen to about £1.7s.6d. a week in the first year, rising to £4.2s.6d. in the fifth year. Labour relations were by then changing fast, and by 1950, though the premium remained at £13, wages were then being fixed as a percentage of Union wages, or as laid down by National Agreements. There was, therefore, from the beginning a realisation that there was always the possibility of apprentices being exploited by their masters which is why the indenture laid down such tight regulations on both sides.

By 1960, the system of apprenticeships was seriously declining to the great detriment of industry and trade. The great benefit of the apprenticeship system was that boys and girls learnt their trade thoroughly from the bottom up and were thus able to set themselves up as independent operators in due course. This was John Clingan's intention, though he would probably have been the first to accept that modern technology required a somewhat different approach and a higher standard of education. Certainly the need for thorough training has never been greater.

Over the years, other changes came about. In 1965, since it was then found that the limits placed on those who could be helped were still too narrow to meet the wider needs of those trying to equip themselves for the modern world, the scope of the Charity was widened still further. The age limit was raised to 25, since training particularly for the professions, tended to continue well after the age of 21, and as already noted, both boys and girls were included. Scholarships, bursaries and maintenance allowances could be held at any university or other proper educational establishment. Help could be given towards the purchase of books, tools, equipment or clothing that were necessary to prepare the student for their chosen trade, profession or calling. Also included was assistance towards educational travel necessary for study purposes, and the study of music, drama, ballet, singing and art. Because both the body as well as the mind need to be exercised, coaching and training of all sorts of sports were included, provided they were not normally provided by the Local Educational Authority. The area covered by the Charity was further widened in 1996 to include both the Parish and Borough of Christchurch. This was partly because the William Arthur and Tom Newman Fund, that was primarily to give similar help to people living in Burton, was consolidated into the Clingan Charity. Consequently, the area covered by the Charity was amended to read *'the former parish of Christchurch and the immediate neighbourhood thereof'*.

The number of apprentices that could be assisted was never limited. In the early years, the numbers fluctuated from one to five, with the occasional year when there were no new apprentices. The limit of assistance was always determined by the amount of money available, and as the funds have steadily increased through prudent and efficient management, so more assistance has been available. Nor should it thought that all the local apprentices were funded by the Trust. Most would have been put through their apprenticeship by their parents or relatives. However, in the early years, one source of candidates would have been those covered by the Poor Law regulations. In 1819 the question was raised as to whether it was possible to extend the Charity to the children in the Parish Workhouse. Council's opinion was sought, and in 1821 *'the resolution to admit such children was confirmed, with the restriction that their cases should not be considered until all other applications are disposed of'.* As a result of this, it was possible to apprentice such children to the fusee chain makers, some of whom went on to set up in business on their own account.

The records of the Trust also contain many of the leases both of the farms and property that John Clingan owned, the earliest of which appears to be land let to John Kerley in 1742. In 1833, the farm at Iford was let for £51.10s., other land at Iford was let at £5, the land at Roeshot was let at £20, and the house in High Street, now Bookends, was let at £25. There was also £200 of 3% Government Stock that yielded £6. By 1855, the Trust also held an acre in Bure Mead, 2 roods and 28 perches on Bernard's Mead, and 16 acres, 2 roods and 6 perches of common allotment land. The Charity also benefited the town in other ways. In 1863, several small parcels of its land on either side of the Stour near Iford, were sold to the Ringwood, Christchurch and Bournemouth Railway so that the line could be extended to the growing Bournemouth. As a Trust, its properties had to be let by tender, so that the best possible price could be obtained. The two major parts, about 49 acres at Iford and 12 acres at Somerford and Roeshot, were advertised for letting in 1862 from the offices of the then Receiver, Mr. Druitt, being the same offices occupied by the present Receiver, David Richardson. So things have come full circle.

The records also contain some interesting insights into early administrative problems that the Charity seems to have experienced. Though the Trustees obviously intended to take care of their property, their efforts do not seem always to have been successful. In 1776 it was ordered that *'a plan and measurement of the whole belonging to the charity should be made'.* However, for some reason this appears not to have been done, since in 1801 it was again resolved that *'such a plan should be provided by two land surveyors named, if a plan could not be obtained from Mr. Webb'.* Four years later, in 1805, there was a minute resolving that *'the Charity's land should be surveyed and properly mapped and marked with stakes',* though by 1810 it was recorded that *'many posts are not sufficiently known and ought to be ascertained by a map or descriptive account'.* Perhaps the Bounds were no longer being regularly beaten as had happened in the past. Certainly it would seem that there is some evidence that during the first quarter of the 19th century matters had become a little lax.

Consequently in 1824, a committee was appointed to review not only the land holdings of the Charity, but also its procedures for choosing and appointing apprentices. The meeting of the Trustees in December 1825 resolved *'That a regular survey and map be made of the Charity Lands and that Mr. Stubbs be written to'* enquiring if he would undertake the work at the usual charges. If he declined, then *'Mr Holloway of Burley be immediately directed to measure and map the estate'.* The Holloway family was well known in the area[1]. The appointment of apprentices and their indenture payments was also re-assessed, it being resolved *'That as to the ages of the Apprentices to be places out, the same shall be between the ages of 12 and 14, except to the Sea Service in which cases the Trustees are to act at their discretion according to circumstances as to the age of such apprentices. That in future before any installment of the Receivers be paid after the first installment, the Master shall produce his apprentice at the time application be made for the payment of such installments and satisfy the Trustees that the Master or Mistress are duly fulfilling the stipulations of the Indenture. That the payment of Ten Pounds Ten Shillings to Apprentices in the Parish of Christchurch be made in three installments, viz. £4.10s. at the time of executing the Indenture, £3 at the end of the first 3 years and £3 at the end of the term on the same regulations as in the last resolution. That all persons applying for Apprentices shall produce costs or otherwise satisfy the Trustees that they were proper persons to have apprentices and qualified to teach them their respective trades and that there be no relationship or connection between the parties likely to lead to any collusion in the application to the Charity. That the Rules when agreed to shall be written fairly on paper and laid before the Trustees at every meeting and corrected as often as any alterations may be made'.* The implication seems to be that all was not always well either with the master or his apprentice.

The conduct of the Trustees meetings was also put on a more regular footing. In future the Clerk or Receiver had to read the minutes of the previous meeting, produce accounts, and report on events over the past year. The Receiver was also instructed to collect and list all the records of the Charity to date, and *'that the books and papers themselves be deposited in a Box and placed in such custody as the Trustees may hereafter determine. And that the Accounts are to be made and exhibited in the form stated in the report. That from and*

---

[1] See chapter 25

after passing these Resolutions all others to the contrary effect standing in the books are rescinded'. The result of these 1825 Resolutions is that there still exists, in what is probably the original steel box, a virtually complete set of records of this ancient charity.

From what can be discovered about John Clingan, it is surely safe to say that he would have thoroughly approved of the present scope of his Charity. He was a man who was very much in tune with the needs of his time. Such needs are equally relevant today. His intention was to help those who needed assistance to make their way in the world by their own efforts, but who lacked the means to do so. The original intention to help those associated with the sea, surely dates from Clingan's experiences at the time of the 1703 storm and the position of Christchurch as a port. As a churchwarden, he would have been well aware of the story of Jacob's Ladder that led from Earth to the Heavens. He wished to provide the young people of Christchurch with such a ladder. In this he succeeded beyond his wildest expectations. Today, the number of young people who have been directly assisted by John Clingan's Charity, is nearing 3,000. Countless numbers have also received indirect help, since at one time grants were made to all primary and secondary schools in the area for the purchase of books to which their pupils would not otherwise have had access. Help towards the purchase of computers was also given. Many of those who have been prepared to climb the ladder that John Clingan provided have prospered in their chosen calling as he would have hoped. Some have obtained first class degrees at their university. Others have risen high in the fields of medicine, the law, engineering, music and elsewhere.

As with the Priory School and Mary Magdalen Charity, John Clingan's Charity demonstrates a coming together of Town and Church for the benefit of both. The two ex officio Trustees, the Vicar and the Mayor, are there to ensure that the funds are put to the best possible use for the benefit of the young people of the town. John Clingan understood the meaning of the word 'charity'. Derived from the Latin word 'caritas', its meaning is esteem for and love of ones fellow mortals. He would also have known the thirteenth chapter of St Paul's first letter to the men of Corinth, which, in the 1611 version with which he would have been familiar, ends *'And now abideth Faith, Hope and Charity, these three; but the greatest of these is Charity'.*

May the citizens of Christchurch today try to follow John Clingan's example, so that the town may continue to prosper.

Chapter 21.

Smuggling and the Battle of Mudeford.

It is commonly assumed that smuggling was largely an 18th century occupation. Certainly the most famous and exciting tales relate to this period, but smuggling has been going on for centuries. It probably began in earnest early in the 14th century when kings started to use two general levies on traded goods as a means of raising revenue on a regular basis to finance their general expenditure, and in particular their wars. These were 'Tunnage and Poundage' first imposed by Edward I in 1275, and primarily concerned wine and wool, though foods were sometimes included. Wine was imported in large barrels known as 'tuns' which held about 250 gallons of wine. A toll of 4d. was levied on each tun at the port of entry. When wine was exported, there was a duty of 8d. per tun. The size of ships was in consequence calculated by the number of tuns that could be carried in their holds, not by their weight in tons. A similar levy was raised on the poundage value of all wool exported to the continent. Wool was handled in 'sacks' that held the wool-clip of 250 sheep. These sacks weighed about 364 lb. and measured about 4 ft long by 4 ft wide and almost 3 ft high. The duty initially was 1d. per sack. Since the trade in these two items was probably greater than any other commodity, the tolls levied provided the king with a very useful source of revenue. Being a charge that effected nearly every trader, there could be no complaint that only a few of the population were effected.

The import and export of goods was controlled through the Staple Ports, where the tolls were levied. Since private enterprise tended to produce results for the king with less trouble than having to use royal officials, it became common practice for kings to farm out the collection of dues to local individuals. They bought the right to collect the tolls and then extracted what they could from the local populace. Such a system had been used since biblical times. St Matthew the gospel writer and disciple was a tax gatherer.

The great sheep rearing areas were originally in the Salisbury Plain and Cotswold regions, although later East Anglia also became a major centre. Initially, the Staple Ports were Southampton, Poole, Melcombe and Chichester. Despite the fact that the Avon was one of the common routes for bringing down wool from Salisbury Plain and the Cots-wolds, Christchurch was never a Staple Port. Those responsible for collecting Tunnage and Poundage on goods passing up and down the Avon and Stour had to make the best they could of their difficulties. The suggestion that Staple Cross may have been a collecting point for goods or even for the tolls due on them does not seem to stand up. As the crow flies, it is at least a mile and a quarter from the town's quay, and over a mile and a half from the rivers' mouth at the Run. The opportunities for bypassing such a collecting point were therefore too great for it to be put to such a use. Indeed, Christchurch must always have been a difficult place at which to levy the royal tolls. Those responsible for collecting Tunnage and Poundage would probably have had to rely on the goodwill of the mayor and burgesses. It is likely that the monies due would have been collected by the town's officers and passed on, less a suitable com-mission, to the royal collectors in due course.

Towns like Christchurch-Twynham that had charters, would have been able to raise a series of levies on goods entering and leaving the town. These were usually listed in the Freedom Certificates that were given to those who were made free of the town. These people would be the mayors and burgesses and other officers and those who were members of any Craft Guild that there might be in the town. Others who had served the town well in some respect, might also be made free men. It was a valuable privilege, since it could involve not having to pay a variety of tolls. These included exemption from the toll on goods bought at the biannual fair; not having to pay a toll for using the town's bridges, that were in constant need of repair; for bringing in laden carts, the sums raised being used to repair the town's walls; not paying tolls on goods sold by the 'last' such as herrings and tar and also on occasions, wool. There were also other advantages that mainly avoided various duties that would fall on the ordinary townsfolk who did not have those 'freedoms'. It was hard to avoid most of the tolls, since they would be levied at the town gates. However it cannot have been unknown for the more enterprising traders to avoid the tolls by surreptitiously slipping goods in and out of the town, perhaps over the walls at night, or by a suitable arrangement with the gatekeeper. Much would depend on how heavy the tolls were and whether the saving made was sufficiently large to warrant the risk of being caught in the act. Since it would be well known that the sums raised would be used to protect the town and keep its bridges in good condition, in other words for the benefit of local people, these tolls were usually accepted as justified, however grudgingly.

The heaviest tolls, as one would expect, were those levied by the king, and it was here that smuggling was most likely to be a risk worth taking. Those who would have to pay them would be wholesale importers and exporters rather than small retailers. Nor would the benefit be felt locally. Indeed, since one of the main uses of the customs duties raised by the kings was to wage war against their continental enemies, many traders could find excellent reasons for not paying them. Certainly Tunnage and Poundage was avoided where the coastline lent itself to such a practice. Such a coastline could be found along the flat marshland of the south coast of Kent and along the sparsely inhabited coast of Dorset, where there were many convenient inlets and plenty of tracks through the heath-land leading well into the interior. Since the trading vessels, usually called 'cogs' carried about 100 tuns, and the duty levied in 1308 was 2s. on every tun, it is clear that it was worth avoiding if possible, since the duty on one tun represented a man's wages for at least a week. The duty of 1d. per sack of wool was also well worth avoiding since the quantities involved were very much larger. There was another advantage. At first, the only official wool importing port in France was Calais, and this was controlled entirely by the English merchants. Since the crossing from Christchurch to the Cherbourg peninsular could take as little as eight hours under favourable conditions, whereas the journey to Calais would take a couple of days or more, depending on wind and tides, there were added incentives to use the short -smuggling- route.

Those responsible for collecting the customs dues did not have an easy task. Local opinion was usually on the side of the smugglers. There is a record of one, John Roger, who lived at Melcombe Regis. Having been caught smuggling wool in 1428, rather than pay the customary fine, he elected trial by jury. This was however refused by the Privy Council on the grounds that no local jury would convict him, whatever the evidence. His fine was fixed at 200 marks 'or more if he can afford it'. It would seem therefore that, as an occupation, smuggling has long had popular support, not only as a way of slighting the unpopular authorities, but also as a means of subsidising low wages.

During the reign of Elizabeth I, privateers, such as Raleigh, Drake and Hawkins, were encouraged to prey on foreign shipping, particularly if it was Spanish. It was but a short step to smuggling, and huge quantities of grain, cloth, powder and shot and even guns and horses went to France without paying any duty. There was also considerable similar trade with the Channel Islands. Tobacco reached England in 1565, but only became popular at the end of Elizabeth's reign. Her successor, James I, strongly disapproved of the habit, which he considered to have been inspired by Satan himself. He therefore first increased the duty from 2 pence to 7 shillings per pound on imported tobacco and then raised the duty several times more over the years. Though this probably made an initial impact on the amount of tobacco smoked, the inevitable result was that from then on, tobacco became a prime commodity for Dorset smugglers and those in Christchurch. It is interesting that it was not until 1999 that the Royal Warrant was finally removed from the main cigarette manufacturers. Tea suffered a similar heavy duty. In 1680, the cheapest tea cost 7 shillings a pound, the equivalent of a labourer's weekly wages, of which 5 shillings was duty. As a result, it was estimated that at the height of the smuggling trade, two thirds of the tea drunk in England was smuggled.

It should not be thought that the citizens of Christchurch were entirely or even mainly dependent on smuggling for their livelihood. There can be no doubt however, that the trade did for centuries make life a little easier for many who lived in and around the town. Since many were involved in fishing, the additional occupation would have come quite naturally to them.

The smuggled goods had to come by sea from the continent. Though the crossing at Dover was the shortest route, it could be kept under observation for its whole distance by a single ship placed mid-channel. Indeed in good weather the French coast is visible from the Kent coast. On the other hand, the crossing to and from the Dorset coast was out of sight of land for over half its distance. It was therefore a better route to use. The smugglers could use the excuses either that they were fishing, or that they were in fact intending to sail east or west to their final destination, and that their cargo was intended for some foreign port.

By the late 18th century, because of the heavy duties being levied on many goods, smuggling had become a very sophisticated enterprise. Since the success of any smuggling operation depended largely on the efficiency of the boats used, great care was taken in their design. They needed to be fast, in order to be able to complete the crossing from France overnight if conditions were favourable, and also outrun the cutters used by the Revenue Service or the Royal Navy. They also needed to be well armed, so that they could out-gun their pursuers. Perhaps most importantly, the boats needed to be roomy, so that the cargo could be sufficiently large to make the often dangerous crossing worth the risk. The favourite design was therefore the lugger. This might be anything from 50 to 300 tons, with a lug-sail that enabled the boat to sail much closer to the wind than the naval craft. The hold was also capacious and could carry up to 3,000 half-anker kegs of spirits, the largest barrel that could be conveniently man-handled, as well as up to 12 tons of tea, carefully wrapped against the effects of salt water. Some boats could even be rowed and the fastest could make the crossing from France in under eight hours. The best-organised groups of smugglers had devised a convoy system to bring over the largest shipments long before the Navy thought of the idea, sometimes under the noses of the authorities that were then powerless to intercept them.

Those most closely involved in the carriage of illicit cargoes were often also fishermen, who knew the waters like the back of their hands. They knew every shoal and sandbar, all the currents, and each cove and inlet. They could also row for long distances if necessary. It was not unheard of for crews to row the full distance across the Channel if there was no wind and the revenue cutters would therefore be unable to give pursuit. Those who distributed the cargoes once they were landed were commonly agricultural labourers, keen to take advantage of an opportunity to supplement their depressed wages. They had access to horses and carts and were themselves prepared to turn out in large numbers if required. They frequently had the backing of their masters, the local squires and other landowners, and on occasion the parson, doctor, and parish clerk. Church towers and even graves were frequently used as hiding places for contraband. Parson Woodforde in his diary for 1777 records buying gin and tea from smugglers, though there is no evidence he stored it for them. Nor is there any evidence that smuggled goods were stored in the Priory. However Kinson Church has grooves in the castellations on the top of its tower, said to have been worn by the ropes pulling up the kegs that were stored there before being taken further inland. The doctor was often happy enough to tend to any injuries, and the parish clerk was an ideal person for keeping the records and accounts of the enterprise. In return, both would be supplied with a present of gin, brandy, tea or tobacco. The whole community could easily find itself involved in one way or another. Provided a major conflict between the authorities and the 'gentlemen' could be avoided - and this was an important proviso - a large proportion of the population felt that the system was justified. The import duties were considered to be unnecessarily high and interfering with people's reasonable pleasures and extravagances, and the only loser was the Government who - as always - was assumed to be taking far too much in tax and wasting it.

Nor could it be said that those responsible for controlling the trade always had their hearts in their job. A common practice was for the smugglers to allow a small proportion of the cargo to be 'captured' by the authorities, while the bulk of the cargo was dispersed through its regular outlets. The preventative officers and riding officers could then be seen to be performing their duties while the rest of the community was pleased to receive their goods at a reasonable cost. Since a riding officer's pay might only be £25 or at most £50 a year, he would be very tempted to avoid a perhaps dangerous confrontation with the smugglers while at the same time satisfying his superiors with a small 'catch' and also having his own free supply of liquor, tobacco and other goods.

There is no doubt that many in responsible positions in the town were involved in the trade as well as more ordinary citizens. Rudyard Kipling summed up the 18th and 19th century trade very well in his Smuggler's Song.

'If you wake at midnight, and hear a horse's feet,
Don't go drawing back the blind, or looking in the street.
Them that asks no questions isn't told a lie.
Watch the wall my darling, while the Gentlemen go by!
Five and twenty ponies,
Trotting through the dark -
Brandy for the Parson,
'Baccy for the Clerk;
Laces for a lady, letters for a spy,
And watch the wall my darling, while the Gentlemen go by!

There was no level of society that was not involved either in bringing in the goods or receiving them - or both.

Smuggling probably reached its peak in Christchurch just after the end of a war against France, Spain and America (when the American colonies were lost) and shortly before the start of the French Revolution in 1789. However its high activity continued until some time after Napoleon's final defeat in 1815. It was in 1784 that the 'Battle of Mudeford', fully described by Mike Powell in his book of that name, occurred. There is no purpose in repeating the contents of his excellent book. Suffice it to say that lives were lost on both sides, and it is clear that on this occasion matters had come to a head. There was normally sufficient respect by both sides to hold back from taking life. More commonly, if the preventative officers were overpowered, they would be bound and immobilised so that the 'run' could proceed uninterrupted. Neither the smugglers nor the preventative officers, nor the soldiers or seamen, relished the thought of being responsible for the death of a fellow countryman. It was particularly for this reason that soldiers used to track down the smugglers were very seldom recruited locally, since they could not be expected to fire on men whom they probably knew.

The Battle of Mudeford was the culmination of a determined attempt to control the trade in this area and involved several vessels on both sides. The extent of the trade passing through Christchurch on this occasion can be gauged by the size of the operation on land. 300 men, 100 carts and 400 horses were involved, many of them New Forest ponies that were ideal for the task. This in itself must have meant that a considerable proportion of the town was involved. It is estimated that the cargoes landed included 6,000 casks of spirits and over 30 tons of tea. There would also have been a quantity of tobacco, lace, silk and other finery as well. The result of the battle would have been a severe blow to both sides. The Revenue failed to capture the cargo and Mr. Allen, the sailing master of the sloop-of-war,

H.M.S. Orestes, died of his wounds, while several sailors were wounded. Though the cargo was saved, the smugglers' boats were captured and they themselves had suffered casualties. More importantly, they knew that one of their number had killed an officer of the Crown in the execution of his duty. It is likely that smuggling became much less common in this area for some time afterwards, since the whole town was badly shaken by the events and the tragic loss of a life and the many injuries sustained on both sides.

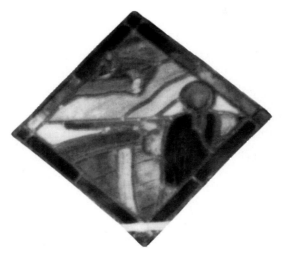

Smugglers watched from the schoolroom in St Michael's Loft.

There are innumerable stories about local smugglers, some of which are true and some apocryphal. Hannah Siller, whose husband had been the landlord of the Haven Inn at the time of the Battle of Mudeford, moved to the Ship in Distress in Stanpit, when her husband died. She soon became known as 'the protecting angel of the smugglers' and it is probable that Mother Siller's Channel that runs through Stanpit Marshes towards her pub in Stanpit was used to transport goods. John Streeter, who was involved in the Battle of Mudeford used the common ruse of bringing in casks of liquor hidden in a cargo of grain, which was to be unloaded, legally, at the town's quay. Unfortunately the 'rummage crew', whose job it was to search ships, discovered the casks, to the feigned astonishment of Streeter, though he later admitted his guilt and was fined and also lost his ship. He then set up a respectable tobacco and snuff manufactory in Stanpit next to Mother Siller's pub, the Ship in Distress. Not surprisingly, most of his supplies came in by night. He used to parcel up his stock and send it throughout the country on the Royal Mail coaches that stopped at the George Inn in Castle Street, and which had an armed guard, thus ensuring that it arrived safely at its final destination. No doubt Streeter was highly amused at the official protection his shipments received. So successful was he that other local tobacco traders complained to the authorities that their trade had virtually disappeared. Ultimately he had to flee to Guernsey, from where he continued to organise supplies of tobacco to his wife who remained in Stanpit. He still visited her, and she had several children by him, who were christened in the Priory with the connivance of the vicar.

The children of the town were well aware of the smuggling trade. There is an account by Richard Warner, who attended the school in St Michael's Loft between 1776 and 1780. He tells how, as a diversion from his Latin and Greek lessons, he used to watch the actions of the smugglers over by Hengistbury Head, through his small telescope. He would see lines of 20 or 30 wagons, each with an armed guard, accompanied by several hundred horsemen with perhaps four barrels of spirits strapped to their saddles, winding their way along beside the harbour. Double Dykes was an excellent place in which to hide the horses until the boats beached and could be unloaded. He also records that the Revenue cavalry were often in attendance to collect their toll of the goods but otherwise to allow the smugglers to pass on their way unhindered. Though it is an account by a schoolboy, who later became a clergyman, it has the ring of truth about it.

One particular smuggler at that time earned the name of 'Slippery Rogers', because of his uncanny ability to avoid his pursuers. He had a particularly fine 120 foot long boat, that was very fast either under her huge spread of canvas sails, or pressed forward by her 40 rowers. To Warner and his fellow schoolboys, they were heroes. But like so many heroes, Rogers became overconfident and his boat was wrecked in a storm, possibly on the Beerpan Rocks off Hengistbury Head. These rocks at the end of the headland were about the only hazard to be avoided along the coastline that otherwise offered gently sloping sandy beaches that were ideal for running in shallow draught craft. From these beaches, tracks ran inland to the New Forest and the Cranborne Chase, which once reached, meant almost complete security for the smugglers to disperse their goods to the main markets as far away as London, Winchester, Salisbury and Bath. The young Warner could let his imagination run riot as he mentally accompanied the 'Gentlemen'. He would have heard of occasions when the Preventive Officers, riding from Mudeford in hot pursuit of the smugglers, arrived at the town bridge only to find their way blocked by a heavily laden farm cart that proved impossible to move, perhaps because the horse had been taken from the shafts. For many reasons, therefore, Christchurch was an eminently suitable place for contraband to be landed.

Dragoons prevented from crossing Town Bridge, Christchurch c.1800

Not all cargoes that were landed were large. It was almost impossible for the Revenue cutters to intercept every boat. There were many small fishing boats that picked up a few kegs of spirits and parcels of tobacco or tea, enough perhaps to fill one covered farm cart, which they brought in beneath their legitimate catch of fish, or landed in some secluded cove. There would be plenty of willing customers, and the chances of being caught by the authorities were slight. At other times, men would sling a line of small casks under their boat attached to the keel at either end and held down by stones or an iron bar. It was simple enough to attach the ends of the rope to the keel and sail into the harbour in all innocence. Alternatively, the line of casks weighted down with stones from the ship's ballast, would be dropped off near the coast, with an anchor at each end, and a single cork float left as a marker. A suitable place to drop them would be perhaps near a line of lobster pots in the vicinity of the Clarendon Rocks or Beer-pan Rocks off Hengistbury Head. The casks could be retrieved by another boat involved in legitimate fishing at a later date. Some boats even went to the expense of having a double deck, the space between being used to pack either tobacco or tea. These and many other devices used by the smugglers must have made the job of the Riding Officers and their men almost impossible.

One of the more diligent Chief Riding Officers, was Abraham Pike who operated in the early years of the 19th century. He lived at 10 Bridge Street, a tall Georgian house with a huge cellar that acted as the King's Warehouse where any captured smuggled goods would be held. His area stretched for 16 miles from Hurst Castle to Poole, and though he had the support of some cavalry based at Christchurch Barracks, it was a thankless task for which he was paid a paltry £25 a year. Only his pertinacity enabled him to have some reasonable success, for the soldiers had considerable sympathy with the smugglers and were not over keen to pursue them, especially at night, and through rivers, mud and gorse in foul weather - and who could blame them! Unlike so many other Riding Officers who died in harness, Pike lived to retire and remained in Christchurch. Despite his profession, he seems to have been respected, perhaps because he took a middle line between enforcement and turning a blind eye and is buried in the Priory churchyard.

However by the 1840's, smuggling was waning. The main reasons were the end of the Napoleonic War in 1815, and the reduction of the level of duty being charged. The former meant that the Navy could now turn its attention to the prevention of smuggling rather than having to concentrate on dealing with French men-of-war. Their success can be judged by the number of smugglers taken to Dorchester gaol. In only three years during the period between 1792 and 1813 were there more than eight such prisoners, and in several years there were none. Between 1813 and 1845 numbers rose dramatically, reaching a peak of 60 in 1822, after which there was a continuous and steady decline. This was also partly explained by the reduction in the potential profit because of the much lower duties being charged. For these reasons, and with a steady rise in wages, there was not so much profit in the enterprise for the organisers, and the need for agricultural labourers to earn a little extra became not worth the risks involved.

The trade did not however cease. It never has and probably never will. Today, because of the various regulations concerning 'Duty Free' goods and the often very different rates of duty imposed in various European Community countries, it is possible to import quite large quantities of alcohol and tobacco at prices far lower than pertain in this country, provided the goods are said to be for 'personal consumption'. This hole in the law would appear large enough to drive through with a pantechnicon and has led to a large 'bootleg' trade. As in the 18th century, legitimate traders are now complaining that their trade is being seriously affected.

During the second half of the 20th century smuggling took on a more sinister complexion. Because of their extremely high street value, drugs became the most profitable commodity to smuggle, with those involved seemingly completely unconcerned about the terrible damage they are doing to those who use drugs, or the number of deaths they cause. Almost equally unpleasant is the smuggling of terrorist weapons with probably even more hideous results in death and injury. Ports and airports throughout the country as well as coast-lines such as Dorset have now to be constantly watched to try to combat these two scourges. Counter methods have rightly become highly sophisticated in an attempt to counter the growing expertise of those who persist in carrying on their deadly trade. Radar, satellite tracking, counter intelligence, X-rays, and sniffer dogs are but some of the methods used today. So what previously was sometimes regarded as a fair game with certain rules which were generally obeyed by the two sides, has now become a vicious and deadly war where no holds are barred. The only winners are the amoral drug barons and international terrorists, while the rest of society suffers grievously at their greedy hands. Nowhere, not even Christchurch where life should be pleasant, is able to escape. Everywhere must now fight to limit, if not yet overcome, these two terrible scourges.

Chapter 22.

Gustavus Brander: 1720 - 1787.

The Brander family came originally from Sweden and lived mainly in London. However Charles Brander, the father of Gustavus, had a house at Nea, between Highcliffe and Friars Cliff where he lived during the later years of his life, so that from his youth, Gustavus knew the area well. Charles Brander had been elected a burgess in 1736 and was a member of the Sixteene probably from then until his death. When he died in 1745, he was buried in the South Choir Aisle in the Priory. There were two sons, the elder, also called Charles, lived in the house at Nea after his father's death, and, like his father, also became a churchwarden. The younger son had for some reason been born in London and lived there for much of his life. His formal education was a not apparently particularly advanced, though it is likely that his tutors were able to inspire his enquiring mind. In addition, many of those with whom he came in contact in the City of London, where he was involved in trade, were men of substance and stature with wide experience of the world. Chief among these was his uncle, Mr Spicker, a man of very considerable wealth, who obviously took to Gustavus and who later left him his large fortune. He was probably inspired to do so at least in part by the young man's obvious acute business acumen.

Gustavus Brander.

Gustavus Brander rose to some eminence in the City and was for many years a Governor of the Bank of England, where his portrait hangs. His enquiring mind led him into other fields of study too. He was a great collector of curiosities, one of the most interesting of which was an imposing iron chair on which were depicted various scenes of events in the history of the Roman Empire. Legend had it that the first Emperor of Germany had used it for his coronation. It had been captured by the Swedish King Gustavus Adolphus, during his continental wars a hundred years before. Brander's interest in it may have been his own Swedish ancestry and the fact that he and Adolphus shared the same name. Another part of his collection consisted of fossils dug from Barton cliffs, many of which were of previously unknown species and one of which was named after him. These he presented to the British Museum of which he later became a Curator. His interests were wide, since he also wrote a tract on the effects of lightning that struck the Danish church in London. His library contained a 1390 cookery book that included perhaps the earliest recipe for curry. In 1754, he was also elected a Fellow of the Royal Society at the age of 34 and he was also one of the first supporters of the Society for the Encouragement of the Arts. Clearly he moved in the most enlightened circles in London and was a man of many interests.

For most of his life Brander was a confirmed bachelor and shared a house in White Lion Court, Cornhill, with Mr Spalding. When this caught fire in 1766, he was, fortunately, able to save both his extensive library and his pictures. According to Richard Warner, who knew him well, he was not particularly charitable towards others, due to 'his ignorance of the wants of those around him'. He did however have 'a sincere and warm piety; a strong sense of divine goodness; and a firm belief in the operations of a particular Providence'. This last was largely due to a lucky escape that he had in London in 1768.

It appears that he was caught in a thunderstorm while driving in his coach near the Thames. His horses took fright, and in his own words, 'my horses ran violently down the Temple Lane, in London, and down three flights of steps into the Thames, in a dark night; and yet neither horses nor carriage, myself or servant, received the least injury: it was fortunately low water'. Warner, commenting on the accident, stated that it was certainly the low tide that saved Brander's life and that of his servants. He also explained that the wheels of the carriage became so stuck in the exposed mud of the river that even the frightened horses were not able to drive the carriage deeper into the river. The shouts of Brander and the whinnying of the horses reached the ears of drinkers in a nearby ale-house who fortunately came to his aid and succeeded in calming the horses and dragging the carriage back to the river bank where everyone was found to be unharmed. Presumably the rescuers were suitable rewarded in spite of Brander's "ignorance of the wants of those around him". Certainly the City authorities soon thereafter erected gates at the Temple stairs, probably due to the pressure that Brander in his respected position was able to bring to bear, to prevent such an accident happening again.

Brander seems to have grown tired of London life and the elegant hospitality of his many talented friends and having lived in Westminster for a few years after the fire at Cornhill, he decided to return to his roots in Christchurch. He had obviously kept in close touch with the rest of his family, staying first with his parents and later with his elder brother who inherited the family home at Nea. How else could he have amassed his important collection of Barton fossils other than by frequent and painstaking excavations on the cliffs there? He also seems to have been interested in the early history of the town, since in October 1773 he discovered and acquired the Baldwin de Redvers charter, which was in a very sorry condition, and had it repaired and restored. For this act alone, the town owes him a great debt. It was logical therefore that in 1781 he should buy a property that was within easy walking distance of Nea. Somerford Grange that had been the home of Prior Draper after he was turned out of the Priory, fell easily into that category. Still an active man, he immediately pulled down the old Tudor house and built a more substantial residence on the site. According to Warner, he maintained there a purely bachelor establishment, the only females permitted into the house being his cook, housekeeper and other domestic servants. However, there seems to be some confusion about this statement in view of his marriage.

Life in the quiet rural setting of Christchurch does not seem to have produced the satisfaction that his active mind required. After many years as a confirmed bachelor, he had finally fallen at the age of 61 for the widow of Vice Admiral John Lloyd. He married the lady, Elizabeth, in the Priory in 1780. He presumably hoped that she would bring him comfort and companionship in his old age, and even though at first he spent most of his time entertaining friends and neighbours locally and from the neighbouring counties, he was soon disabused. She had been used to the exciting life of a senior naval officer's society, though this would have been interspersed with fairly long periods of enforced grass widowhood while the admiral was away at sea, not that this need necessarily have interrupted her gay social life. In order to try to re-create the sort of life she had been used to, Brander took the opportunity to buy the Lordship of the Manor of Christchurch Twynham from John Compton of Harbridge in Hampshire. The Lordship also brought with it the right to hold a fair on the feast of Corpus Christi, though it is doubtful if he ever exercised that right. The estate included amongst its lands, the area once occupied by the conventual building to the south of the Priory. On that site he built the substantial south-facing mansion that we know as Priory House, laying out the grounds as beautiful gardens. There he hoped to provide suitable entertainment for his bride. He may have hoped that the proximity of Priory House to the artillery barracks would enable his wife to become acquainted with the officers' wives. Unfortunately she probably felt that their comparatively junior rank was too far beneath hers as the widow of an admiral for her to be able to receive them.

Her new house was indeed extensive. A few years later it was to be described as having several large rooms on both the ground and first floors and *'seven good chambers six servants rooms and other apartments. The offices and out-buildings are convenient and useful'*. There were also an ice house and 30 acres of rich meadows and pasture land next to the house, that was presumably Convent Meadows. It was certainly a house that had many attractions to offer, being *'in a good sporting country, within a good neighbourhood and near the church'*. It could hardly be nearer. Life in the town at that time was well summed up in the advertisement of 1792, when the house was offered for letting. *'In point of prospect, bathing, sailing and fishing are remarkably well situated, being near the sea and close to the rivers Stour and Avon. A good bathing machine on a fine shore, about a mile and a half distant is in constant use during the summer and autumn'*. Elizabeth Brander might perhaps have described it as being well situated for outdoor pursuits but in an area that lacked cultural stimulation. However, Christchurch was obviously then, as now, considered by many to be an excellent place to live and for a time the house was occupied by the Duke of Orleans, father of King Louis Philippe of France - an event that might have warmed Mrs. Brander towards it.

Things did not work out as Brander had hoped and as most of his friends could have told him. The lady, who was accompanied by her son, took immediate command of everything. She sacked his old servants, refused to entertain his friends and made his life a misery. The son seems to have been little better, and though Brander tried everything he could to win him over, even to the extent of offering to leave him his considerable fortune, it was to no avail. Since he had no children of his own, Brander therefore wrote a fresh will, leaving his estate back to a cousin of John Spicker whose wealth he had inherited. As was common in such circumstances, he changed his name to Brander. His son was given the name Gustavus after his benefactor and later also lived in Somerford Grange.

185

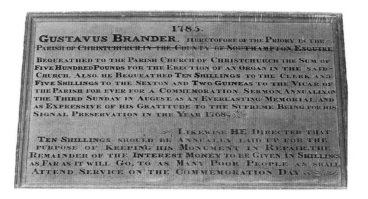

Brander's plaque in Christchurch Priory.

While the site of Priory House was being excavated, the builders came across several ancient stone coffins that had to be dug up. In another place they also discovered a large flat stone, about 33 inches by 24 inches in size that had been cemented with lead into the pavement that surrounded it. When this was lifted it revealed a large cavity filled with quantity of bird's bones that Brander identified as belonging to herons, bitterns, hens and cocks, all of which seemed to be well preserved. His conclusion was that they suggested the site of an ancient Roman temple, though for once it is probable that his conclusions were faulty. Another theory is that the bones came from the prior's kitchen.

Many local people today regret that Brander built his house on the site of the old conventual buildings, though it must be admitted that he chose the site well with its extensive views towards the Isle of Wight. However, as Lord of the Manor, there was no one who could then oppose him. Had he lived today and applied for planning permission, as is now required, it is quite possible that he would have been successful. The site he chose was very near, if not actually on, the site of the prior's lodging. As such he would have been able to claim that there had been a dwelling house on his chosen site for several hundred years, the foundations of which still lay beneath the surface of the ground. Indeed there are large areas of paving slabs that were once part of the monastic buildings lying beneath the floors of Priory House. Some may regret the presence of the house today, though it is now put to great use, not only by the parish for choir practices and parish meetings but also for arts exhibitions and many other uses. We should perhaps also regret that being built on old Priory land, it did not have a more benign effect on Elizabeth Brander.

However, because of his close proximity to the church, Gustavus seems to have come under its spell as so many others have done, both before and since. One of his many interests seems to have been music and he would weekly have heard the singing and music provided by the orchestra at the services. There was at the time no organ in the Priory. He therefore decided to leave in his will of 1785, the sum of £500 to the Priory to pay for the building of a suitable pipe organ. There was however a caveat. The parish had to raise the funds to pay the organist. In view of his considerable wealth and the fact that he had no direct heir to inherit his fortune, one may wonder why he did not extend his generosity to cover the salary of the organist as well. Perhaps he felt that the town should be encouraged to acknowledge its responsibility to support the church. When the organ was built by Alexander Cumming, the leading pipe organ builder of his day, it was installed over the screen that separates the nave from the Great Choir. Unfortunately this effectively blocked the impressive view down the length of the church to the Jesse Screen beyond the High Altar. Fortunately, in the nineteenth century, the organ was re-sited to where it now stands above the South Transept and at the same time rebuilt and enlarged by the eminent organ builder, 'Father Willis'. In 1951, it was further rebuilt and electrified. Finally in 1999, having been silent since 1973, the original pipe-work was completely restored, the instrument considerably enlarged and re-cased by the Nicholson organ builders, to become one of the finest pipe organs in the country. Since it is from the first beautiful though small organ, paid for by Gustavus Brander, that the present magnificent instrument is descended, it is clear that the town owes him an enormous debt.

Brander's organ gift to Christchurch Priory 1788

Gustavus Brander made another bequest to the Priory. Remembering his happy deliverance from his potentially tragic accident in the Thames, he left £200 to the Priory. The interest was to be used to pay the clerk ten shillings, the sexton five shillings and the vicar two guineas, so that a sermon could be preached annually on the third Sunday in August, *'as an everlasting memorial, and an expression of gratitude to the Supreme Being, for my signal preservation in 1768......'.* He also willed that individual shillings should be given to any of the poor of the parish who attended church that day to hear the sermon. The sermon is still preached annually on what is known locally as "Coach and Horses Sunday". Brander also left funds for a suitably large and impressive monument to be erected to him after his death, with an endowment to see that it was properly maintained.

Whether Brander enjoyed sailing is not known. However there is a large mud flat between Grimbury Marsh and the Marine Training Centre, where the rivers begin to open out into the harbour, that bears his name. Though it is possible to sail round it, many dinghy sailors have gone aground on it in low water and thereby probably not blessed his name.

Towards the end of his life in 1786, Brander returned to London. Matrimony, he found to his cost, did not suit him. That winter he purchased a house in St Alban's Street, but whether his wife accompanied him is not known. Certainly he was by then a sick man, possibly suffering from a malignant prostate infection. He died on 21st January 1787.

Though in his lifetime, Christchurch could well have basked in the reflected glory of his fame and achievements, Gustavus Brander seems to have been largely a self-centred individual. Warner's comment that *'his charity and benevolence was bounded only by his ignorance of the wants of those around him'* seems to sum up his character well enough. But he was no different from many of his class in that age. His portrait shows a distant man, well dressed in the fashion of his time, but seemingly unconcerned about the fate of those beneath him. Though Gustavus Brander left his mark on Christchurch in several ways, his generosity did not match that of others in the town. It was left to later generations to improve on some of the things that he had begun. Perhaps his importance was that he produced the seed corn that others could cultivate.

Chapter 23.

The Fusee Watch Chain Makers.

From time immemorial, men have always wanted to know how much of the day had passed and how much daylight remained. The reasons are many and obvious. How much longer would a man have to work at his daily task. How long would it be before the light failed, so that he could no longer see either to work or travel. How soon would it be time for him to meet his neighbour, or even when could he cease work and eat his frugal meal. If the sun was shining, he could have some rough idea of the passage of time through the day and his stomach would certainly tell him when it was time for his meal, though in times of famine this would be always. Man, being an inventive creature, made early efforts to resolve this problem of time.

As early as 3500 B.C. there are records of simple shadow clocks, or gnomons, which acted much like a sundial, though these were only of use if the sun was shining. Later it was discovered that they were inaccurate to the extent of up to sixteen minutes a day, depending on the season of the year and the position of the sun. However, it is doubtful if such a comparatively small inaccuracy was of much concern to our forefathers. In any case, since the inaccuracy would be the same for everyone in the same place, it was irrelevant. Sand and water clocks had been invented by 300 B.C. These were accurate, provided the flow remained even and there was someone constantly available to invert the hourglass as soon as it had emptied. By the 14th century a device had been constructed whereby a 500 lb. weight slowly falling for a distance of 32 feet pulled a lever round a dial that could be calibrated in hours. This was fairly inaccurate because the strength of pull varied on the amount of cord that had unwound. The instrument itself could of course not be moved. It did however have the advantage that it was attached to a large bell which struck on the hour. This meant that anyone within earshot in the town or surrounding fields would know the hour of the day. Not unnaturally, such devices tended initially to be in church towers and monasteries, where they were of particular assistance to the priests who had to say their various offices at set times.

What is probably the oldest working clock in the world, having been made about 1380, may be seen in Salisbury Cathedral. It was made entirely of hand wrought iron, the downward pull of the weights being originally controlled by a verge escapement and foliot balance and there was no pendulum. Though this clock had no dial, it did strike the hours, which was its main purpose. A few years later, a similar though more advanced clock that also struck the quarter hours, was installed at Wells, almost certainly made by the same man. Since Salisbury is less than 30 miles from Christchurch and communication between the two towns both by land and river was frequent, Christchurch folk would have been well aware of the wonderful time-piece at Salisbury. It is also possible that something similar may have been installed at Christchurch early in the 16th century, not long after the West Tower was added to the Priory in the 1480s. Obviously both the canons and the inhabitants would have welcomed such a facility.

It was not until the 1660s that Robert Hooke invented the escapement that allowed the use of a swinging pendulum on a small arc to be controlled accurately and thus regulate the rotation of the hand on the dial of the clock. He also invented the spiral hairspring for the balance wheel that greatly increased the accuracy of the mechanism, particularly in small portable timepieces. At the same time, additional hands were added to the clock face to denote first minutes and then seconds. Such was the perceived need for greater accuracy. This need led to other inventions. John Hanson developed a means of compensating the changes in the length of the pendulum due to temperature changes - pendulum clocks tended to go too fast in winter and too slow in summer. This he rectified by using metal with different co-efficients of expansion, such as steel and copper, a discovery used later in the manufacture of chronometers, where accuracy was essential for mariners.

All these devices made telling the time more accurate and were increasingly important with the advent of the Industrial Revolution. The length of the working day, dinner breaks and train timetables for example, could now be accurately recorded.

Oddly enough, much earlier in 1525, Jacob Zech, working in Prague, had invented a device for use in small portable timepieces. This was a spiral pulley to equalise the varying pull of the spring inside a watch. This was the origin of the fusee chain, though it does not seem to have been adopted generally until much later. It probably tended to slip off the spiral if it was shaken or dropped. In addition, the 'chain' used was gut made from animal fibre that had a tendency to stretch or contract as the humidity varied. Consequently the greater accuracy created by the spiral pulley was counteracted by the in-accuracy produced by the gut. Nor at that date was there generally any great need for such accuracy in telling the time, so there was little need to find an alternative to the gut. The Clockmakers Company, one of the many City Liveries and Guilds, had been established in London in 1630. Thirty years later, Monsieur Gruet of Geneva, who had by then invented a minute chain to replace the gut, was working in

London. where he presumably started to manufacture fusee chains for watch spirals. He would presumably have been acquainted with Robert Hooke and known of his inventions. since both men were working on increasing the accuracy of small portable timepieces.

Manufacturing fusee chains involved several processes. First the figure-of-eight links of the chain had to be punched out of a thin bar of steel. These had to have a minute hole punched into the centre at each end. Hooks for each end of the chain also had to be punched out and a hole made in the wide end. Fine wire was cut into very short lengths and flattened at one end to form the rivets to hold the links of the chain. Each part. links. hooks and rivets. were filed smooth and polished before they could be passed on for assembly into a chain. The links were assembled three deep. the centre link overlapping the two outer ones rather like a bicycle chain. with each set of links being held together by a fine wire rivet. When the rivet had been inserted through the three links. its end was flattened to prevent it slipping out again. The whole chain then needed filing smooth and burnishing and reshaping if necessary before being tempered in hot oil. Finally it had to be polished so that it shone and to remove any last trace of roughness that might prevent its smooth operation before it could pass its final inspection. Quality control was certainly vital. One of the most important people in the factory would have been the tool-maker. since upon him rested the quality of the work that could be produced. Such fine chains involved equally minute and well-finished tools. Hammers. punches. files and pliers all had to be precision made. The whole industry was yet another example of the extraordinarily high quality of 19th century engineering that was the hall-mark of the Industrial Revolution upon which so much of the prosperity of the country was to grow.

Because the work was so fine - the finished chain could be as thin as button thread - it placed a terrible strain on the eyes and even then could only be done by constantly using a magnifying glass. The most common way of alleviating the pain was to bathe the eyes in clean cold water. Though there were plenty of springs and water pumps from which to draw water in the town. it was found that the spring beside the harbour at Purewell gave the greatest relief. Chemical analysis would probably show that there are certain trace elements in its water that are particularly soothing to eye ailments. Certainly local people have believed this to be the case for some centuries. Though this well-spring is no longer used. and was capped off some years ago. there are local people who still remember drawing drinking water from it. The site. which is on open common land. is well known and marked with an inscribed plaque.

Fusee chains

It was essential to have as much light as possible by which to work. For that reason, William Hart, of whom more will be said later, designed his factory with its huge windows. In the early days of the industry, women would either sit in a window, or else work by candle-light. To increase the quantity of light from a solitary candle, it became customary to fill a glass globe, about four inches in diameter, with water and place it between the candle and the workbench. This had the effect of magnifying the light source. It was also common to place a mirror behind the candle. This threw all the light forward and effectively doubled the quantity of light available. Even with these simple aids, the strain on the eyes must have been enormous. It was not surprising therefore that those who worked for years at home or in the factories, went blind. Nor should one be surprised at the number who took the earliest opportunity to escape from work into marriage, domestic service, or any other employment they could find.

Robert Harvey Cox seems to have been fairly typical of the growing number of entrepreneurs that the Industrial Revolution produced. It seems likely that he had served his apprenticeship as a watchmaker in London, where he would have been aware of the latest technology, which included fusee chains. In an age of innovation, he saw the potential of this particular invention that had still to be exploited. He returned to his native Christchurch, where it is known that in 1776 he was repairing, selling and probably making clocks and watches, though the location of his first workshop is not known. He appears in the 1784 Sadler's Directory of Hampshire as a clock and watchmaker. Although Christchurch was a small town, there would have been a reasonable demand for his wares from amongst others the gunnery and cavalry officers at the military barracks. He therefore needed to employ several artisans in order to satisfy the demand. Because it was such a specialist trade, it is likely that he also found a ready outlet for his watches in towns such as Poole. Southampton, Winchester and Salisbury and other places even further afield. By the middle of the 19th century, fusee chains as a separate item were being imported and sent to major watch manufacturing centres such as London, Birmingham and Liverpool. This was to become an important industry in Christchurch.

It was not until 1790 that the manufacture of fusee chains finally came to Christchurch. The reason for its arrival was probably due to the French Revolution and our subsequent war with France. Fusee chains had been made in Switzerland for some time, but with the turmoil existing on the continent, trade was becoming increasingly difficult and the import of such luxury items as minute chains for the internal workings of watches would probably have been abandoned.

By 1789, the year the French Revolution began, Robert Cox had prospered to such an extent that he took a lease of a house, later described as a house and workshops, next to the Ship Inn in the centre of the High Street. This move was probably necessary in view of the way his business was expanding into the manufacture of the fusee chains that he could no longer import. He therefore decided to manufacture them himself. Because of their small size, the greatest need was for good eyesight, nimble fingers and the ability to concentrate. What better workforce could he have than children, and preferably girls. Of these there was a plentiful supply, particularly amongst the poorer families in the town.

Initially, Robert Cox probably trained his artisans and the children himself, though once he had created a competent workforce, the necessary skills would be passed on by the more experienced girls to the younger ones. This was similar to the system then operating in schools, where the older girls taught the younger ones. An article in the Hampshire Repository of 1801 states that *The children of the poor inhabitants of Christchurch have been for some years past very usefully employed in the manufacturing of watch-spring chains. By the spirited and laudable exertions of Mr Robert Cox, Watchmaker, between forty and fifty children who would otherwise have been a burden not only to their families but perhaps to the parish, are now earning, on an average four or five shillings per week each, contributing most essentially to the support of their parents, and acquiring habits of industry, duty and affection'.*

One may question the Victorian morality expressed in forcing young 'idle hands' to work and it is doubtful if the wages of 4 or 5 shillings were ever achieved. Since the records for 1801 of the Christchurch Workhouse - now the Red House Museum - show that 39 children were involved in chain-making and received a total of £2.18.6d. it seems that the more usual wage was only 1s.6d. for an average of about 70 hours work a week. The higher wage mentioned in the Repository would have been more acceptable to its readers as would its sentiments concerning the relief afforded to the parish rates. Nor would the wages have been paid to the children themselves, since the Workhouse claimed the wages to offset the cost of keeping the poor children. The final assembly of the fusee chains would probably have been done in Robert Cox's own workshop, by the more skilled girls and young women who quite possibly did receive wages nearer the figure mentioned in the Hampshire Repository.

The Workhouse records show that Robert Cox was made a member of the Workhouse Vestry Committee largely, one imagines, because he was providing employment for between one third and a half of the inmates. As such the town would have been very grateful to him. Unfortunately the wages paid seem to have decreased three years later and one may well wonder if the two events were in any way connected. However, part of the reason may have been the decline in workmanship, perhaps due to poor working conditions. Another explanation may have been the frequent recurrence of smallpox that would have lowered the vitality of those lucky enough to survive. There was a particularly severe epidemic in 1807 as a result of which 96 paupers were inoculated at a cost of 5 shillings each.

Such was the growing need for fusee chains for watches, that in 1806, Robert Cox not only opened up a factory in his own house in Wimborne, using children from the Workhouse there, but also made a similar agreement with New Milton. Employing children in both these towns began to draw the work away from Christchurch. Two years later, in 1808, Robert Cox was enquiring if he could employ children at Boldre. By that date wages seems to have increased since he was offering 1s.6d. to children as young as nine years old, in the first year, rising to 2 shillings in the second year and 2s.6d. in the third year, by which time it was assumed that they had become quite skilled. Thereafter he even claimed that the children would be able to earn up to ten shillings a week for piecework. If such wages could indeed have been earned and paid to the recipients, they would have been well pleased.

The following year Thomas Barrow came from London to join Robert Cox and help in the making of the dies that were needed to produce the links of the fusee chains that were now being universally used in both watches and clocks since their accuracy had been widely proved. Three years later children from a further workhouse, in Fordingbridge, were added to the labour force. Conditions were also beginning to improve. Whereas in 1802, the children that Richard Cox employed from the Christchurch Workhouse were to be taught to read for ten minutes in the morning and afternoon, and *'that they and other poor shall have two hours out of the 24 for air and exercise'*, ten years later in 1812, at Fordingbridge, and probably elsewhere too, *'the children be allowed half an hour at Breakfast and one hour at dinner and in order for the children to have some time for learning to read, they are to leave work at four o'clock in the afternoon'*. It was also laid down that the teacher was to be of a good moral character - an interesting comment in view of recent scandals in some children's homes.

There were several reasons not only for this philanthropic morality, but also for the relationship between factory master and employee. The Sunday School Movement, started by Robert Raikes in 1780 had led by 1801 to there being 2,290 such schools. This grew to 23,139 schools in 1851, with an estimated two thirds of working-class children between the ages of 5 and 15 attending. Wesleyan Methodism and its offshoots were becoming an increasing influence on Christian morality, though its application to everyday life tended often to be to the advantage of the ruling classes. Thus the Commandment *'Honour thy father and thy mother'* led easily to 'do as you are told unquestionably' if you were an employee. *'Six days shalt thou labour .....but the seventh is the Sabbath ....'* meant not only 'work hard for all the daylight hours for six days', but also for domestic servants, 'attend church with the master and mistress even if it does mean getting up two hours earlier than usual, in order to light the fires and clean the house first'. For the children of the middle class household, it often meant not playing a game, but sitting in one's uncomfortable best clothes reading 'improving' books or learning the Catechism.

Perhaps the worst biblical misinterpretation was to be found in the division of the world into the 'Chosen Race' and 'Hewers of Wood and Drawers of Water'. This led, particularly in Africa and North America to the concept of the 'White Man', as the 'Chosen Race', exploiting the 'Black Man' as the 'Hewer of Wood'. To a lesser extent this was also shown in the growing industrialised parts of Britain in the relationship between master and worker. Though charity was practised, particularly in the country districts and small towns, where the lady of the manor would take food and clothing to the sick herself, in the major cities it was often at a distance. Too often, the lady of the house would drive to the slums in her carriage with her basket of food or cast-off clothing - and send in her maid to distribute it, lest she be contaminated by its recipients.

That there were of course many genuine and caring employers and their wives cannot be denied, but life was harsh and strict. Christchurch was a garrison town and its inhabitants would be accustomed to hearing about and witnessing the results of the flogging of soldiers - Waterloo was still some years in the future. The stiff upper lip amongst all classes was considered a virtue, so that suffering by the poor would be accepted as the norm. Thus, what would now be considered exploitation of young children, was then regarded as providing work and training for them. This becomes clear from an 1813 Vestry Agreement drawn up by Robert Cox, in which he agreed *'That after the child has been six months in his opinion, they should not be discharged except in cases aforesaid, namely, on leaving the workhouse, going into service, or some other reasonable or just cause'*. Since the number of girls in the workhouse involved in fusee chain making continued to decline, it is clear that as many as possible found ways of leaving, either to get married at the earliest opportunity, or go into domestic service, for which there was a constant demand, or to set up as self-employed chain makers, once they had learnt all the necessary skills. As a result, fusee chain making tended to become increasingly a cottage industry. The Post Office Directory shows that in 1855 there were 500 people engaged in making fusee chains, nearly all of them in their own homes. They were selling piece-work to Robert Cox until his death in 1815, and afterwards to his widow, Ann, who continued in partnership with Thomas Barrow, and others who had by then also set up factories in Christchurch to supply the major watch manufacturers in London and elsewhere.

Of the others who entered the trade, the best known were Henry Jenkins, both father and son, who employed 100 people and William Hart, who employed 104 females and two men. Henry Jenkins is first recorded as a manufacturer of fusee chains in 1833. His factory was in Rotten Row, which now forms part of Bridge Street, opposite the present gas holders. He appears to have been a pillar of the town, being elected a burgess in 1831, mayor in 1857, and churchwarden in 1837-8. He seems also to have been a good employer, for the Christchurch Times records that on his death in 1869, *'the deceased gentleman has been for nearly fifty years a large employer in the Town as a Watch Chain Manufacturer - he was followed to the grave by a large number of his workpeople'*. It is worth noting that the ages of those employed ranged from 9 to over 60, so that, despite the difficulties of the work, women were prepared to continue at it for much of their lives. For some, this was probably because they had no alternative if they wished to keep out of the workhouse.

William Hart only became involved in fusee chain making in 1845, having made his money first as a taxidermist in Purewell. His late arrival into the industry was all the more remarkable since he had no experience of the trade, though he must have had particularly sound business acumen as well as advanced ideas on employment conditions. To establish his business, he first built the still extant factory in Bargates between the present Conservative Club and the recently closed Magistrates Courts. This was built to the most advanced design, with particularly large windows on both sides. Though the building was 74 feet long, it was only 18 feet wide, which meant that the employees had the maximum possible light for their intricate work. Perhaps unusually, all aspects of chain making were carried out in the factory - wire drawer, wire cutter, link cutter, chain rivetter, chain polisher, chain finisher, chain examiner and tool maker. It may reasonably be regarded as an early example of mass production on an assembly line. William Hart's son, Frederick, took over the factory on his father's death until Swiss and American watches made more cheaply without the need for fusee chains, began to be imported in 1875. Though fusee chains continued to be made until the turn of the century it proved to be death knell of an industry that had been one of the major employers in the town during a period when other employment was hard to find.

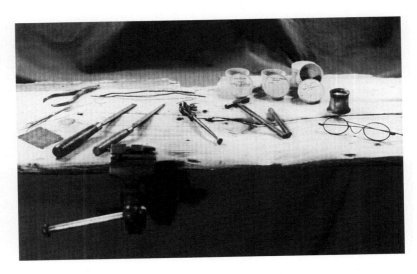

Fusee chain making tools.

Had any alternative large-scale employment been available in Christchurch, then the fusee chain industry might not have prospered as it did, since those involved in it risked, and often suffered blindness. However, it should be remembered that conditions in the cotton and woollen mills and in the mines and iron-works were probably even worse. Health and Safety understanding and legislation remained far in the future. It was still the era of *'See-saw, Margery Daw, Johnny shall have a new master. He shall earn but a penny a day, because he can't work any faster'*. Though few factory owners were deliberately cruel, many gave insufficient thought about how they might improve the welfare of their workforce, probably adopting the attitude that life was harsh and in any case there were plenty of other potential employees who would be prepared to work under the existing conditions.

On the positive side, one may speculate on the fine skills and manual dexterity acquired by so many women in the town who worked to produce the fusee chains up to the end of the last century. These skills may have been passed on to create a similarly skilled workforce that was needed in the electrical and electronic factories that sprang up and prospered at the beginning of World War II and which are today such major employers in the town. If this is so, then we owe the fusee chain makers a great debt.

Fusee chain in a watch mechanism.

Chapter 24

The Military Barracks – 1794-1996.

Before 1792, the country possessed hardly any purpose built barracks to house soldiers. It was the common custom to billet them either in alehouses, in hired buildings, or sometimes on the local population. The former were naturally popular with the soldiers themselves since they were then as close as they could get to an almost unending supply of liquor and probably also female company. Hired buildings might or might not be popular, depending very much on the magnanimity of the officer responsible for finding the accommodation. To be billeted on the local population was also a haphazard affair whose success depended very much on the relationship between the soldiers and the householders. Sometimes it worked well and led to good relationships and friendships between the two. At other times, if little consideration had been given to placing men in suitable quarters, all kinds of trouble could arise, leading to theft, damage and molesting of the females in whose houses the sometimes uncouth soldiery were forcibly thrust. Much might depend on the calibre of the officer in charge or more frequently the sensibility of the billeting sergeant, as to whether the billet was a success or a disaster.

Official government policy was against the formation of a large standing army. This was largely on grounds of cost but also because people were aware that Bonnie Prince Charlie had died less than 5 years previously. The 1745 rebellion and the battles of Falkirk and Culloden were also still living memories in the minds of the older generation. If there was no body of trained soldiers upon which a pretender to the throne could call, there was less likelihood of efficient armed support rallying to him again. He did not die until 1788 and his brother, Henry, survived into the next century. According to William Pitt, the Prime Minister, Europe had every reason to believe that peace would continue for at least another 15 years. He therefore reduced taxes, to the delight of those that paid them, and cut down on armaments and the number of regular troops. Blackstone, in his 'Commentaries on English Law', echoed the widespread feeling in the country that, *In a land of liberty it is extremely dangerous to make a distinct order of the profession of arms. Soldiers should be enlisted for short periods, and live intermixed with the people; no separate camp, no barracks, no inland fortresses should be allowed'.*

The execution of Louis XVI of France on 21st January 1793 changed everything, particularly as ten days later France declared war on Britain and Holland. Before the end of the year, Belgium had fallen to the French and the Duke of York's army had been driven out of Dunkirk and Flanders. Raw recruits, hastily enrolled, needed to be trained and the threat of invasion had to be countered by the presence of troops along the South Coast. Though of little concern to those living south of the Thames, there was also social unrest in the industrial Midlands and North, fanned in part by the revolutionary creed that was spreading out of France.

To counteract the invasion threat, the Master General of Ordnance who was responsible for such few barracks as did exist, concluded that *in order to effect the movement of troops to the coast, it would be necessary that steps should be immediately taken for hiring of a great number of places to convert into barracks for the Infantry, for the Cavalry and the Horse Artillery.* Since only engineering and artillery barracks were under the control of the Board of Ordnance, it was necessary to establish a separate Barrack Department to be responsible for building new barracks for the cavalry and infantry. The new department's first Superintendent was Colonel Oliver Delancey, who had the previous year toured the Midlands to assess the causes of unrest there. According to Sir John Fortescue's 'History of the British Army', *Delancey was empowered to purchase or hire plots of land, to contract for the erection of buildings, for the supply of bedding and so forth, and to conduct financial operations on an enormous scale without the slightest supervision or control. ....No doubt there were a few officers in the Army qualified to wield the powers to the newly created Department, Delancey was not one of them*. Ten years later it was found that £10,000,000 of public money, a huge sum in those days, had been issued to the Department, for which no account could be produced! Though a large number of subordinate barrack-masters were appointed where there were no barracks, yet the department did ultimately build 203 barracks to house 1,700 cavalry and 146,000 infantry, one of which was at Christchurch.

There had been smuggling along the south coast of England especially since the 14th century when the excise duties of Tunnage and Poundage on the import of wine and export of wool made it profitable for sailors and local traders to evade the duties. It was however not until the 18th century, when heavy import duties were placed on such items as brandy, lace, tobacco and silk, that smuggling became rife. In areas such as Dorset and Somerset, it was regarded as almost respectable with the squire and parson often heavily involved. To try to control this trade, it had become the custom to station bodies of mounted troops at convenient places along the coast and billeted in hired quarters, to try to intercept the smugglers that had evaded the revenue cutters which patrolled the coastal waters. One such body was already stationed in Christchurch, so that it was natural that one of the new barracks should be built here. It could if necessary house both the 'preventative officers' and also a troop of Horse Artillery to be used in the defence of the coast against the threatened French invasion.

A suitable site for the new barracks was found about half a mile outside the town to the west on the edge of the Portfield. Here, according to Tucker's Guide to Christchurch published in 1832, *'About midway between the town and Iford Bridge is an extensive range of barracks erected about 40 years since, containing stables and gunsheds for the accommodation of Horse Artillery; a troop of which was generally stationed here during the last war against Napoleon; since which they have been occasionally occupied by detachments of Dragoons from headquarters at Dorchester'.* The 1844 tithe map of Christchurch shows the barracks as being near the edge of the cultivated strips of land farmed by the local people. It was bordered on one side by a narrow road that led over the bridge at Iford towards the neighbouring town and port of Poole, and on the other by the River Stour. It was sufficiently far from the houses of the town, not to be a nuisance yet near enough for the soldiers to reach the alehouses and other entertainment that the town could provide. It was also conveniently placed to enable the riding officers to patrol the coast both east and west, and for the artillery to ride their guns to convenient locations along the coastal cliffs to drive off any potential attacking ships.

The threat of attack was taken seriously, since in addition to the artillery already stationed there, a Marching Order dated 17th July 1794 orders part of the 92nd Regiment of Foot stationed at Devizes *'to take up quarters at Christchurch and Christchurch Barracks'.* This involved a march of over 50 miles along unmade roads in the heat of summer and would presumably have taken two days. No doubt the columns of soldiers, perhaps two hundred strong, led by their fifes and drums, would have made a brave sight in their scarlet tunics, even if they were dusty, hot and probably footsore, as they entered the town. Many a heart must had fluttered in maidenly breasts, while their Mammas suffered fits of the vapours as they imagined their daughters suffering what was then considered to be "a fate worse than death". Those fathers who were involved in commerce would probably have rubbed their hands in delight at the prospect of considerably increased trade from the new arrivals. One can also imagine their sons, as has always happened, copying the drill of the soldiers with broomsticks for muskets.

Initially these new arrivals would have been accommodated in tents, since the barracks as then built were too small to house them all. The officers would probably have taken the opportunity to find comfortable billets with some of the genteel families in the town and parties and other entertainment would have soon been organised to the delight of all and profit of the tradesmen.

Building continued for some years, for it is recorded that Thomas and John Pilgrim, the builders, who were both carpenters and joiners, were paid a total of £3,600 between December 1795 and the end of 1798. By 1800, the Barracks are recorded as having accommodation for 210 N.C.O.s and soldiers.

In 1809, the Barrack Department was wound up and control of those establishments reverted to the Board of Ordnance, whose Assistant Inspector, Captain Close, compiled what is probably the earliest detailed plan and full description of the barracks. The main barrack block housed besides the Commanding Officer's married quarters, both officers and men on the first floor, with stabling for their horses on the ground floor. It stood two and a half storeys high and was well built of red brick with a hipped slate roof. The stalls for the horses were separated by some of the earliest cast iron columns to be used in such a construction, and the floor was cobbled with a central drainage gully. Beneath the ground floor of the officers' quarters was a small cellar that one can imagine was used as a wine store. It seems that they were very conscious of the risk of fire with so much straw and fodder about, for the upper floor had long lengths of rope attached to hooks by the dormer windows for use as fire escapes. The remainder of the buildings were single storey. The west side housed the canteen, engine house, hospital stables - there is no mention of a similar facility for the men - and artificers' shops. The east side housed the gun sheds and magazine, while between these two stood various storage buildings for coal and beer for the men, and forage and grain for the horses.

It appears that the Barracks at that time could only accommodate half a troop of Horse Artillery, rather than a full troop that was considered necessary. Captain Close's report was less than complimentary. Although he found that the buildings were well built, and some of them were later to receive Grade II listing, he considered that enlargement 'was essentially necessary for the good of the service, the preservation of the horses and the Discipline of the soldiers'. His order of precedence is interesting. He further reported that 'the Quarters at Christchurch are so notoriously bad that it has been, and still is, found almost impracticable either to preserve the soldiers from participating in much of the licentiousness of a Borough Town inhabited by a people who are at all times tempting soldiers to disobedience of orders and to the dishonest treatment of their horses.' How accurate a representation of the behaviour of the citizens of Christchurch is this report, must be open to question. Presumably the contents of the report was confidential, or the town's elders would have remonstrated vehemently at the slur that it cast upon the morality of their town.

Captain Close reported that the Barracks held only 5 officers, 57 men and 63 horses, which was well short of the 210 men quoted by Colonel Delancey for the temporary infantry barracks in 1800. Perhaps that accommodation had by then been removed. The recommendation was that more accommodation should be erected, by Mr Pilgrim as previously, to house an additional 88 men and 86 horses. Also to be built was the Guard House, that is now Grade II listed, and still presents a pleasing landmark beside the road. All this was finally approved the following year by the Chief Royal Engineer, Major General Eveleigh, who also recommended that there should be accommodation for an extra officer and that the work should be carried out by the Barrack Master using local labour as well as the resident soldiers. How well the two labour forces co-operated is not known but it seems that the work was successfully completed by October 1812. The bricks for the new buildings came by sea from Hilsea near Portsmouth and were unloaded at the Haven at Mudeford. This is surprising since there was a quay at the town besides a mud-berth at the Quomps, both of which are much nearer the Barracks site than Mudeford. Indeed it is probable that vessels which could reach the Town Quay could also have been taken up the Stour as far as the Barracks site itself. This would have avoided the necessity of hiring carts and carters to transport the bricks the two miles from the Haven. Perhaps, however, the town insisted on this added transport as a means of increasing local employment. It is indeed recorded that permission was given not only to purchase 'frocks' or protective overalls, for the soldiers who were to handle the bricks, but also that horses and carts could be hired locally to collect the bricks from the beach before the local inhabitants removed them! Were the local inhabitants really so dishonest?

By 1857 it appears that further buildings had been added. These were a house for the Commanding Officer and a building to house a school with accommodation for a schoolmaster. There must therefore have been a considerable number of married soldiers who had their families with them. Presumably, the school in the town was too small to take the 22 soldiers' children that there were in 1861 and there were to be more later when the extra married quarters were built. Or was it considered undesirable that the children of the "licentious soldiery" should mix with the supposedly more refined children of the town? Such was the low opinion of the general population of the British soldier who had most recently fought successfully in the Crimea.

Christchurch Barracks c. 1900.

Twenty-five years later, a further range of buildings had been added. These comprised a new range of officers' quarters and a further block of married quarters complete with a washhouse near the river. The latter however were demolished in the 1950's to be replaced by an office block needed for the increasingly complex design requirements of the modern Engineers. Little however changed until the first World War, when a series of temporary buildings were erected both outside the perimeter wall and on what had been the Barrack Square.

Between the wars, the town itself began to expand westwards. In consequence, the Barracks became enclosed by housing and the open spaces within, became increasingly filled with temporary buildings. Though the Barracks were originally built for the Artillery and was also used to house Cavalry, as time passed and needs changed, more space was used by the Military Engineers. This became particularly important with the advent of the Experimental Bridging Company shortly before the first World War, and its successor establishments, culminating in the Military Engineering and Experimental Establishment (M.E.X.E.) and finally the Military Vehicle Experimental Establishment (M.V.E.E.). Important engineering developments for both military and civilian use, continued in the Barracks until the mid 1990s, when, with the end of the Cold War and the general run-down of military expenditure, it was finally decided to close the establishment. Thus ended a 200 year history of military association with the town. There can be no doubt that some of the experimental work carried out, particularly by the Engineers, played a major part not only in winning wars, but also in helping to win the peace and improve the lot of under-developed countries. The presence of the engineering barracks also attracted much civilian technical expertise to the town that found other outlets in the local aircraft. electrical and electronic industries. Between them they have helped to build up the world-wide reputation that Christchurch enjoys as a centre of both civil and military engineering excellence.

The effect of the presence of military personnel in Christchurch was considerable. As has already been said. from the end of the 18th century they inevitably brought increased trade to the town. Not only were there profitable building contracts but also a continual demand for supplies for both men and horses. In addition, both grazing land for livestock and rented accommodation were in constant demand as were the services of such men as farriers. The Summer Fair also saw the sale of surplus horses and their equipment. No wonder the *Christchurch Times* recorded in February 1882. *'We hear that the Artillery now stationed at Dorchester have been ordered off to Christchurch Barracks. We only hope the report is accurate'*. Two months later it was further reported that 46 men. 45 horses and four guns had arrived at the Barracks. due in large measure to the good offices of the local Member of Parliament. Mr. Horace Davey. No doubt the soldiers also helped to provide entertainment. whether by holding balls and dances or horse races. There were also frequent football and cricket matches that were played and watched with the customary enthusiasm. Likewise. there were reports of drunkenness and other disorderly behaviour. including an assault on a police constable – a rare case in those days. A newspaper report of 1889 reports that at one of the frequent N.C.O.'s quadrille parties. which were held either at the Barracks or in the Town Hall. *'the proceedings were characterised by much pleasantness. Dancing commenced at 9 p.m. and extended about 8 hours.'* It appears that by then. public opinion of the Military had considerably improved. Indeed the barrack fire engine was used to put out several fires in the town and the town bought the military fire engine called 'Ye Deluge' in 1863 and used it to put out a bakery fire the same year. In 1928 the then resident 18th Medium Battery Royal Artillery turned out to help fight the fire that raged over 600 acres of heath land in the St Leonards and Matchams area. There are also records of many mixed civil and military marriages over the years. However the Cavalry who were periodically stationed in the Barracks were not universally popular. Since one of their main duties was to try to control the smuggling that for some years formed a major element of the trade in the town. this is not surprising.

So for 200 years the presence of the Barracks in Christchurch has had a notable impact on the life of the town. Not only did the town increase in prosperity and size as a result, but also many families became intimately connected with those who served there. The town can justifiably take vicarious pleasure and pride from many notable people who have lived and worked there. There was Sir Augustus Fraser, who ultimately commanded the Horse Artillery at Waterloo with great distinction and then became Director of the Royal Laboratory at Woolwich. Then there was General Sir John Dupuis who served in the Crimea and Indian Mutiny and who, while at Christchurch, obtained a proper artillery training ground between Somerset and Wolverton Roads. Then in more recent times there was Sir Donald Bailey, who invented and developed the famous bridge that bears his name.

Town and Barracks have developed hand in hand to their mutual benefit, defence and support. Nor should it be forgotten that a thousand years ago, when Twynham was a Royal Burgh, we know from the earliest Saxon Charters that its inhabitants were all involved in military service, fortress work and bridging. So it has continued down the ages.

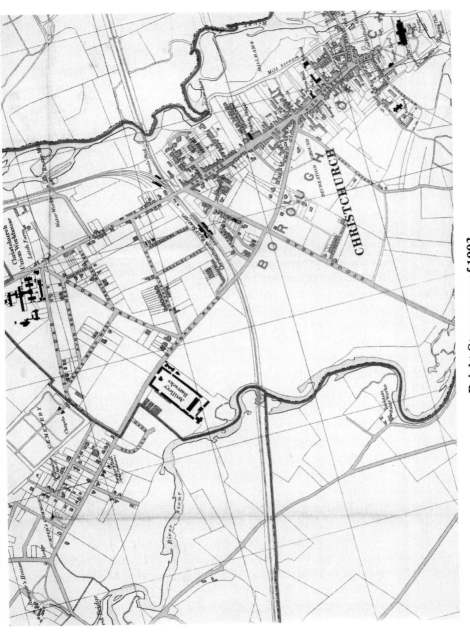

Bright Stores map of 1903

207

Chapter 25.

The Earl of Clarendon, J.E. Holloway and Hengistbury Head.

Throughout its long history, Christchurch Harbour has always provided a safe anchorage for ships. The Romans established a small port under the lee of the headland and it became one of the chief trading posts between the continent and southern England. However, its entrance has also presented mariners with problems. The earliest maps show the entrance as being very different from the shape it now presents. There was no long sand spit with which we are familiar, but rather a wide entrance partially obstructed by a series of islands and sandbars, through which vessels had to find their way. This meant that only shallow draught ships could enter and it was advisable to employ a local pilot to guide one in. Once within the shelter of the harbour, it was an easy sail up to the town quay, though, if the wind was light or from the wrong direction, it might be easier to pole the vessel up stream. Unless the rivers were in full spate and the tide was running out fast, this probably presented little problem. In any case, it was always better to come in on a rising tide, so that in the event of the vessel running aground on one of the many shoals at the entrance, it would only be necessary to wait a short time before it floated off again. There was also the possibility, if there was little cargo to be off-loaded or be taken on board, that the vessel could make a quick turn round, and sail out before the second high tide fell away.

When Edward Hyde, Earl of Clarendon bought the Lordship of the Manor of Christchurch in 1665 from Lord Baltimore, he decided to try to resolve the problems of the difficult entrance to Christchurch Harbour as part of his general plans for the improvement of the town and its trade. It cannot be said that his motives were entirely altruistic, since, as Lord of the Manor, he would have profited greatly from the tolls and other duties he would have been able to extract from his enterprises. Clarendon already knew that quite large vessels could navigate the Avon as far up as Salisbury. Raleigh had towed a large merchantman up to Downton, where he had it broken up and the timbers used to enlarge his house for the proposed visit of Queen Elizabeth, though he must have chosen a high Spring tide and stripped the boat to its bare hull to achieve this. Later, in 1625, John Taylor, a London wherryman sailed a large shallow draught boat up the Avon from Christchurch to Salisbury in order to prove that the river could be used as a trade route. Though the voyage created considerable local and even some national interest, the idea did not catch on immediately. During the Commonwealth, there was a scheme to use 30 ton flat bottomed craft that only drew 3 foot as a means of transport between the two towns. This too came to nothing.

Clarendon had heard of both these ideas. He also knew about Andrew Yarranton's survey "England's improvements by Land and Sea (to outdo the Dutch)". Clarendon had brought him down from Salisbury to Christchurch and also had him survey the coastal waters off Hengistbury Head as well as the harbour. Yarranton reported *'I found in the sea great quantities of Iron Stones lye in a Ridge. For in the Sea, pointing directly upon the Isle of Wight, observing it at low water, I found that the ridge of Iron Stones was the cause that forced the ground Tide about the point, which has carried and lodged the Sands so, as it had choaked up the Harbour; but the Stones near the shore lay so great and thick, that they were the occasion of lodging the Sands by them, near the Western Shore, and so of preserving a place which is very deep and good Anchorage, and within a hundred Yards of the Shore, which gives unto that River the advantage of making there as good an Harbour, as to the depth of Water it will draw, as any in England, where a Boy (sic) and a Cord two inches diameter will be sufficient to hold a Ship; the Harbour being a great inland Lake or Pool, and well defended from all winds'.*

Yarranton then outlined the advantages of the area for ship-building and the manufacture of guns. He pointed out how easily defensible Hengistbury was, adding that if £2,000 were spent on a fort to defend the headland, it would probably be impregnable. He stated that small fifth or sixth rate ships could easily be built there.

He then stressed the economic advantages of the area. *'The King may have all his Iron made and Guns cast at very cheap Rates. There is Iron Stone in the Sea, by the Harbour mouth, and the king hath vast quantities of Woods decayed in New Forest, of which at this time Charcoal is made, and shipt away to Cornwall and other parts. If two Furnaces be built about Ringwood to cast Guns and two Forges to make Iron, and the Iron Stone be brought from the Harbour mouth out of the Sea up the river to the Furnaces and the Charcole out of the New Forest to the works, there being sufficient of decayed woods to supply four Iron-works for ever; by these means the King makes the best of everything, and builds with his own timber being near and convenient, whereas now the charge and carriage makes the Timber of no use to him. And having Iron Stone of his own for gathering up, and Wood of his own for nothing, he will have very cheap Guns and Iron'.*

As a result of this report, the Earl devised a scheme for making a new entrance to the harbour in the middle of what is now the sand spit and then dredging those parts of the Avon that were particularly shallow between Christchurch and Salisbury. In consequence, there was proposed in 1664, *'An Act for the making of the river Avon*

Navigable from Christ-Church to the City of New-Sarum'. Its object was. *'Whereas the making navigable and passable with barges, boats, lighters and other vessels, the River Avon in the Counties of Wilts. And Southampton, from the Town of Christ-Church ... ...to the City of New-Sarum; ... ...and the making of a new Haven, may with god's blessing be of great advantage and benefit not only to the said Counties, but also to the publique, by import and export of commodities, and increase of Commerce and Trade, and of able Seamen and Watermen, and most profitable and necessary for the said City of New Sarum for the conveyance thereby of Fewel [fuel] and other necessities to the said City, whereof there is great scarcity, and far greater likely to grow, if some help therefore be not provided, besides the extraordinary preservation of the highways in and near the said City and County'.*

The enterprise would create considerable employment, not only for the construction of the new havens but also the river works. There would be ongoing employment, since in places it was estimated that horses and men would be required to draw boats up-river. There would also have been tolls, berthing dues and other payments that would have been to the advantage not only of the landowners through which the improved river highway passed, but also of the owners of the wharves at each end. Earl Clarendon of course owned the Christchurch end. He was also to be the Chief Commissioner of the project. If it succeeded, then Clarendon would have been one of the main beneficiaries.

However, the Act came to nothing. Perhaps Andrew Yarranton's enthusiasm outran his business ability. Perhaps also Clarendon discovered that he would not be able to claim payment for the ironstone that would be removed from the shore that formed part of his manor. He may therefore have decided not to press the advantages that Yarranton stressed, even though the scheme would have helped to increase trade in the two centres of population. It would certainly have moved heavy traffic, such as the carriage of coal for fuel, from the roads. Even in those days, they were anxious not to clutter up the roads unnecessarily with heavy and slow moving vehicles. The 17th century also had its public transport problems.

Though creating such a transport route might have brought considerable advantages to both Salisbury and Christchurch, there would have been disadvantages too. Creating a new entrance to the harbour could have had a serious effect on the salmon run, besides altering the flow of the rivers. This would have produced unexpected and undesirable results, particularly upon the rest of the surrounding shoreline. However none of this was appreciated at the time.

Earl Clarendon did however make the initial moves to demonstrate the feasibility of the scheme by starting to lay down a line of rocks on the western side of the new entrance that he also had dug. The stone used was partly ironstone doggers that were deeply strewn all along the base of Hengistbury Head and the foreshore, and partly Portland stone shipped round. Without the authority of the Act, he was unable to make much progress and allowed the work to lapse. In the event, as so often is the case, nature took a hand. In November 1703, a terrible storm hit the country, doing damage that far exceeded that of the storm in 1987. Clarendon's new cut into the harbour was silted up with sand washed round from the south shore of the headland, and his rock groyne severely damaged. So ended a brave attempt to make Christchurch into a thriving entrepôt. Other schemes were put forward over the next 150 years, but all foundered on what were seen to be insuperable difficulties.

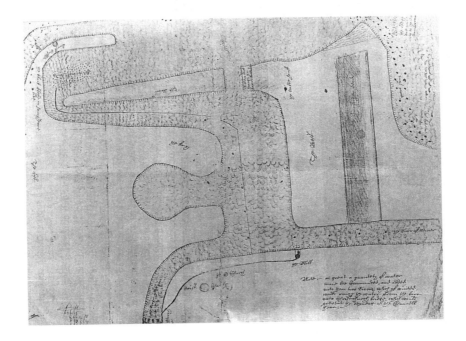

Clarendon's scheme for Christchurch Harbour 1671.

There are however good reasons for being thankful that Clarendon did not press harder for Yarranton's scheme to be implemented. Had the scheme to remove the iron doggers gone ahead, it is likely that Hengistbury Head would have long since disappeared, as it was in danger of doing two hundred years later. In any case, by the time that Yarranton came to publish his report in 1676, the Dutch Wars had been over for two years and negotiations were in progress for the Dutch William of Orange to marry Princess Mary, the daughter of James II. Peace was agreed with Holland in 1674, the year that Christopher Wren started to build St Paul's Cathedral, using stone that came from Portland. Some of the stone was probably carried in Christchurch ships.

The threat to Hengistbury arose once more in the 1840s. The quantity of coal being shipped into Christchurch was increasing, much of it being brought round to Southampton by sea from the South Wales, Northumberland and Durham coal-fields. From there it was collected by George Holloway in his smaller ships and delivered mostly to Town Quay, for final delivery to houses in the town by cart. However, some was delivered from flat-bottomed barges to individual houses that had jetties along the harbour's edge. George Holloway had already established himself as a boat builder in the area of the Black House at the eastern end of the sand spit. There was no shortage of skilled labour on which he could call, since boats had been built in the area for centuries. During the reign of Edward I, the prior had built, and probably manned, a boat that sailed with the fleet against the Scots and most of the local fishing boats would have been built in or near the town. Indeed, boat building remains a natural occupation for Christchurch men with such names as Elkins, Purbrook-Rossiter, Lack, Stride and Bob Hoare, who built an Olympic Gold Medal winning dinghy.

Before 1842, another member of the Holloway family, John Edward, had been shipping limestone locally. He used to collect the ironstone doggers that lay off the shore of Hengistbury Head to use as ballast for his return journey. Had not some of these same stones been used to form part of Clarendon's breakwater? Holloway now found that these doggers had a market since they had a particularly high iron ore content. He could sell the ironstone to the colliers, who then took it back to the coal-fields, there to be used in the growing iron and steel industries of Wales and the north. He approached the then Lord of the Manor, Sir George Gervis, for a lease to collect the doggers from the shoreline and the Head itself. This was granted in 1847. At that time, Hengistbury Head was a scrub-covered area, seldom visited by anyone, with the southern shoreline almost impassable because of the huge piles of doggers that littered the beach. Even Double Dykes was seldom visited, except by the few who were interested in its antiquities. The headland's chief claim to fame would have been as an area used by smugglers. Certainly there were no holidaymakers there, since there was nothing to attract those few who were able to visit the seaside. Sir George Gervis would have been only too delighted to be able to derive an income from what would previously have been regarded as an area of no value. Holloway however now found that he had a highly profitable enterprise waiting to be exploited.

Five years later, in 1852, Holloway had removed all the loose doggers from the foreshore and then began mining the base of the cliffs themselves. Though the general public did not visit the area, it was already becoming apparent to the authorities that as a result of Holloway's activities, a serious alteration was taking place in the coastline. Hengistbury Head was seen to be shrinking alarmingly, and Old Harry Rocks were now visible from what had previously been safe anchorages, but were now exposed to the direct force of the south-westerly gales. In addition, the sand spit that had previously stretched little further east than the Black House was lengthening alarmingly towards Highcliffe Castle. There was also some confusion as to whether the rights of the foreshore belonged to Sir George Rose or Sir George Gervis who had granted the lease to Holloway. Nor was it clear whether the conditions of the lease were being adhered to or exceeded, particularly when Holloway started mining at the foot of the cliffs. Though Holloway was providing considerable employment for general labourers, opposition to the works on the Head was growing from the fishing community and others, because of the effect on the southern and western shorelines. Sir George Rose wrote to the Admiralty expressing his fears, but not until three years later did Captain Vetch investigate the matter on behalf of the Admiralty. His report was damning, stating that the damage already done far outweighed any benefit obtained from the sale of the ironstone. In spite of this report and the efforts of James Druitt, who acted for Sir George Rose with the strong support of the local Council, work continued on the Head. Indeed, mining from the harbour side was also carried out for several years, with Holloway cutting through a channel from the harbour's edge to the foot of the headland, to form what is now known as Holloway's Dock. From there, his barges were loaded with ironstone that he was mining from the middle of the headland. So deep into the headland had he gone, that had it not been finally stopped, the end of the Head would have been cut off and become an island. The size of the operation can be gauged from the fact that in 1856 alone, thirteen thousand tons of stone were removed, while the spoil was piled up to one side.

150 years ago, there was virtually no knowledge about the effects of tides and currents on the shoreline, nor how erosion took place or could be controlled. In times of storm, beaches came and went in an

213

apparently unpredictable fashion. Attempts were sometimes made to hold back the sea with earth and stone barriers, with the best engineering expertise coming from the Netherlands. Though this had been applied successfully in East Anglia, there seemed to be little similarity between that coast and Hengistbury Head. The lessons of the effects of altering the composition of a shoreline had to be learnt the hard way.

Over the years, Holloway had become a man of some importance locally. He was a town councillor, Justice of the Peace, and finally mayor for two years in 1865 and '66. Whatever justification he might give for his actions was therefore likely to carry some weight. He could argue that he was certainly providing employment to many people and bringing trade and wealth to the town. He could presumably claim that there was at that time little or no conclusive scientific evidence that his activities were the direct cause of the changes to the western shoreline of the headland. He could perhaps question whether reducing the width of Hengistbury Head was of any great concern, since it was not an area that was much visited, there being no proper road at its base, and the top being far too windy for pleasant exercise. Indeed, many of the elder generation in the town would remember the headland primarily as a haunt of smugglers, with hardly a house between the headland and Poole many miles to the west.

That he finally ceased operations was probably due to the opposition that James Druitt, Mayor in 1850, '59 and '67, was able to galvanise. Since he succeeded Holloway's two-year mayoralty in 1867, it may be that the strength of the opposition to the mining operations was by then sufficiently strong for pressure to be brought to bear on Holloway to cease operations. But by then the damage was done. Not only was the width of Hengistbury Head reduced by several hundred yards, but the effect on the coastline for several miles eastwards was radically altered with unknown damage to the harbour entrance, the beaches and the cliff faces to the east. During the 1880s and '90's, the Run extended for about two miles to Steamer Point, causing great difficulties to the fishermen and others trying to use the harbour. It was only with the construction of the Long Groyne off the western point of Hengistbury Head that the erosion was finally checked. This has led to new beach forming off the end of the headland that has slowed the erosion of the cliffs, though there are still falls in rough weather. Nor is the damage confined to the end of the headland. As recently as the 1980s, a serious storm washed out several metres of the land adjacent to Double Dykes. This caused fears that there might be a breach through to the harbour, since the land there is low-lying and consists of only compacted gravel. Fortunately, remedial works were carried out to stabilise the area and remove the threat. though at considerable cost.

It could be argued that both Clarendon and Holloway were bent on exploiting Hengistbury and that neither knew what damage their schemes would do. since present scientific knowledge was not available to either of them. However. there would seem to have been a difference in their approach. Clarendon seems to have taken a wide view of the benefits that his scheme would produce for Christchurch, Salisbury and all places between. though he cannot have been unaware of the financial benefit that would have come his way as Lord of the Manor. Though Holloway could plead ignorance of the possible effects of his actions on the coastline. it can be argued that he should have taken more notice of the fears raised not only locally. but also by the Admiralty Inspector. In his defence. he could say that his lease gave him the right to act as he did. But it is hard not to conclude that once there was clear evidence of the damage caused by his activities. as a leading citizen of the town he should have ceased operations. More particularly so as there seems to have been some doubt about the terms of his lease. rather than, perhaps. let the profit motive assume precedence.

It has taken many decades for the scars made by Holloway on Hengistbury to be almost hidden. Since his depredations. the efforts of local conservationists and nature lovers have done much to turn the damage he did to good effect. The ponds Holloway created for his cart horses to drink from have been turned into attractive lily ponds. and the area where he was in danger of cutting right through the headland has now been dammed to form a wild-life lake. The sand spit itself is probably now wider that before he started and can therefore accommodate many more beach huts than would have otherwise have been possible. In this way. Holloway can be said to have helped the tourist industry in the area. What cannot be put back is the loss of so much of the width of the headland itself. and even part of the ancient fortifications of Double Dykes.

It is clear that it has never been practical to develop the harbour as a port for anything other than very shallow craft. so that there has been no danger that it would be developed as a busy. and polluted. commercial port. The constantly moving bar at the entrance to the Run and its fast tidal flow in both directions. means that unless one has personal knowledge of the channels. it is always advisable to call for local assistance before attempting to enter. Once within the harbour entrance. the many sandbars make sailing. even in dinghies. an interesting experience. Being effectively landlocked as well as shallow. the harbour with its low speed limit for motorised craft. is ideally suited for wind-surfers and dinghy sailors. and particularly children.

Those who now have the responsibility of caring for the whole of the headland, use their best endeavours to improve all aspects of area. There is far greater knowledge of environmental issues available today than there was 150 years ago and even the damage that the sheer numbers of visitors can do to a sensitive area, can now be assessed. Though there may be some restriction of use on the headland that perhaps initially causes resentment, when set in the wider context of the benefit of the many, the policies become logical. As a result, Christchurch folk, as well as the countless visitors who flock to such a pleasant place, can therefore continue to enjoy the pleasures of an area that not so long ago they were in grave danger of losing altogether.

Chapter 26.

James Druitt: 1816 - 1904.
Herbert Druitt: 1876 - 1943.

The Druitt family came originally from Wimborne. The earliest record of the family appears to be that of Philip Druitt who was born in 1675 and died in 1736. The family was well known in the town, since James was the second son of Robert Druitt, one of the town's doctors. The family was also closely involved with the Grammar School there, since both James's maternal grandfather, Revd. James Mayo and his son, who was also christened James, taught at the school. When James Druitt's father died in 1822, his Mayo grandmother took in the six-year-old boy and put him through his formal education in Wimborne Grammar School, where the annual cost of schooling was £1.11s.6d. a year besides stationery. Life at the school has already been described in chapter 18, and comes from James Druitt's autobiography. The curriculum at Wimborne consisted almost entirely of Latin and Greek Grammar, Mathematics and some French. It therefore covered the subjects that would enable the brightest boys to obtain a double first class degree at Oxford, in Classics and Maths, such as was obtained by William Gladstone in 1831.

With this scholastic training, it is not surprising to find that James acquired a good grounding in the subjects that would be of use in his career. When he left school in 1831 aged 15, he was articled to Henry Rowden, a solicitor in Wimborne, who also acted as Clerk to the local Justices. James acted as his clerk and as such was able to gain wide and varied experience not only in criminal matters but also in civil law. By 1838, he had gained sufficient knowledge and experience to enable him to be admitted as an attorney. Almost immediately he was offered the Christchurch practice of Mr. Dibsdall, who wished to retire. This he accepted, and when Dibsdall died a few months later, Henry Rowden joined him as a partner in Christchurch. From that date onwards, James Druitt became increasingly involved in the town.

It is clear that he quickly prospered. At first he lived at 1 High Street where his eldest child was born in 1844. That year he was able to buy 15 High Street and build there the imposing mansion that we know as the Druitt Library. There he not only lived but practised from 1841 to 1877. Later, he took his nephew, Robert into partnership. He was to be Mayor for four successive years, in 1910, '11, '12 and '13. Another member of the family, John, always known as Jack, who was a son by James's first wife, also qualified as a solicitor and was Town

Clerk of Christchurch from 1892 until 1925. He had to return temporarily to that post in 1928 on the untimely death of his successor, Albert Harley.

In 1858, James acquired an interest in the next door property, No. 16, that had for a time been the National School. It was an ideal location for a solicitor, having large rooms and being centrally placed in the High Street. From 1859 it was also opposite the Town Hall that had been moved from its previous Market Square site on the corner of Castle Street and Church Street. With the centre of the town's administration on the other side of the road from his office, James Druitt was ideally situated to capture much of its official business. He had also purchased for £15, a small cottage that formed part of the West Marsh Farm buildings that was occupied by Mrs Cull. This he owned for over 50 years, its importance being that it qualified him to vote under the property qualifications existing at the time.

Over the years, he took on a large number of official duties. His offices also housed the town's impressive archive of ancient manuscripts. James himself was what in modern parlance would be called the Secretary of numerous official bodies. These included the old Corporation of the Mayor and Burgesses and later the new Municipal Corporation when that was formed; the Board of Guardians of the Christchurch Union and Assessment Committee; the Superintendent Registrar; the Christchurch Rural District Council; The Christchurch Burial Board Joint Committee; the Bournemouth Improvements Commissioners from 1861 until 1877; the Mary Magdalen Leper Hospital Charity; and the receiver of both Brown's Charity and Clingan's Charity. He was also Clerk to the Petty Sessions from 1838 and Registrar and High Bailiff of the Christchurch and Bournemouth County Court. Finally he held from Sir George Meyrick, in whose gift it was, the franchise Coronorship of the Hundred of Christchurch and Liberty of Westover - an area that covered most of Bournemouth as well as all of Christchurch. There were therefore few official organisations in the area that he was not connected with and in all of which he took a great interest. In addition, James also became a director of the South Western Railway Company that was responsible for the railway coming to Christchurch. He was also a promoter and a director of the Tuckton Bridge Company that was responsible for linking the town to Southbourne. Inevitably he was elected a burgess quite early on and served the town well in that capacity for many years. He was also elected Mayor five times over a period of 46 years; in 1850, 1859 and 1867, under the old system of election of Scot and Lot, and in 1888 and 1896 by the Town Council, under the new system of election. In 1892, the year he retired from business, he was elected an Alderman, an office he held until his death.

James had other interests too. He was a member of the Priory choir and also a staunch supporter of the Sunday School. In 1839 he became a Freemason, and was Master of the Lodge of Hengist for two years in 1844 and '45. This lodge met originally in the temple in High Street until it moved to Bournemouth, whereupon the building was taken over for a time to house the school. His was surely a worthy record of service that few people in the town's long history could equal.

All these posts helped to swell his already successful practice that, as a consequence, prospered greatly. As a result, James Druitt became extremely wealthy. In 1865 he was able to take a lease with Peter Tuck on about 90 acres of what was still fairly desolate heath land in the Liberty of Westover in an area that would become Springbourne. On this they built as artisans' houses in the area now bounded by Windham, Ashley and Holdenhurst Roads to meet the growing demand of the expanding population of the infant Bournemouth. Three years later, in 1868, he finally acquired the freehold of 16 High Street and in 1870 he was able to enlarge his main property at No. 15. Over the years, he extended his property to the rear, and thus began to lay out an extensive garden.

James Druitt with two of his daughters.

As one would expect of a man who was so closely connected with the affairs of the town, where something detrimental appeared to be happening he took action. Nowhere was this more important than in the case of Hengistbury Head, as described in the previous chapter. Had he not persevered through all the legal channels at his disposal, it is likely that the headland would have effectively disappeared. This would not only have deprived the inhabitants of Christchurch and Bournemouth and the many visitors to the area, of a wonderful place of recreation and interest, but it would probably have destroyed the local fishing industry. The other great debt that the town owes to James Druitt is his preservation of the town's archives in his office. Such priceless records were frequently discarded as irrelevant in other towns or else were destroyed by damp or rodents. He made sure that the town's records were preserved, though it was left to his son, Herbert, to catalogue them.

James Druitt's health inevitably began to decline towards the end of his long life and his funeral in 1904 was a major event in the town. Newspapers from the whole region published long and glowing obituaries describing in detail his many contributions to the life of the town for well over half a century. The funeral procession, led by the town's police and fire services, stretched almost the length of the High Street. It was generally felt that a notable figure had passed from the town.

Herbert Druitt was the second youngest of the ten children of James's second marriage (to Matilda Mayo) and was born when his father was aged 60. Like his father, he was a solicitor, and took over the Christchurch practice from him. In 1916, his mother left him the building that we know as the Red House Museum. It had been built in 1768 as the Christchurch Workhouse. Like his father's house at 15 High Street, where he himself lived for many years, it was spacious, since it had housed 120 inmates, 60 men and 60 women, though so many would surely have found the quarters cramped. Herbert used the building largely as a store for part of his growing collection of items of local interest.

Herbert Druitt.

Inevitably, Herbert acquired not only much knowledge of the town from his father, but also a keen interest in it and everything connected with it. He was however a very different character from his father. Though he took over many of the official duties that his father had carried out, he never became either the town's Mayor or Town Clerk, though he was for a short time a councillor. He did, however take great interest in the town's archives. These he had meticulously listed by one of his clerks in a huge book. When the task was completed and each document carefully lettered and numbered on the back in red ink, he then personally checked each entry and initialled it. His neat pencilled 'H.D' can still be clearly seen against the description of each document listed in the book and this formed the basis against which the Dorset Record Office catalogue of the town's archive was checked. He likewise had the documents of the Mary Magdalen Charity similarly numbered and lettered. He probably had these catalogued also, but this record is now missing. However the Dorset Record Office has remedied this loss with its own comprehensive catalogue. Apart from the Cartulary, the fact that the two most important archives of documents referring to the town have come down to us so well preserved, is in large part due to the meticulous care of Herbert Druitt.

Researching and recording the town's history was a major part of Herbert Druitt's life. He was an avid collector of anything and everything that was connected with the town, since it was his intention that Christchurch should if possible have its own museum, art gallery and library. As an early step towards this goal, he founded the Christchurch Historical and Scientific Society in 1918 with his friend Russell Oakley, and was its first secretary and honorary editor. He was also the secretary of the Scientific Art and Technical School, whose headquarters was in the Town Hall. Though both have now ceased to exist, in their day they did much to widen the interest of citizens in their town. The present Local History Society may be said to be the successor of Herbert Druitt's earlier society, and much of its material is what he himself collected.

By 1919, Herbert had acquired sufficient material to enable him to open his first museum. Opened by his Aunt Mary on 2nd April, a selection of the more interesting items were displayed in a couple of rooms in his property in Quay Road until 1922. Material continued to pour in, and dealers and collectors soon realised that if they had anything that had even a remote connection with Christchurch and its surroundings, there was a ready purchaser in Herbert Druitt. Booksellers, particularly, supplied him, often taking advantage of his sometimes uncritical acquisitive nature. They found that they could pass off whole collections of their unwanted stock, provided it contained perhaps a single volume that Herbert needed. In consequence, his house became a store of huge quantities of material that was of little use to him, but which he had neither the time nor the energy to catalogue. He realised this, and his diaries have frequent comments about the mass of material that he was accumulating but had not the time to sort through.

Herbert collected everything. Fossils, stones, shells, artefacts unearthed in excavations in and around the town, memorabilia, books, papers, paintings and drawings; anything that might have a connection with the town. The growing collection soon overflowed his house and had to be stored elsewhere in his other properties. After a few years, it became almost impossible to locate material, let alone catalogue it. That task had to be left to his executors. On one occasion he records in his diary that a woman brought him an old and cracked violin with a label inside which read "Antonius Stradivarius Cremonentis Anno 1745". Unfortunately, Stradivari had died in 1737. However, since Herbert only paid the woman £7.10s.0d. for the instrument, he presumably knew what he was doing and may have bought the instrument partly to help the woman, who was extremely poor and partly to encourage others to being him things that might be of value. Certainly Herbert managed to collect an immense amount of fascinating material pertaining to Christchurch.

Herbert was always a public-spirited man. In November 1913, he delivered a lecture in the Adult School in Millhams Street on *"Some Rights of the Inhabitants of Christchurch and our Duty in Preserving them"*. He was also for a time the editor of the Christchurch Times and in subsequent years, much was to flow from his pen that was of interest to the town including well-researched works on costume and brasses. But probably his most important writings were his regular four-page contributions to the Christchurch Parish Magazine from 1919 until 1932 that together have been compiled to form the Christchurch Miscellany, extracts from which have been used in this book.

Fortunately, Herbert also kept a diary in which he noted down not only his more interesting purchases, but also comments on conditions in the town at the time. A few extracts from his diaries help to give a flavour of life in Christchurch in the first half of the 20th century. In 1916, he noted that the postal service was being reduced to two deliveries a day, since the 10.30 a.m. and 2 p.m. deliveries were being cut. In future there would only be the early morning delivery (well before breakfast) and the 5.30 p.m. delivery. On June 9th 1924, he recorded the result of a traffic census in Barrack Road, where by then he was living and in consequence had a proprietary interest in the local conditions. He recorded that 413 cars passed in one hour, thus proving that the town's present traffic problems are nothing new. That same year, in December, he bought one dozen claret, one dozen half-bottles of champagne and a bottle of rum for £4.10s. One may be sure that it was all of good quality. This provides an interesting comparison with prices at the end of the century, when a single bottle of cheap claret costs more than Herbert's 25 bottles. Two years later, he noted that the cost of a High Court case that involved the Priory was £1,800, while in 1928, he wrote that he bought 14 High Street for £1,200. Though Herbert made no comment on these comparative costs, from his profession, he would have been well aware of the high cost of litigation. That same year he recorded that a house off Kings Road and Stour Road, known as Homelands had 15 acres of garden full of fruit trees. The house, originally built by Admiral Douglas, had been called Portfield House and for a time had been the vicarage before the vicar moved to the present house in Quay Road.

In 1930, he noted that Bournemouth bought Hengistbury Head from Gordon Selfridge for £25,000. The land had been offered first to Christchurch, since Selfridge had lived at Highcliffe Castle for a time. Unfortunately the Borough Council took a short-term view of the financial situation and decided not to take up the offer. It is probably the decision that all subsequent councillors have most regretted, not only for the loss of a magnificent amenity for the borough, but also for the huge loss of income that the sand spit with its hundreds of beach chalets in particular continues to generate.

In 1931, Herbert moved his office from 15 High Street to 6 Castle Street, probably so that his younger sister, Charlotte, who had continued to live there since the death of her father in 1916, could live more peacefully in the High Street. Two years later he bought more land behind 15 High Street in order to extend his garden behind the house. Herbert and Charlotte continued to buy more land over the years, until the garden stretched as far back as Creedy Footpath near Wickfield Avenue. His keen interest in vegetable gardening as opposed to flowers was clear from the entry in May 1933 that he harvested no less that 2,020 sticks of asparagus. His friends must have been delighted. However, he was not particularly gregarious, preferring the company of the large number of stray cats that he fed daily in the High Street garden. These became so numerous that at times they caused a problem to the immediate neighbourhood.

It is also clear that Herbert preferred the old days to the new. In July 1934, he was one of those who strongly disapproved of Alan Cobham's air display, described in chapter 27. He commented *'All day the beastly Cobham Air Circus making the day hideous, flying low over the church and High Street. God curse them'*. He recorded that January 20th 1935 was the last day for the organ blower in the Priory, adding that *'it is now superseded by a damned machine'*. However his interest in conserving what was best in the town caused him to comment the next year very unfavourably on *'a preposterous scheme to demolish 15 High Street and build a square of houses'*. This matter was raised again in 1938, when he was approached by a well-known developer, who was offering to buy 15 and 16 High Street. The proposal was to *'demolish the existing premises and erect a handsome new Building consistent with modern day requirements which would be a credit to the Town'*. This offer too received short shrift. Herbert cared too much for Christchurch to submit even to a highly profitable proposition. It is all the more unfortunate that he was not alive in 1958, when the impressive Palladian style Square House on the corner of High Street and Wick Lane was pulled down. The house took its name from the fact that it faced the town hall that had stood in the old Market Square. He would certainly have raised opposition to its destruction. Entries in his diaries refer to five paintings on one of its ceilings, said to be by Cipriani, and plaster work by the Adams brothers. It is likely that modern techniques would today have been able to save a building that commanded such an important position at the beginning of the High Street, which is the poorer for its destruction.

The diary has two references to a house bordering the harbour in Mudeford, called Rushford Warren. The first was in July 1936, when he visited what was then a nudist club. It is recorded elsewhere that young boys and girls playing tennis on the adjacent property owned by Miss Hamilton, used to peep through the knot holes in the fence to see what was going on next door. Herbert's second reference to Rushford Warren was on 4th September 1940, when he records that a stick of high explosive bombs fell on the garden of Rushford Warren, the greenhouse of Willow Lodge, by the gate of Willow Lodge and that the windows of Mudeford House were blown out. It seems, however that damage was fairly insignificant, since he made no comment about it.

There is little doubt that what could be described as Herbert's collecting mania ultimately got the better of him. He accumulated so much material that by the time of his death, on 13th November 1943, the material completely filled not only most of the rooms in his house in Quay Road, but also several other large buildings in and around the town. Not till after the war was it possible for those whose task it was, to begin sorting through the material and decide what should be on display.

In 1951, sufficient progress had been made, for his property in Quay Road was opened as the Red House Museum, an event that would have pleased him greatly. The best material that he had collected over the years formed the core of the exhibits of what is a very interesting museum that explains much of the long history of the town, its surroundings and life as it was lived here over the centuries.

One ambition Herbert was not able to fulfil was that he was never able to purchase sufficient good quality paintings or drawings to form the basis of an Art Gallery. Such a task was beyond the resources of all but the wealthiest patrons of the arts. Nor were the borough councillors themselves willing to spend the large sums necessary to establish a worthwhile collection such as could be found in major cities like Birmingham or Manchester. In this they were probably right, since fashions in art are fickle and prices can rocket or plummet according to the mood of the moment. The town had however acquired a number of paintings and drawings, probably the best of which were a collection of 53 original watercolours by the accomplished amateur artist Louisa, Marchioness of Waterford, who spent most of her summers between 1867 and 1890 at Highcliffe Castle. Unfortunately, during the Second World War the whole collection was apparently put into store and at the moment there seems to be some doubt as to their present location.

Charlotte Druitt with guests in her garden.

When Herbert died in 1943, he left most of his estate to his sister, Charlotte, who was already ill. She died a few years later and gave to the town, as her brother wished, the house in the High Street where she had lived for so long and where the family had practised as solicitors, and also its extensive gardens. The house was to be used as the town's public library, thus satisfying another of Herbert's ambitions. The gardens were to be kept as a quiet open space for the citizens of Christchurch to enjoy for all time. This too was his wish. The Druitt Library in its present form, with the archives of the Local History Society housed in an upstairs room, would surely meet with his satisfaction. The Druitt Gardens have now been taken over by the Dorset Wildlife Trust, whose object is to improve its appearance. Though it is no longer laid out as the flower and vegetable gardens of the Druitt's time, it will hopefully become once more a haven of peace that will help to play its part in continuing to make Christchurch a place "Where Time is Pleasant".

Chapter 27.

Christchurch Airfield 1926 – 1966.

It is difficult to realise that in the short space of half a lifetime, Christchurch Airfield came and went. Now, 35 years later, and the fact that the area was once an airfield can only be identified by street names – Airfield Way and The Runway for example. The companies involved are likewise remembered in De Haviland Way and Airspeed Way, and the planes that were made or flew from here have given their names to Anson and Ambassador Close, Comet Way, Wellesley Avenue, to name but a few. During the last 70 years, a considerable area of the Borough has changed from open fields to housing and mixed industrial development and the airfield has both come and gone.

During the early 1920's, the land on the north-east side of Mudeford Lane, known then as Burry's Field, was used for horse racing. Probably the first such use was by the cavalry or horse artillery based at the Barracks that had been built to the west of the town near the River Stour. However in June 1926 the Surrey Flying Services began offering 5/- flights from an area two fields further to the north east that was also bounded by Somerford Road, then known as Street Lane to the north and Highcliffe Road to the north-east. Shortly afterwards, the Hampshire Flying Club, which was based at Hamble, began to use this larger field as the landing ground for weekend trips to Bournemouth.

Though three fields away Burry's Field was still being used as a landing site, it was not until 1930 that the airfield at Somerford could be considered properly to exist. That year, Francis F. Fisher, who was already flying regularly, having then bought an Avro 504K, rented a field towards the eastern end of Somerford Road, where he set up his base. With no hangers or any other buildings there, planes kept overnight had to be securely pegged down to prevent them being blown over in the not infrequent high winds. Fuel, 80 gallons at a time and costing 5d. a gallon, was transported in cans from Campbell's Garage a mile away at Purewell. When Fisher's plane needed an overhaul, it was towed with its wings folded to a garage at Iford. The landing field was often used by those appearing on stage in Bournemouth, such as Will Hay, and others who needed to save the time taken by more conventional means of travel. Another frequent visitor was the film star James Stewart, who changed his name to Stewart Granger. His sister, Iris Stewart, was married to Francis Fisher. There were also occasional small aerobatic displays given, more to advertise the concept of flying than anything else. The enterprise appears to have been successful, for between 1930 and 1933 the Fisher Aviation Company advertised *'Exhilarating fascinating safe flying every day from 10 a.m. till dusk at Somerford Bridge, main London Road, Christchurch'*, offering *'Generous circular flights from 5/- which you will never regret'*, with longer trips and stunt flying by arrangement. He wisely added that *'Hants and Dorset buses pass the entrance, or Corporation Buses to Purewell terminus'*.

FLYING
June   AT   1926
CHRISTCHURCH
MUDEFORD LANE, MUDEFORD

The SURREY FLYING SERVICES
beg to announce they will shortly pay a visit
to your town.
PASSENGER TRIPS DAILY
11 a.m. TILL DUSK.

From . . . **5/-** per Passenger.
IN ADDITION
Special Stunt Flying Displays
Will take place, including
The Great Death-Defying Spectacle:
Walking the Planes in mid-air at 1000 feet.
ALSO
Thrilling <u>Parachute</u> Descents.

Admission **6d.**   Children **3d.**

<u>The Flying Display Advertisement</u>

There appears to have been little opposition to the flying activities until a Sunday in April 1933. That day, Sir Alan Cobham's Air Circus arrived to be watched by 8,000 spectators who came in over 1,000 cars. This caused Canon Gay, the Vicar of Christchurch, to remonstrate from the pulpit, though whether it was *above the roar of the aeroplanes' engines* as the local paper claimed, may be open to doubt. The vicar considered it to be unthinkable that the display should be held on a Sunday and made a vigorous complaint to the Air Ministry, invoking the Lord's Day Observance Act of 1677. However, it appears that on this occasion the Town was against him, since later in the day the Deputy Mayor and many of the Aldermen and Councillors enjoyed trips round Christchurch.

When Fisher's lease of his field from the Grange Estate expired in December 1933, he had flown 19,000 passengers, two at a time, from his original site over a period of four years. He therefore sought planning permission and obtained the consent of Mr. Burry to extend his operations onto his fields. Planning permission was, as always, not a straightforward matter, as was reported in an article in Flight magazine, dated 26th April 1934:-

'*PROPOSED AERODROME AT MUDEFORD. One of the first cases of its kind has recently been decided in connection with the proposal of the Fisher Aviation Company to establish an aerodrome at Mudeford, on the outskirts of Christchurch.*

The Company, the partners in which are Mr F.C. Fisher, R.A.F.O., and Mr. H. Clive Smith, submitted plans for an aerodrome to the local authority. These were rejected by the Council on the ground that they conflicted with the local Town Planning Scheme. The company promptly appealed to the Ministry of Health, and a public inquiry was held at Christchurch on 27th March, presided over by Mr W.D. Lockhart of the Ministry of Health.

The main points raised by those opposed to the airfield were:-

(a) *That the establishment of an aerodrome would spoil the development of the area for residential purposes.*

(b) *That the noise of the aeroplanes would seriously interfere with the amenities of the district and would be injurious to public health.*

(c) *That the site selected was too far away (6½ miles) to serve Bournemouth, and at the same time too near (one mile) for the comfort of Christchurch.*

(d) *That it would have an injurious effect on a local nursing home about 1,000 yards away.*

(e) *That the aeroplanes would be a danger to Christchurch's historic buildings.*

(f) *That the aeroplanes would interfere with Divine Service.*

The report enlarged on this last objection with reference to the previous year's Air Circus.

It was alleged that the machines on this occasion had repeatedly flown round the church tower during the hours of Divine Service at a very low height, and that the owners had explained, in answer to complaints, that the direction of the wind made this unavoidable, notwithstanding the fact that church was nearly three quarters of a mile away from the flying ground. There was also strong opposition by local builders, who were afraid of the effect of an aerodrome on their building schemes'.

Those supporting Mr Fisher's proposed aerodrome included Mr. I. McClure of the A.A., who was also an aerodrome consultant, and Mr. Forder, editor of the *Christchurch Times*, who gave evidence as to local feeling in the matter. The oldest councillor, Mr. F. Clarke, a local builder, said he was in favour of aviation and progress generally. The report also commented,

'In this connection it is interesting to note on the cross-examination of witnesses opposing the aerodrome that all of them claimed to be in favour of the development of flying and the establishment of aerodromes - provided that the aerodrome were not established near them!'

It would appear from this that the 'not in my backyard' syndrome is nothing new. The Appeal was allowed, and as the report concluded,

'This will presumably mean that the local authorities of Christchurch will have to alter their town planning scheme and give the proposed area full benefit and protection of being scheduled as an aerodrome.

It is interesting to note that at last year's Airport Conference the Minister of Health gave assurance that his department appreciated the importance of aerodromes and landing grounds, and this case may be taken as an indication that the Minister is prepared to implement his assurance in all proper cases'.

To some degree, therefore, it seems that Christchurch Airfield was a test case. Certainly it was to have a considerable effect on the development of the eastern side of the town.

Much work had now to be done to make the new airfield serviceable for even small aircraft. The ground had to be levelled with heavy rollers, which Fisher did himself, while he and his wife built the first Club House. By 1935, the Flying Club was up and running with one Gypsy Moth 60 and half a dozen other Moths.

Apart from conventional flying, the aerodrome was used for local advertising. During the summer months, planes would fly over the beaches from Poole to Christchurch with advertising streamers stretched out behind them. On days when there was little wind and a clear sky, other planes produced smoke 'sky writing' that required great expertise and would stay legible for up to five minutes. Other more daring flyers indulged in the thrill of parachute jumping. In February 1936 there was also a demonstration of the extraordinary

'Flying Flea'. Designed by a Frenchman, Henri Mignet, it was intended to be a do-it-yourself plane for the man-in-the-street. Powered by a motor cycle or car engine, it had a rudder but no elevators or ailerons and achieved its lift from the hinged centre section of one wing. It was certainly one of the more unusual planes to land on the airfield.

Christchurch Airfield c. 1937.

The airfield quickly became popular, partly because it was easy to identify. This was the era when navigation was in its infancy and was often referred to as 'Flying by Baedeker'. Almost all flying had to be done in daylight, and pilots would look out for large towns and other clear landmarks. One of the favourite methods was to follow the railway lines that could be clearly seen cutting their way across the countryside. This worked well so long as no other pilot was following the same line in the opposite direction. In bad weather it was not unknown for a pilot to come down in a farmer's field and knock on the door of the farmhouse to enquire where he was. The airfield at Christchurch was easy to pick out. From the sea it was midway between The Needles and Old Harry Rocks off Swanage. On land, the surf breaking on the shore, and Hengistbury Head and the harbour were easy to see. Finally, the gasometers near the centre of the town both had **CHRISTCHURCH** in large white letters painted on their tops. The early aviators really were 'daring young men in their flying machines'.

Over the following years until the outbreak of war, a series of small companies operated local services, with aircraft capable of taking no more than ten passengers, using the still limited facilities that the aerodrome had to offer.

The great change came in 1939, when, with the prospect of war looming ever greater, the government decided to disperse aircraft production throughout the country in order to limit the damage that could be caused by any one attack. The Airspeed Company took over the shadow factory that was built in 1940, beside the airfield, next to a series of other small factories that had been built to the south of the Somerford Road. One of these was occupied by Gardners Transformers who played a significant part in supplying equipment for air navigation.

In April 1940, the Special Duty Flight arrived at Somerford. This unit was highly successful in helping to develop a variety of navigation and intercept devices based on RADAR, a task it continued to perform when it moved to Hurn Airfield a year later. This was linked to the R.A.F. Ground Control RADAR Interception Unit, known as R.A.F. Sopley, that was adjacent to but separate from the Advanced Landing Ground at Winkton.

During the war years, the Airspeed factory produced 559 'Oxford' training aircraft, over 700 'Horsa' gliders used for carrying troops on 'D' Day, and 100 'Mosquito' fighter/bombers. In addition 100 Spitfires were converted to 'Seafire' fighters for the Fleet Air Arm. There were also continuous repair operations carried out on damaged aircraft, patching them up and returning them to their bases in the quickest possible time. Also built towards the eastern end of the airfield was a RADAR Research Establishment, which, along with the rest of the airfield, was photographed from the air by the Luftwaffe late in 1940. Fortunately it appears that the site was not considered sufficiently important to attack. The photograph shows that by then the camouflage arrangements used later to disguise the airfield were not in place. These were rudimentary and consisted of spraying strips of creosote, the width of a hedgerow, to divide up the large grass area, and then mowing the 'fields' thus made at different times and in different directions, to make the area appear to be a series of small fields. At the Mudeford Lane end of the airfield, a different method was used. Strips of tar and gravel were laid at the ends of three roads to give the impression that these roads continued across the grass runway, so that it appeared to be too short for use as such. How effective these devices were, is not known.

The airfield was also used extensively by the adjacent Air Defence Research and Development Establishment (A.D.R.D.E.), later to become the Signals Research and Development Establishment (S.R.D.E.), set up beside the Highcliffe Road, midway between Somerford Bridge and Humphreys Bridge. Together they tested the efficiency of their equipment, by flying various types of aircraft up and down the coast off Hengistbury Head, taking care that no enemy aircraft were aloft. For this they used the Special Duty Flight which was made up of about a dozen and a half different types of aircraft.

One result of this co-operation was the discovery of the ability to 'bend' and widen the enemy radio beams that directed their aircraft, while flying blind, to their targets. Interestingly, some of the equipment used was produced at Gardner's Transformers, who were situated just over the perimeter fence of the airfield.

So secret was much of this work, that for about 18 months during 1940-41 there was no defensive guard on the site, to give the impression that nothing of any moment was being carried out. In fact, men like Sir John Cockroft were developing devices to track U Boats and enemy aircraft, which were areas of supreme importance to our survival. The large white plastic 'Golf Balls' that for many years stood on the cliff at Steamer Point were all part of this work, which was based at Worth Matravers. In February 1942, their work was greatly aided by a daring parachute raid on Bruneval on the French coast that succeeded in capturing and bringing back a complete German Radar station. When in May 1942, the Special Duty Flight moved it operations to Malvern, for greater safety, they were replaced by H.M.S. Raven, who took over developing RADAR for the Fleet Air Arm.

Because of the extensive use of the runway, it was necessary to lay down a Sommerfeld Tracking System of wire mesh to hold the ground together. This was greatly improved when in March 1944, the use of the airfield changed once more. First, the U.S. 833 Engineering Battalion arrived and set up a tented encampment near Bure Homage House, which they used as their headquarters. They laid fabric and square mesh tracking to make a solid runway 150 yards wide and 1,400 Yards long for their heavier planes. Then 950 United States officers and men of the 405th Fighter Group, 9th Air Force descended on the airfield. The effect on the town was immediate and considerable but short lived. Having arrived on 9th March 1944, their first flight took place on 12th April and then finally moved to a more advanced airfield in France on 11th July. At first they used 80 American P47 Thunderbolt fighter/bombers, to be followed shortly afterwards by Mustangs. Both of these aircraft were used extensively from Christchurch to destroy selected targets in France during the months before 'D' Day. 405 Fighter Group, 9th U.S.A.A.F 'also took over Winkton Advanced Landing Ground from which their 80 Thunderbolts flew on similar missions. When the Americans finally left, their commanding officer presented a Stars and Stripes flag to the town to commemorate their stay here. The flag was laid up in the Priory Church, to hang along side other ancient Colours of the Christchurch Volunteers. Fifty years later, the same officer, now an Air Force General, returned to re-present the flag at a service conducted by the Chaplain in Chief to the Royal Air Force.

Christchurch Airfield in the late 1940's

Once peace returned, the factory, which was owned by Airspeed, was able to turn its attention to supplying the growing needs of civil aviation. For this they were well suited, since Airspeed had developed in 1943 as a replacement for the American 'Dakota', the Ambassador. The first of these was delivered to British European Airways in 1951, the year after the de Havilland Company took over Airspeed, and production continued until 1958. Military aircraft also continued to be built. First there was the Vampire, of which over 100 were built for the home market as well as overseas. Between 1958 and 1962, when the factory finally closed, over 100 Sea Vixens were also built, as well as parts of the first jet airliner the Comet.

In 1954, it was found that the American runway would no longer take the greater weight of the larger aircraft. It was therefore re-laid, about 4,500 feet long and 100 feet wide, by the Military Engineering Experimental Establishment (M.E.X.E.) situated in Barrack Road, using a technique they had developed of mixing the concrete direct with the existing soil. It proved a great asset in continuing the efficiency and popularity of the airfield. The Christchurch Flying club continued to use the grass field next to it until well into the 1960s, but it was known that it could not last. In 1966, de Havillands finally decided to close the factory and move away. At the far end of the airfield, however, the enlarged Signals Research and Development Establishment (S.R.D.E.) continued to develop communication equipment, until they were taken over by a succession of civilian companies. These have continued to refine and develop vital electronic equipment for the armed forces and also civilian use and with other factories in the vicinity have played their part in making Christchurch a centre of excellence in this field.

An important effect of the presence of the post-war aircraft factory and S.R.D.E. was the need to provide housing for their large workforces. During the war, there had, naturally, been no house-building, since all efforts were directed towards the war effort. There had been a certain amount of temporary accommodation built on Holmsley and elsewhere in the neighbourhood but after the war, this was not considered suitable as permanent housing for those working in the local factories, let alone for the returning war heroes and their families. It was therefore decided that the large area bounded by the Somerford Road and the railway line should be developed as a new housing estate. At the time it was open fields with part of the areas used for allotments. There was a narrow track running across it for which there was considerable pressure and many letters to the Borough council, to provide some street lighting. It was alleged that there had been several incidents of people being approached – though not harmed – while using the path. It crossed the direct route to the town from Somerford Grange, which was where Prior Draper lived out his life after being removed from the Priory in 1593. Since many people believe that they have also seen the figure of John Draper in the Priory itself, some were under the impression that they may have seen him going there from his last home at Somerford Grange. If this were so, then it appears that the Prior is well satisfied with what has been built, since he no longer seems to walk there.

The first houses to be built were Canadian steel-framed pre-fabricated homes, erected in 1946 on Slinn Road, named after the then mayor. Like other post war 'prefabs' they were quick to erect and intended to last ten years until more conventional properties could be built in the future. They were highly efficient and are still occupied over 50 years later. In 1948/9, the houses in Amethyst Road were built, the name being taken from the Royal Navy frigate that made a dramatic escape from the Yangtze River in China. Later, in 1953/4, Everest Road and others adjacent to it were named after those involved in the successful ascent of that mountain shortly before the coronation of Queen Elizabeth II. St Mary's Church followed in 1956 to cater for the needs of the some 2,000 properties that by then comprised the estate. Infant, primary and secondary schools were also built at the same time.

Thus from the small beginnings of a grass airstrip in 1926 developed an airfield, factories and a large area of houses with their attendant facilities, that came to play an important part in the development of the town. Though the airfield itself has now gone, remembered only in the names of the roads, its influence remains. There is also a tangible reminder of the airfield. A Fleet Air Arm Sea Vixen – the last one made - with an explanatory plaque now stands at the entry to Wilverley Road beside one of the remaining aircraft factory buildings. Nor should the other airfields nearby be forgotten. Sopley, with its underground communications centre, was later used as a camp for Vietnamese refugees. For a few years it was also used as a holiday camp for the Household Cavalry horses, thus renewing the towns' 18th and 19th century links with the cavalry. Also within the boundaries of Christchurch lies Hurn Airport, now re-named Bournemouth International Airport. It should be remembered that much of this neighbouring town was carved out of the old Parish and Borough of Christchurch in the early 19th century. Christchurch is secure in its ancient history and like a good parent, is content for its offspring to fly the nest and make its own way in the world. The part played by the airfields of Christchurch was important in many ways, before, during and after the war. Bournemouth should be proud to have such distinguished parentage and the country should be grateful for what happened here.

Chapter 28.

Sir Donald Bailey Kt. O.B.E. & The Bailey Bridge.

There is on the pillar in the Priory Church nearest to the War Memorial chapel in the south nave aisle, a memorial tablet which reads as follows:-

IN MEMORY OF
SIR DONALD COLEMAN BAILEY, Kt. O.B.E.
(1901 – 1985)
INVENTOR OF THE WORLD WAR II
BAILEY BRIDGE
AT THE EXPERIMENTAL BRIDGING
ESTABLISHMENT, CHRISTCHURCH.
Remembered by his Comrades of
The Corps of Royal Engineers.

Beneath the inscription is a representation of a painting by Edward Cuneo showing the Royal Engineers constructing an 80 foot Class 30 Bailey Bridge across the River Rapido at Monte Cassino in Italy under constant direct fire on the night of 12-13 May 1944.

Probably the greatest impediment throughout the ages to man's movement across land has been the presence of either a chasm or river standing in his path. Provided it was sufficiently wide and deep to prevent him stepping across if he was in any way burdened, it was necessary for him to find some method of creating a bridge over which he, his burden and his pack animals or transport could pass. Though this was important at all times, it became critical in time of war. As has already been recorded, the three Saxon charters in the Cartulary, dating from A.D. 956, state specifically that the duties from which their recipients were not excused were military service and fortress work for the defence of the realm, and also bridging, necessary for the free passage of trade and to ensure mobility at all times. This need was further emphasised in the three indulgences dating from 1331[1], whereby men willing to help repair the town's bridges could obtain remission from their sins. Such has always been the importance of bridges.

After the Great War of 1914-1918, the Army decided to re-examine their resources for providing bridges. With the new ability to

---

[1] See chapter 10

destroy bridges from the air as well as by land and with the advent of the tank and other heavy transport, it became necessary to re-assess the means for constructing or replacing crossings of natural or artificial obstacles. This was vital to obtain and maintain mobility and speed. The basic method of constructing a bridge that was more than a simple plank or log over a gap had changed little over the centuries. A basic box section is unstable unless braced across its opposite corners. It then becomes rigid and capable of bearing considerable loads in safety. Given time and sufficient timber, the most readily available raw material, huge structures could be put up to cross wide gaps. In wartime, neither timber nor time might be available. To address these problems the Army decided to establish a research establishment.

There had existed in Christchurch since the 1790's, a military barracks that had originally been built to house troops to defend the south coast against a Napoleonic invasion. When that threat receded, it housed mounted troops to control the smuggling that was then rife and highly profitable. Such a need no longer existed. It was decided in 1919 to use the facility in Barrack Road to establish the Experimental Bridging Company Royal Engineers, whose purpose was to develop a method of bridge construction that would be quick, flexible, easily transportable and if possible partly pre-fabricated. All these factors were considered to be pre-requisites for modern warfare. Fortunately, the Bridging Company was then commanded by an enterprising and very gallant soldier, Major, later Lt. General Sir Gifford, Martel. He discovered a useful loophole in Army Regulations that allowed him to retain on strength 'pivotal men', and was thus able to retain his Sappers in the Bridging Company, when it appeared likely that they might be posted to Russia. Bridge design and construction was thus able to continue at Christchurch. However, by 1925, due to the general revulsion of war, the campaign for disarmament and economic stringency, the unit was disbanded and replaced by the Experimental Bridging Establishment, or E.B.E., which contained both civil and military staff.

Three years later, in 1928, a young man who had been educated at the Leys School in Cambridge, and then taken an engineering degree at Sheffield University in 1923, came to Christchurch to join E.B.E. as a civilian designer. He had some useful experience. After working first for Rowntrees at York, he was employed by the L.M.S. Railway. He then joined the City Engineer's Department at Sheffield, where he was involved in bridge design. This establishment like all military development units, was operating under severe financial pressure. Indeed at one time he feared for his job because of the economic restraints. Luckily common sense prevailed, so that developments already in hand could continue. This became increasingly important with the design of new and heavier tanks that would have to pass over such bridges. By the outbreak of war, the main bridges being used were small and large Box Girder bridges capable of taking loads of up to 30 tons, both of which were slow to build. Much of this equipment was lost in the evacuation from Dunkirk.

In early 1940, a prototype of a new 'Inglis Bridge', designed by Professor Inglis of Cambridge University, based upon his successful World War 1 design, buckled under an increased test load that was considered necessary to bear the new and heavier tanks then being built. Returning from witnessing a failed trial of the proposed new bridge, Donald Bailey, by now chief designer at E.B.E. and Major S.A. Stewart, the Superintendent, discussed the problems that had occurred. Donald Bailey had been experimenting in his mind with various new ideas, and now produced the legendary envelope from his pocket on which he proceeded to sketch out his idea for a new style of bridge constructed of ready made panels. In some ways the concept already existed in the children's construction kit, Meccano. Experience learnt over the years had thrown up the shortcomings of various bridge designs. It was however agreed that the basic requirements were flexibility of use; readily available materials; ease of manufacture by almost any engineering firm; each part to fit into a standard 3 ton lorry; and no part to exceed a six man load. It was also important that the basic unit should be securely welded. It was immediately seen that Bailey's revolutionary but simple design was likely to fulfil all these requirements. Bailey and Captain H.A.T. Jarrett-Kerr and his by now increased number of staff immediately concentrated on detailed design work.

The design of the bridge consisted of a basic panel 10 foot long by 5 foot high. The top and bottom girders were 4 x 2 inch rolled steel channels, welded either side of 3 x 1½ inch rolled steel joist web and diamond bracing members. At each corner of the panels were fitted male and female jaws, drilled to take steel securing pins. In this way, the panels could be quickly secured to each other to make a bridge of any desired length. Similar fixings enabled the panels to be secured up to three panels wide and three panels high, so that a bridge of massive strength could be easily constructed once decking had been fitted between the main side girders. Using this simple method, it was quick and easy to construct anything from a 90 foot span bridge capable of carrying 9 tons, to a 240 ft. bridge to carry a load of 70 tons.

The speed of the development was also impressive. Bailey sketched out his initial design in December 1940. The pilot model was ready for testing by May 1941, production started in July and the first bridge was with the troops in North Africa by December 1941. It was found to be an immediate success in practice. Initially these bridges were built away from enemy fire. Since each section only required six men to manhandle it, the structure could be completed in a matter of a few hours using less than a platoon of men. However the first of many bridges to be constructed under enemy fire was a 100 ft. triple-single bridge, capable of carrying 40 tons, thrown across the Medjerba River in Tunisia, on November 26th 1942, after the first bridging convoy had been set on fire by enemy action. This bridge enabled heavy tanks to breech the enemy's river defences and overcome their position.

The Bailey Bridge was also adapted to be a pontoon bridge. An early example of this was a 370 ft. bridge of three floating bays and two landing bays across the River Volturno in Italy. This was completed in 48 hours on 17/18th October 1943 and at its peak carried almost 500 vehicles an hour. It was also found possible to adapt the bridge to cross high and wide caverns by erecting vertical piers to support the horizontal span. On 26-27th August 1944, a class 40 bridge 694 feet long was thrown across the Seine, and on 24-25th March 1945 a 1200 ft. Bailey pontoon bridge was thrown across the Rhine at Xanten. Later that year a semi-permanent bridge 2,391 feet long and capable of carrying 24 tons was constructed over the Rhine at Dusseldorf, to replace a pre-war construction that had been destroyed in the fighting. Designs for a suspension bridge were also developed at E.B.E. in 1942/3, to be used later by the Americans to build a 440 ft. long suspension bridge across the Shweli River in Burma.

Some idea of the importance of the Bailey Bridge can be gauged from the fact that in the Italian Campaign of 1943-5, 2,500 bridges were built. In N.W. Europe, over 1,500 bridges with a total length of 29 miles of normal Bailey and 3 miles of floating Bailey Bridges, were built between 1944-5. They were also extensively used in the Far Eastern campaigns. Nor was there any limit to size or weight. A pontoon bridge over the Maas in Holland which, with its approach spans measured almost 4,000 feet, could carry 40 tons, while the semi-permanent 40 and 70 ton bridges over the Rhine at Rees built in April and May 1945 measured about 5,000 feet. They are reputedly the longest military bridges in the world. Some of the bridges in Germany were still in use after 20 years and played a major part in assisting Germany's post war economic recovery.

The success of the Bailey Bridge design can perhaps best be assessed from its production figures. During the last three years of the Second World War, over 490,000 tons of Bailey Bridge was manufactured, with production reaching over 25,000 panels a month, produced by a large variety of manufacturers. Yet of over 700,000 panels produced, of which 70% were proof tested, only 140 panels were rejected for welding defects and another 130 for substandard steel content. Such was the safety margin of the design. It was also estimated that if the total Bailey Bridging sections constructed during the war were laid end to end, they would stretch from Christchurch almost to Leningrad. According to Field Marshall Montgomery, *'Bailey Bridging made an immense contribution towards final victory in World War II. As far as my own operations were concerned, with the Eighth Army in Italy and with 21 Army Group in NW Europe, I could never have maintained the speed and tempo of forward movement without large supplies of Bailey Bridging'.*

Donald Bailey had been awarded the O.B.E. in 1944 but was rightly knighted in 1946 for the valuable contribution his bridge made to the Allied victory. The same year, his old university, Sheffield, awarded him an Honorary Degree of Doctor of Engineering, an honour of which he was justly proud.

With different post-war needs, the Experimental Bridging Establishment at Christchurch, where it all began, changed its name and function to the wider Military Engineering Experimental Establishment, or M.E.X.E. of which Sir Donald first became Assistant Director and in 1957 the first civilian Director. He continued to oversee other interesting and important developments there until he was appointed Dean of the Royal Military College of Science at Shrivenham. There his prestige and reputation did much to enhance the standing of the college.

Sir Donald Bailey.

When in 1966. Sir Donald finally retired, he returned to Christchurch, where he had first come 38 years before. Here he lived until his death in 1985. an honoured and valued citizen of the town where he had carried out his greatest work for the country.

Christchurch acknowledged the debt that the country owed to M.E.X.E. as the successor to E.B.E. by granting the Freedom of the Borough to the Royal Engineers unit in 1969. It was widely felt that a similar honour should have been conferred on Sir Donald himself, but this was not to be. The Royal Engineers have cemented their link with the town by two further actions. The apprentices at the Barracks made the pair of gates that are placed at the entry to the north choir aisle in the Priory Church. The Royal Engineers also made and presented to the town a silver mace that is always carried, in company with the town's older gold mace, on all civic occasions. Thus Town, Church and the Barracks were bound closely together to their mutual benefit.

What then was the importance of Sir Donald Bailey's life and work? The brilliance of his 'back of an envelope' bridge design certainly played a vital part in hastening the Allied Victories both in Europe and the Far East. In addition after the war, his bridges were able not only to restore but also to create communications in many parts of the world with incalculable benefit to the economies of the countries concerned. Not to be forgotten is the employment that was created in a host of engineering firms throughout the country as a result of his invention. As late as the early 1960's, the work force at M.E.X.E. was approximately 1,000 strong, with a Royal Engineers element of only 15 or 16 R.E. Officers and a dozen or so other ranks. This largely civilian workforce was engaged in the development of all types of equipment for the Royal Engineers, from bridging, to trackways, water supply equipment and a wide range of plant for road construction. Nor was this equipment used only for military purposes. Much of it was of immense value to developing countries both to improve their communications and also their general infrastructure. It was sad therefore when it was finally decided that the establishment should be closed in 1994.

The Bailey Bridge itself is still in use with the British Army over half a century after it was invented, and a bridge panel now stands by the roundabout in Barrack Road opposite the site where it was first tried and tested. Though the military barracks have now been sold and redeveloped as housing and commercial premises, some of the older buildings remain and a new public house and hotel on the site has been named after the bridge and its inventor. There is also a small Bailey Bridge that crosses Mother Siller's Channel – an old smuggling route - on Stanpit Marsh. What better location to place a bridge designed in the Barracks that in its early days had been used to combat smuggling.

Bailey Bridge on Stanpit Marsh.

Chapter 29.

Cecil Gardner of Gardner's Transformers.

It all began in Westcliff on Sea, in Essex, when Cecil Gardner's headmaster gave him a special prize for services to the school. The school was renowned for its emphasis on the individual and there is little doubt that the headmaster was a very far-sighted man who was able to estimate the direction in which each boy might develop. For this reason, instead of choosing an improving work by some dull though perhaps famous nineteenth century author, or even a stirring tale about the heroes of the British Empire, young Cecil received in 1925, a book entitled 'The Boy Electrician'. This was obviously a particularly suitable choice since it was already clear that Cecil Gardner's interests lay in things scientific rather than literary. In this prize he soon found something that particularly appealed to him, - how to make a battery charger. This was in the early days of wireless broadcasting. The B.B.C. had been founded only in 1922. The idea of being able to receive music and speech over the airwaves was of obvious appeal to almost every schoolboy. However the early radio receivers were all battery powered by direct current. As every schoolboy quickly discovered, the accumulator soon went flat, and had to be taken to the nearest electrical shop for recharging. This was both inconvenient and expensive. Cecil Gardner therefore decided to see if the instructions in the book were effective. To his great delight they were and he made his first accumulator charger. His success quickly spread through the school, for several boys had their own simple radios and were intrigued to see Cecil's 'invention'. At this point, the entrepreneur in Cecil became apparent. He found himself approached by other boys to re-charge their radio accumulators, which he was happy to do at 3d. a time. It seems that the headmaster had an interest in this new method of communication, for he had a large wireless receiver which needed much greater battery power to operate it. Cecil Gardner was able to re-charge this for his headmaster at 1s.6d. a time to their mutual satisfaction. His future course was set.

At the age of 15, Cecil Gardner left school and set up in business. He rented a garage for 7s.6d. a week, put up shelves in it and installed a workbench and began to contact those whom he knew had wireless receivers. The need was there, and by word of mouth news soon spread that he could provide a much needed and growing service. Before too long, he bought a motor bike with a sidecar, with which he was able to collect and deliver accumulators for re-charging and his small business began to thrive.

In 1930, two years after his mother died, Cecil and his father moved from Westcliff, where they had been living, to Southbourne and opened up a shop. It was the time when E.K.Cole was developing the all mains radio at Southend on Sea, which meant that radios could be operated by A.C. current. Cecil, who was then joined by his brother Harold, started building radio sets himself and selling them, though he continued with the battery charging business. The next year, their father retired and handed over his shop to his sons, who moved into larger premises. There they opened 'Gardner's Radio', one of the first wireless shops in the area, which quickly became well known.

There was certainly a market both for his radios and for re-charged accumulators amongst the fairly opulent residents in the area. There was also a growing need for transformers to convert the Direct Current radio receivers to Alternating Current that was then becoming universal. So much so, that in 1934, Cecil was approached by the Bournemouth and Poole Electric Supply Company, who had a D.C. generating station in Bargates, where the Electricity Museum is now situated, to take over the conversion of all the wireless sets in the area from D.C. to A.C. He accepted the challenge. One problem that quickly became apparent was the need for suitable transformers, since the main suppliers seemed unable to produce a satisfactory product. He overcame the problem by producing his own which were highly efficient. At the end of the Bournemouth and Poole contract, he had to find another outlet for his goods and turned to mail order. This too prospered, and by 1936 he opened a small factory in Carberry Row, Southbourne, which employed 25-30 young men. Within a few years, this enterprise outgrew its premises, and Cecil had to look round for somewhere else.

During the summer of 1939, he found what he was looking for at 65 Somerford Road in Christchurch. This was a purpose built factory, situated on a main road, adjacent to the airfield from which Sir Alan Cobham, who was a pioneer of re-fuelling aircraft in flight with Flight Refuelling of Wimborne, used to give highly successful aviation and aerobatic displays. Cecil Gardner moved into his new factory on Saturday 2nd September 1939, the day before the Second World War started.

Fortune must have been smiling on him that day, for there landed on the grass runway of Christchurch Airfield, an American. His first request was for equipment to give him a supply of 110 volt electricity. For this he needed a transformer to convert the British 230 volts supply. Was there anyone in the area who could oblige? Those at the airfield were aware that Cecil Gardner was just moving in next door, and suggested that he might be able to help. He could and he did. Delighted, the American enquired if Cecil had any spare capacity that could supply such equipment. Indeed he had, and this led to a contract being drawn up. Since the factory was at that time largely involved in making lighting transformers for air-raid shelters, a demand that would soon be satisfied, the additional work was invaluable.

At this time, the population of Christchurch was much smaller than it is now. None of the Somerford Estate had been built, so that Cecil could see the trains entering and leaving Christchurch on the embankment across the fields towards Burton. During the first six months of 1940, particularly during the time of the evacuation from Dunkirk, most of these trains carried large red crosses, for they were hospital trains, full of wounded soldiers brought back from France whence they had sailed to Poole and Weymouth. There can be little doubt the constant sight of these trains had a considerable effect on those working in Gardner's Radio Factory, making them feel that their work for the war effort really was important. The factory operated seven days a week, only closing on Saturday mornings to allow the women to do their weekly shopping.

Other work soon began to come in, largely to do with the war effort. The Telecommunications Research Establishment at Worth Matravers invited Cecil to visit them to discuss supplying them with transformers, as did scientists from the Ministry of Aircraft Production. The result was that he was soon undertaking a series of highly important, and often secret, contracts for various government departments. These involved devices needed for a variety of projects such as RADAR and other communication systems connected with offensive and defensive weapons, which played an important part particularly in the successful operation of the war in the air.

One device that went under the code-name 'H.2.S', was a blind bombing instrument, which enabled aircraft to see their targets through cloud and was to be fitted to all bombers. Initially, a major national electrical manufacturer was approached to produce the equipment, but they said they required two years to set up the tooling and complete the contract. The Ministry of Aircraft Production obviously could not wait that long so they set up a factory to produce a small number of basic units and Cecil was asked to manufacture the transformers that were needed for each unit. These and the rest of the equipment were then screwed by hand onto 'breadboards' fitted into a limited number of Mosquito aircraft that were used as Pathfinders. They went ahead of the main bomber formations to locate through the clouds the intended targets, which they then illuminated with incendiary bombs. For each of these highly complex hand-made units, Gardner's had to make no less than 17 transformers of different descriptions. Though it was inevitably labour intensive, each unit taking several people at least twelve hours to make, it was successful and delivery was quick, which was of the essence, if the bombing raids were to succeed and the lives of many airmen were to be saved.

At the same time, the Ministry of Aircraft Production gave Cecil a blanket contract for the supply of transformers, which were needed in great numbers and in all sizes. The factory soon grew in size to about 150 employees, the majority of whom naturally were women, since most able-bodied men were away at the war. It is also fair to say that women often had the greater manual dexterity necessary to produce high-grade equipment and were in any case only too keen to play their part in the war effort. This was probably particularly true since what they were producing would be of considerable benefit to their men-folk in helping them perform better in the air and on the field of battle, and no doubt saved many of their lives.

When in 1942, the Telecommunications Research Establishment moved from Worth Matravers on the coast to the greater safety of Malvern, Cecil found himself making weekly journeys to Malvern and back, by car. These journeys were hazardous in the extreme, with effectively no headlights, since these were largely blacked out leaving only a few narrow slits of light directed towards the road a few yards ahead. Many of the roads by which he had to travel were very narrow, and it was not uncommon to be confronted by a convoy of tanks approaching from the opposite direction who might well not see him and who would probably not give way even if they did.

It was also in 1942 that Cecil had an urgent request – though it was one of many. This message came through during the morning from T.R.E. at Malvern. It was most important that a particular and unusual type of transformer should be available for pick-up at 3 p.m. the same day. Was it possible? Cecil went to see Peter, the man involved in its manufacture. Could he do it in the time? By working all through the lunch hour, Peter was just able to meet the deadline. The transformer was collected and immediately rushed to the Isle of Wight where it was hastily installed. It had been learnt, no doubt as a result of the success of breaking the Enigma codes, that a 15 plane bomber raid was due on Southampton docks that night, which could have had disastrous results had it succeeded. But the equipment for which the transformer was required was able to 'bend' the directional beams that guided the enemy planes to their target, away from Southampton to open fields outside the city where fighters were waiting for them and half of the bombers were shot down.

When the war finally ended, there was inevitably a change in requirements, though, the defence contracts continued for some time to provide Gardner's Transformers with work. By then the Telecommunications Research Establishment employed about 3,000 people, many of whom then moved on to different employment with civilian commercial enterprises. However they took with them the knowledge of the high quality work that Cecil Gardner's firm could produce. so that peacetime contracts began to come in from a wide variety of places. These ranged from the Atomic Energy Establishment at Aldermaston. the Admiralty. and budding electrical and electronic enterprises. But the manufacture of transformers of all types remained the backbone of Gardner's Transformers. which grew in size to employ about 270 people. Of these. about 40% were men. now released from active service. and 60% were women. their manual dexterity still being of considerable importance. The only serious competitor in the field was Ferranti. who had their factory in Dundee. Scotland.

Realising the need to diversify in a field which was expanding in so many directions. in the 1950's Cecil started experimenting with the transformers needed for microwave ovens. Such kitchen equipment was novel in those days. and there seemed then to be little demand for it. so the project was put to one side since he was in effect ahead of his time. However. during the 1970's. as the Cold War eased. the defence contracts began to fall away and it became important once more to look for other work. The most obvious field was the microwave oven operation into which a considerable amount of effort had already been invested. A suitable location was found in Cardiff. a place of high unemployment. and a factory was opened to cope with the demand for microwave ovens. It became apparent that the market was considerable. both at home and overseas. The factory became successful and by 1980. it was employing some 70 people. The same year Gardner's Transformers was awarded the Queen's Award for Export Achievement. a highly coveted distinction that was not lightly earned. Cecil. accompanied by a representative chosen from the workbench. went to Buckingham Palace to receive the award that was signed both by the Queen and the Prime Minister.

Unfortunately this expansion into a new field to meet a known demand proved to be the turning point in the life of the company. Serious consideration was given at this time to going public. and floating the company on the Stock Exchange and brokers and bankers were consulted with this in view. The move however came just too late and it was decided that a flotation might well not be successful in such a cut-throat market. The decision was largely based on the fact that others too realised the need for the microwave. Like so much of modern day electrical and electronic equipment. the main threat came from the Japanese. who could mass-produce the goods. Using low-cost transformers imported from Taiwan. the Japanese were able to undercut British-made goods to such an extent. that it became impossible for Cecil to compete in the same field except at a loss.

Having invested heavily in the Cardiff enterprise as well as in the Christchurch factory which also diversified so far as was possible, Gardner's Transformers was faced with difficult choices. At Christchurch particularly there were a large number of employees who had been with the firm for many years, some since shortly after the last war. Many were immensely loyal and almost part of the fabric. A ruthless employer might well have dispensed with their services, paying the minimum legal redundancy. This might have saved the day, but it was not Cecil's way. He felt that if he had to 'downsize', then full compensation should be paid, which would involve a prohibitive cost. The alternative was to struggle on, reducing the workforce through 'natural wastage' and retirement and hope for an upturn in price and demand. This course he adopted, though in the end it proved unsuccessful in the face of foreign competition.

Cecil had by now reached and indeed passed the normal retiring age but was still struggling to keep the factory alive for the sake of the highly skilled workforce. The possibility of a management buy-out was seriously considered, in the hope that new and younger blood could turn the enterprise round once more. In the end, this too was seen not to be a viable proposition.

Finally a purchaser was found for the goodwill. This was a considerable asset, since over the years, the firm had built up a wide client base and a reputation for prompt delivery, particularly of specialised and often 'one-off' items. The new owner tried to tap new markets, but this too ultimately proved unsuccessful and the factory finally had to close.

Gardners Radio Ltd.

This was indeed a sad end to an enterprise that had brought so much good to Christchurch. Not only had Gardner's in its hey-day been a major employer in the town, but being one of the first factories involved in the budding electrical and electronic field, it also attracted others to the area. In consequence other firms, such as Penny and Giles and Plessey opened factories in the immediate vicinity, to take advantage of the workforce that already had proven ability in the field of electrical equipment manufacturing. The skilled employment spin-off was therefore considerable and added greatly to the prosperity of the town.

The final chapter was more positive. At the end of 1997, the factory building, that Cecil still owned, was sold to a growing firm that was already manufacturing small plastic items, mouldings and electronic robots on the industrial estate that had been built on what had been the site of Christchurch Airfield. This was the site where the American had landed on 2nd September 1939 and found that Cecil Gardner was the man to provide him with the transformer he needed. The factory layout suited the new owner's needs, and more importantly, there was a pool of labour with the necessary skills available, which they had learnt at Gardner's. For Cecil, this was perhaps the most important aspect of the sale.

It also highlighted an important aspect of life in Christchurch. Local people, and more particularly the female half of the population, seem to have been blessed with particularly skilled manual dexterity as can be seen in the success of the fusee chain manufacture[1]. Another example is to be found in those working at Gardner's Transformers such as Rose Goddard, who, as a young girl, entered service as a housemaid at Highcliffe Castle in 1939. There she was one of eleven servants looking after Miss Violet Stuart Wortley at a wage of 5 shillings a week. Early in the war, she left that employment to work at Gardner's, where she became one of their best coil winders. As such, she joined a specialist group working on the top-secret components of the highly successful Dam Buster bouncing bombs, for which she was ultimately especially commended. Today, similar and more advanced skills are to be found in the several electronic factories that make up such an important part of the employment pattern in the town.

What then was the importance of Gardner's Transformers to Christchurch? Moving, fortuitously, into its new factory the day before broke out, the factory was able to play a not unimportant part in the war effort, particularly the war in the air, by producing equipment, much of it secret, both for offensive and defensive use. After the war, the factory was able to expand and diversify and by employing over

---

[1] See chapter 23

300 people directly, and many others indirectly, became one of the town's major employers.

Gardner's Transformers always remained a family business. During the 1960's, it became the custom for Cecil to throw a large party for all the workforce and their wives or husbands in the King's Arms, the main hotel in the town centre. As many as 400 people would be present, with a leading group to provide the music. In 1965, it was The Seekers, who then were topping the Charts. Later, when the popularity of a big party began wane, Cecil changed to providing a large and carefully chosen Christmas hamper for every employee, that contained everything that was necessary for a good feast. The 'family' spirit of the firm is well illustrated by a simple incident connected with these hampers. A temporary employee was away on a very extended holiday that covered the Christmas period. Imagine his delight therefore on his return, when he found that a hamper had been kept for him – because he was an employee like all the others, despite his lengthy absence.

Cecil always believed in keeping his workforce fully informed about what was being produced, so that they should know how they fitted into the scheme of things. This helped to maintain the family atmosphere in the firm, particularly when there was a special order to be produced. A particular example of this, which was in no way unique, occurred during one normal working week. An urgent request came in for a special transformer needed for a baby's incubator, without which the infant would die. The workforce was told over the well-used Tannoy system what was needed and that several people were being taken off their normal work in order to concentrate on this special order, which had to be completed that day. Though this meant interrupting the schedules of other work leading to loss of production elsewhere, there was universal agreement, and immense interest in the special order. The task was successfully completed in time and it was broadcast to everyone that the baby had been safely installed in the incubator to their great delight.

It is therefore fair to say that, in its day, Gardner's Transformers played an important part in the development of the town. Not only was it a large employer, but it was also a place where good working practices were paramount, people were well trained, and men and women were valued for themselves. Such an environment surely helped to make Christchurch a town 'Where Time is Pleasant'.

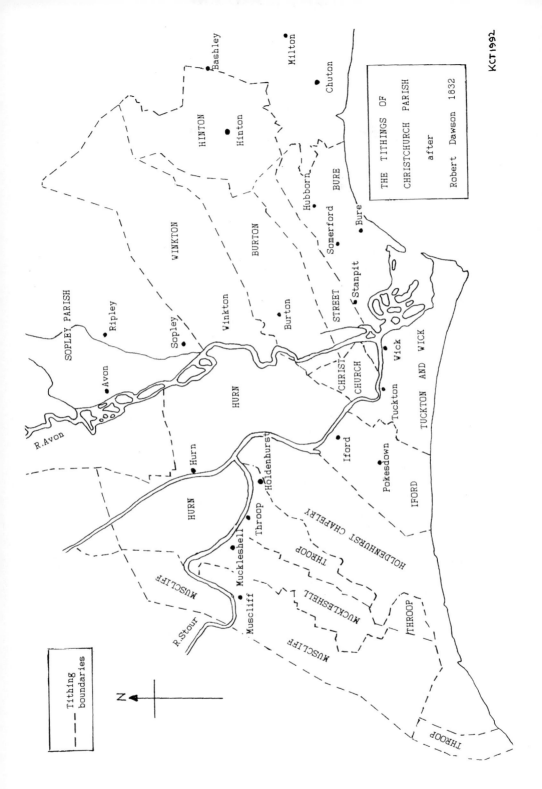

THE TITHINGS OF
CHRISTCHURCH PARISH
after
Robert Dawson 1832

KCT1992

Tithing
boundaries

Chapter 30.

The Manors of Christchurch.

"The Manor of Christchurch" is not one but three. The most important and extensive was the Honour of Christchurch. The term "Honour" was used to define an extensive manor, whose lord granted several of the subsidiary manors on his lands to others. In many cases, the Lord of the Honour was the King himself, with his greater and lesser nobles holding subsidiary manors within the Honour, for which they owed allegiance and service to the King. Tweoneam, whose name later became written as "Twynham", was one of the Honours owned by the King. In due time there came into existence the lesser Manor of the Borough of Christchurch, and also the Manor of Christchurch Twynham, both of which owed allegiance to their overlord the King.

It is not clear exactly when the name "Christchurch" was finally adopted to the exclusion of Twynham, but both names were used in tandem for some centuries. It would certainly be more accurate to describe the early Honour or Manor as "Egheite" This is the term used in the Domesday Record of 1086 to describe the Hundred of which the Burgh of Twynham was a part. Since this was eight years before the start of the building of the Priory Church, it is clear that at that date, the name Christchurch would be wholly inappropriate.

It is likely that the Honour of Twynham had belonged to Saxon kings at least since King Alfred had caused the place to be fortified as one of his series of burghs along the South Coast, probably about the end of the ninth century. The earliest record we have that seems to confirm the ownership of the Honour or Manor is in the charter of King Ethelred, dated A.D. 985. As mentioned in chapter 2, he gave some of his land at Bosley and Portfield to Sulfric the Priest, one of those who was ministering to the population in and around the burgh of Twynham. The later charter of Edward the Confessor, dated 1053, in which he gave some of his land at Bashley to Lutrise his thegn, probably confirms this royal ownership of the Honour. On Edward's death, the Honour, with all the other royal lands, passed to his successor, Harold, until his defeat at Senlac by Duke William of Normandy in 1066.

By 1086, when King William had the great Domesday Record compiled, the boundaries of the Honour become much clearer. The centre of the Honour was the Burgh of Twynham, with its simple fortifications across the neck of land between the two rivers, and its church and chapels, all of which comprised a tithing. The rest of the

Honour consisted of a series of other tithings: Hoburne, Stanpit, Knapp, Hurn, Bosley, Holdenhurst and Bashley. Attached to the Honour were the lands to the west, over the River Stour, known as the Liberty of Westover. These comprised North Ashley, Muscliff, Muccleshell, Throop, Iford, Tuckton and parts of Holdenhurst. There were other tithings to the east of the Stour that were also closely linked to the Honour: Ashley, Avon, Arnewood, Boldre, Bure, Burton, Chewton, Efford, Hinton, Hordle, Hurn, Keyhaven, Milford, Sopley, Street, Sway and Winkton.

Over the centuries, the lords of the three manors have included kings and queens, several of their chief advisers and many distinguished people, who have often taken a great interest in wellbeing of the manors and their inhabitants. Until recent times, the lordship of the manor carried many duties as well as benefits. Today, however, the position is almost entirely honorary.

The arms of the Norman kings.
Gules, two leopards or, passant gardent.

The arms of de Fortibus.
Gules, a cross vair.

The arms of Montacute.
Argent, a fesse indented of three points gules.

The arms of de Redvers.
Or, a lion rampant, azure.

The arms of Edward III.
Gules, three lions or passant gardent.

The arms of Nevill.
Gules, a saltire argent and a label gobony argent & azure.

253

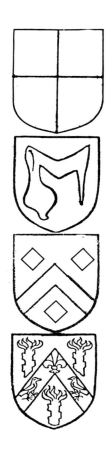

The arms of Margaret.
Countess of Salisbury
See below

The arms of Hastings.
Argent, a sleeve sable.

The arms of Clarendon.
Azure chevron between three
lozenges or.

The arms of Meyrick.
Sable, a chevron argent between
Three ragged staves or aflame with
a fleur de lys gules between two
Cornish choughs on the chevron.

The arms of Henry VIII.
Gules, three lions or passant
gardent quartered with azure,
three fleur de lys or.

The arms of Arundell.
Sable, six hirondelles argent.

The arms of Tapps.
Azure, a fesse or between three
rhinoceroses argent with three
scollops gules on a fesse.

The arms of Malmsbury.
Azure, a chevron erminois between three hedgehogs or and a
chief augmentation argent with
a black eagle of Prussia therein.

The arms of Margaret Countess of Salisbury are Quarterly.

Ist Quarterly: France Modern and England, a label of three points argent each charged with a canton gules (Clarence).

2nd Quarterly: Gules a saltire argent, a label of three points gobony argent and azure (Neville) impaling Gules, a fess between six crosses crosslet or (Beauchamp).

3rd Quarterly: Chequy or and azure, a chevron ermine (Newburgh) impaling Argent, three lozenges conjoined in fess gules (Montacute).

4th Quarterly: Or an eagle displayed vert (Monthermer) impaling Quarterly I and IV, or three chevrons gules (Clare): II and III, Quarterly, Argent and gules, a fret or, overall a bendlet sable (Despencer).

The arms of Pole are: Party per pale or and sable, a saltire engrailed counter changed.

It is clear from Domesday, that some of the lands within the boundaries of the Honour already belonged to the priests running the church in the burgh. In 1092, William Rufus granted the burgh only to Ranulf Flambard, though on his fall from grace, it reverted to Henry I, who then granted it to Baldwin de Redvers. This became the Manor of the Burgh (later Borough) of Twynham. In 1100, Baldwin de Redvers, to whom Henry had already granted the superior Honour of Twynham, quickly transferred part of it to the newly appointed canons of the partly built Priory. These lands became the Manor of Christchurch Twynham, and were added to those lands already held by the priests.

Thus, by about 1100, the three Manors had been established with separate identities. The Honour, which included most of the lands in the other two manors, covered a very considerable area. Even leaving out the eastern tithings, it covered an area that is now both Christchurch and much of Bournemouth. The Lords of the Manors have included kings, their advisers and many distinguished people.

The Honour of Tweoneam, that had belonged to the Saxon kings, remained in royal hands until the reign of Henry I. On ascending the throne, and in order to strengthen his position, he gave the Honour to his relative, supporter and friend, Richard de Redvers, who already held large estates in the West Country. It descended through several generations of the family, who became Earls of Devon, finally ending in the hands of the daughter of the seventh earl, Isabella de Fortibus, whose story is told in chapter 7.

That chapter also recounts how the Manor came into the ownership once more of the Crown in 1293. Edward I then granted it to his wife, Margaret. On her death, Edward II granted it to his wife Isabel. The former was the sister and the latter the daughter of Philip III of France. Such a French connection would surely have greatly benefited the trade between Twynham and the continental ports. The royal connection ceased when Edward III granted the Manor to his friend and supporter William de Montacute, the 3rd Baron, in 1330, in whose family the Manor remained until 1541.

The Montacutes were one of the most powerful families in the land, being not only advisers to successive kings, but also their leading generals and ambassadors. William, the 3rd Baron, was made Earl of Salisbury and also became King of the Isle of Man. Few towns can claim the distinction of have one king as their lord while at the same time owning allegiance to their own sovereign. The story goes that it was the wife of the 2nd Earl to whom Edward III addressed the words *"Honi soit qui mal y pense"* and consequently created the Most Noble Order of the Garter, which is the oldest Order of Chivalry. The 4th Earl fought at Agincourt, and two generations later, through the female line the Lord of the Manor was Richard Nevill, Earl of Warwick, known as the King-maker during the Wars of the Roses. Two generations later, the Lord of the Manor was Margaret Countess of Salisbury, whose story is told in chapter 14.

In 1541, the Manor reverted to Henry VIII on the execution of the aged Countess. When the eleven year old Edward VI inherited the Manor from his father in 1547, he gave it - perhaps he was persuaded to do so - to his uncle Edward Seymour, the Protector, to administer. But on Edward's death, the Manor reverted to Queen Mary in 1553. The next year she gave the Manor to Catherine Pole the granddaughter of the executed Countess Margaret. She married Francis Hastings, Earl of Huntingdon. It remained in that family until 1601, when Henry Hastings sold it to Thomas, Earl Arundell, whose interest in the town is recounted in chapter 9. On his death in 1636, great confusion followed, since he left the manor to be shared equally between his six daughters. Eventually it was agreed that the best claimant to the Lordship, was Lord Baltimore, who was living largely in America, having founded the colony of Maryland in 1632. Not until 1665 did the various claimants finally resolve the situation by selling the Manor to Edward Hyde, Earl of Clarendon and Lord Chancellor of England. His efforts on behalf of the town are told in chapter 25.

In 1708 Henry, the son of Edward Earl of Clarendon, sold the Manor to Sir Peter Mews. This enabled him to become one of the Borough's Members of Parliament, when the town was still a Rotten Borough, returning two Members. When Sir Peter married Lydia Gervis, he settled the Manor on her as a dowry. Since she had no children, the Manor passed twice through the female line until it was inherited in 1778 by George Ivison Tapps, who was knighted in 1791. His son, who inherited the Manor added Gervis to the name. During his lifetime, there were several local Inclosure (sic) Acts, the most important of which was in 1802. This Act noted that *'the said Waste*

Grounds consist of large tracts of Commonable Pasture Land, partly covered with Furze and Heath, of very little Value, and in their present Situation are incapable of any considerable Improvement, but if the same, or certain Parts thereof, were divided into specific Shares, ... might be considerably improved'. The areas involved all formed part of the Honour of Christchurch and lay within the Parish of Christchurch and its chapelry of Holdenhurst. They all lay to the west of the River Stour and were: Muscliffe, Muckleshell, Throop, Holdenhurst, Pokesdown, Iford, Tuckton and Wick. All these areas were separated from Christchurch so that the land could be developed and houses built to create what was to become the new town of Bournemouth. However the land remained within the Lordship of the Manor. Other parts of the Honour at Hurn, Winkton and Hinton Admiral were also separated at the same time so that they too could develop into villages.

When Sir George Tapps died in 1842, his son Sir George Elliott Tapps Gervis, added the further name Meyrick. By the time he died in 1896, the new town of Bournemouth had become a municipal borough and was rapidly making a name for itself as a seaside resort. However, the Honour or Manor of Christchurch still includes land in both towns that remains today under the lordship of the Meyrick family.

The second manor is the Manor of the Borough of Christchurch. This formed part of the Saxon royal Honour of Tweoneam and consisted largely of the ancient burgh that lay within its walls and centred round the Priory, and parts of the Portfield and Bargates. Originally this would probably have been known as the Manor of the Burgh of Tweoneam. As already noted, in 1100 Henry I gave it to Richard de Redvers as part of the larger Honour. It remained in the same ownership as the Honour until 1791, when Sir George Ivison Tapps sold it to the Right Hon. George Rose, who was Treasurer to the Royal Navy. Ownership of the Manor enabled him to become one of the two Members of Parliament for the Rotten Borough of Christchurch. On his death in 1796, his son, Sir George Henry Rose inherited the Manor and held it till his death in 1863. It was then sold to the Earl of Malmesbury, whose family hold the Manor to this day.

The de Redvers family gave many of the privileges that were attached to the Manor to the burgesses and these may be traced in some of the charters in the Cartulary relating to those times. They have been held by burgesses ever since and were originally of considerable importance. The privileges included amongst other things the after pasture of Bure Mead, Bernard's Mead and Stocker's Mead, besides the Commoning Rights on St Catherine's Hill and elsewhere as described in chapter 15, and the tolls of the weekly market and of the October Fair of St Faith that was held outside the Bar Gate on the

Fair Mile. For these privileges, the burgesses paid a 'fee-farm' rental to the Lord of the Manor, known as "Castle Rent". The Steward of the Manor annually swore in the Mayor at the Court Leat, that was held in the Court House that stood behind the property in Castle Street described in chapter 8. The Lord of the Manor was also able to nominate one of the two Members of Parliament as noted above. One of the early duties of the Lord of the Manor was to see that the town's bridges were maintained in good condition for the passage of people and their goods. This led to the Montacutes obtaining the indulgences described in chapter 10.

The Lords of the Manor of the Borough have frequently taken an active interest in the affairs of the town, viewing their position as being one of considerable responsibility. However over the centuries the rights and duties attached to the Lordship have decreased. In particular, the right to appoint a Member of Parliament disappeared as a result of the first Reform Bill of 1832 that swept away the Rotten Boroughs and began the slow transition to universal suffrage and greater democracy. But other rights and duties still remain and the borough still pays an annual rental to the Lord of the Manor for the privileges attached to the common lands. The present Earl of Malmsbury still claims his rent from the Borough to maintain his ownership and rights, though it is not great burden on the Borough. The annual rental has for many years been fixed at one penny and can be equated with the medieval token peppercorn rent that is still used elsewhere. Thus do customs dating back a thousand years continue even today.

The third manor is the Manor of Christchurch Twynham. This should not be confused with either of the other two, since it refers only to some but not all of the property and lands granted to the church in Twynham that was dedicated to the Holy Trinity. Lands had been given to the church over several centuries, the first of which may well have been the grant made by the Saxon King Ethelred in A.D. 985 as mentioned in chapter 2. However the greater part of the property came from the Richard de Redvers and his son Baldwin, after they themselves had been granted both the Honour and the Manor of the Burgh of Tweoneam by Henry I in 1100. Because the lands were given to the Church, the tenure was known as *perpetual alms'* so that there were very few duties attached to them, other than those mentioned in the Saxon charters, though they carried many valuable rights. These can be found in the two charters, dated about 1100 and 1150, in the Cartulary. The Manor took its name from the church itself whose high altar was dedicated to Christ the Saviour and was held of the Lord of the Honour of Tweoneam. Its full title was probably "The Manor of Christ's Church at Twynham", though inevitably this was shortened to "Christchurch Twynham". The parish altar that stood in the nave of the Priory Church was dedicated to the Holy Trinity just as the earlier Saxon church had been. The Priory continued to own the Manor until its suppression by Henry VIII in 1539, the details of which are described in chapter 13. At that time, the estate comprised the church, its churchyard, all the land between the rivers to the south of the church including Place Mill and the Mill Stream, the 'werkes' - an area between the graveyard and the present bowling green - the present vicarage and its garden and the Red House Museum and its garden. There were also various properties in the burgh itself and other lands at Knapp, Stanpit, and on the Portfield, including probably the site of the Leper Hospital outside the Bar Gate and also the Manor of Somerford. These properties did not form part of the Manor, but were additional lands that had been given to the Priory over the centuries. Amongst the benefits that were attached to the Manor from the original grant of Baldwin de Redvers in about 1150, were the rights to hold a fair on the Thursday after Trinity Sunday, large quantities of turf and heath for the fires, a tithe of all salmon caught locally on the lord's rivers, a tithe of new plough-land and exemption from paying tolls on goods brought in to the burgh.

From the time of Henry I, the Manor was held from the overlord as the Honour of Twynham until it was seized by Henry VIII. In 1539. Not only were the Manor's lands taken, but also all the rights attached to it as well as the other properties, such as the Manor of Somerford and other lands in the neighbourhood that had been given to the Priory over the centuries. As was explained in chapter 13, Henry returned the church and its yard to the town the following year, but the rest of the Manor he granted to Thomas Wriothesley, the then Lord Chancellor, in 1545. Henry's daughter, Queen Mary, granted the Manor to Thomas White, who died in 1565. Thereafter the Manor seems to have reverted to the Crown, for in 1610, James I granted it to his son Henry, Prince of Wales, who died in 1612. His younger brother, Charles, took over the Manor in 1617. The Tudor and Stuart Lordship of this Manor may explain the royal interest in appointing the Master of the Mary Magdalen Leper Hospital, as told in chapter 9.

However it appears that Charles I, being short of funds, mortgaged the Manor to the Lord Mayor of London. The City in turn sold it in 1630 to one of their aldermen, Richard Fenn. His family held the Manor until 1683 when it passed to a sister, Jane, who married John Tregonwell. Seven years later, she passed the Manor to her daughter who married Sir Jacob Bancks, of Milton Abbas. His son sold it in 1736 to Edward Lisle of Moyles Court, whence it was sold in 1754 to James Willis of Ringwood. His son bequeathed the Manor, to his nephew John Compton of Harbridge, who, as recounted in chapter 22, sold it to Gustavus Brander in 1782, he having already bought the Manor of Somerford that had once belonged to the Priory.

Finally, in 1830 the Manor passed once more by sale to Sir George Ivison Tapps, who had previously owned the Manor of the Borough. It has remained in that family, which by addition of names as explained above, is now the Meyrick family. The present Lord of the Manor of Christchurch Twynham is Sir George Meyrick.

For the last 300 years, this Manor has been held by local people, though the benefit to them has been small, since the early rights had long since been surrendered. So the three Manors relating to Christchurch Twynham date back for over 1,000 years. May they continue at least for the next millennium.

Appendix 1.

The Mayors of Christchurch.

The civil administration of the town of Twynham and later Christchurch was from earliest times carried out by the burgesses. The chief amongst them was first known as the Reeve, or sometimes Portreeve. This title was still used occasionally until at least 1591. However the present title of Mayor was being used certainly as early as 1435 to denote the chief citizen of the town and the representative of the Lord of the Manor and Sovereign. In addition to the mayor and burgesses, there were several other officers who had an important part to play in the administration of a town. Chief amongst these were the constables, bailiffs, aletaster and hayward. The names of many of these men, as well as many of the burgesses, can be found in the Borough's archives in Dorchester and cover several centuries. Not unnaturally, the names of certain families keep cropping up. Though the list of mayors is unfortunately not complete, it does cover a period of 700 years. From an early date, probably soon after the office of Justice of the Peace was created in 1361, the Reeve or Mayor would also have held that office. The last Mayor to be ex officio a magistrate was James Bell in 1964.

The ancient seal of Christchurch-Twynham.

Mayors have customarily been elected during May and therefore sit during two years. For simplicity, the date of their mayoralty is given as the year in which they were elected. Until 1964, it was not uncommon for the sitting mayor to be re-elected the following year. Where, in the early years, one or two years appear to be missing, it may be that the incumbent continued to sit as mayor the following year.

261

The list of presently known mayors reads:-

1297	John Leshelm.	1550	John Frayle.
1299	John Randouf.	1554	William Mareat.
1301	John Randouf.	1556	Thomas Hancock.
1320	John More.	1557	Richard Carter.
1397	Robert Tankard.	1559	Henry Pawson.
1398	John Walker.	1561	Thomas Hancock.
1399	William Savayn	1562	William Nutkyns.
1400	William Savayn.	1563	Richard Inwood.
1401	Thomas Pyke.	1565	Thomas Petye.
1418	John Vyrley.	1566	William Nutkyns.
1428	Thomas Poure.	1567	Richard Inwood.
1435	Richard Doget.	1569	Alban Whyte.
1437	Thomas Covent.	1570	Thomas Nashe.
1438	John Bonbyle.	1571	Richard Colgill.
1452	Thomas Parke.	1572	William Jerman.
1471	John Vytrok.	1573	Thomas Hancock.
1483	Richard Lowen.	1574	Thomas Pettie.
1488	Robert Baker.	1578	Richard Inwood.
1489	John Parlett.	1581	Thomas Pettey.
1490	John Peynter.	1582	Richard Colgill.
1496	Thomas Crokker.	1583	William Nutkyns.
1497	Thomas Crokker.	1584	Pancheridge Genge.
1502	Thomas Crokker.	1585	Henry Pawson.
1516	John Bevyle.	1586	Robert Carter.
1526	Robert Farrant.	1587	Joseph Frayle.
1527	John Bevell.	1588	Richard Inwood.
1535	James Trym.	1589	Robert Carter.
1536	John Imberly.	1590	John Clare.
1537	Robert Farrant.	1591	John Nutkyns.
1538	John Imberley.	1592	Thomas Pawson.
1539	Richard Genge.	1593	William Colgill.
1540	John Godwyn.	1594	John Clare.
1541	Robert Westbury.	1595	Joseph Frayle.
1542	Edward Lewen.	1596	Nicholas Gregory.
1547	William Meryet.	1597	Thomas Pawson.

1598	William Colgill.	1635	Henry Rogers.
1599	Nicholas Gregory.	1636	John Hildesley.
1600	Joseph Frayle.	1637	Samuel Butcher.
1601	Joseph Frayle.	1638	Henry Pawson.
1602	Robert Waterhouse.	1639	Henry Rogers.
1603	Thomas Pawson.	1640	John Kempe.
1604	William Colgill.	1641	Samuel Butcher.
1605	Joseph Frayle.	1642	John Williams.
1606	John Pitman.	1643	James Colgill.
1607	Robert Waterhouse.	1644	John Rogers.
1608	Thomas Pawson.	1645	John Rogers.
1609	William Colgill.	1646	William Pawson.
1610	Robert Waterhouse.	1647	Jesse Standard.
1611	Thomas Pawson.	1648	James Willis.
1612	William Colgill.	1649	John Willliams.
1613	Joseph Frayle.	1650	John Earle.
1614	Thomas Pawson.	1651	Thomas Crewe.
1615	Henry Rogers.	1652	Richard Oliver.
1616	Willliam Colgill.	1653	John Kempe.
1617	John Templeman.	1654	William Pawson.
1618	Thomas Pawson.	1655	John Williams.
1619	Henry Rogers.	1656	John Willis.
1620	Willliam Colgill.	1657	Jesse Standard.
1621	John Templeman.	1658	William Pawson.
1622	Thomas Pawson.	1659	John Earle.
1623	Henry Rogers.	1660	Thomas Crewe.
1624	Willam Colgill.	1661	John Welshman.
1625	John Kempe.	1662	Henry Hastings.
1626	John Templemman.	1663	John Blake.
1627	Henry Rogers.	1664	Henry Rogers.
1628	Henry Pawson.	1665	Christopher Fabian.
1629	Edmund Newsham.	1666	Nicholas Emberly.
1630	John Templeman.	1667	Thomas Stevens.
1631	Henry Rogers.	1668	Richard Pawson.
1632	Willliam Colgill.	1669	James Dewy.
1633	John Kempe.	1670	Henry Hopkins.
1634	Henry Rogers.	1671	John Welshman.

1672	Robert Stokes.	1709	Thomas Stevens.
1673	Edward Odber.	1710	Thomas Stevens.
1674	William Earle.	1711	James Stevens.
1675	Anthony Carter.	1712	Thomas Stevens.
1676	Henry Hopkins.	1713	Joshua Stevens.
1677	Thomas Coffin.	1714	Thomas Stevens.
1678	Peter Smith.	1715	Joshua Stevens.
1679	John Imber.	1716	Thomas Stevens.
1680	John Stevens.	1717	James Stevens.
1681	Henry Rogers.	1727	Samuel Hookey.
1682	Henry Rogers.	1728	John Hancock.
1683	John Welshman.	1729	John Hinxman Jnr.
1684	Henry Hopkins.	1730	John Tarrant.
1685	John Blake.	1731	Thomas Jeans.
1686	John Blake.	1732	John Dale.
1687	John Blake.	1733	Edward Hooper Snr.
1688	John Blake.	1734	Thomas Jeans.
1689	John Stevens.		Edward Hooper.
1690	John Stevens.	1735	William Goldwyer.
1691	John Stevens.		Edward Hooper Jnr.
1692	Henry Hopkins.	1736	Richard Samborne.
1693	Henry Hopkins.		Edward Lisle.
1694	James Stevens.	1737	Thomas Jeans.
1695	James Stevens.		James Stevens.
1696	Thomas Wyndham.	1738	John Dale.
1697	Edward Seymour.		William Forbes.
1698	Francis Swanton.	1739	Thomas Jeans.
1699	Thomas Stevens.	1740	Robert Dale.
1700	Thomas Stevens.	1741	John Pollen.
1701	Thomas Stevens.	1742	James Stevens.
1702	Thomas Stevens.	1743	Samuel Hookey.
1703	Thomas Stevens.	1744	Thomas Jeans.
1704	Thomas Stevens.	1745	Simon Witherington.
1705	Thomas Stevens.	1746	Samuel Roy.
1706	Thomas Stevens.	1747	Thomas Jeans.
1707	Thomas Stevens.	1748	John Reeks.
1708	Thomas Stevens.	1749	Richard Holloway.

1750	Edward Hooper.	1788	William Dean.
1751	John Dale.	1789	Steven Holloway Jnr.
1752	Thomas Jeans Jnr.	1790	Thomas Beckley Jnr.
1753	Edward Hooper.	1791	Thomas Hyde.
1754	Thomas Mews.	1792	Thomas Beckley Jnr.
1755	Thomas Jeans.	1793	Thomas Heathcote.
1756	William Newsam.	1794	George Rose M.P.
1757	Joshua S. Jeans.	1795	Thomas Beckley Jnr.
1758	Edward Hooper.	1796	George Rose M.P.
1759	Thomas Mews.	1797	William Chamberlayne.
1760	Edward Hooper.	1798	William Stewart Rose.
1761	Thomas Harris.	1799	George Rose M.P.
1762	Thomas Mews.	1800	William Chanberlayne.
1763	Richard Samborne.	1801	William S. Rose.
1764	Benjamin Woodroffe.	1802	Thomas Beckley Jnr.
1765	Thomas Mews Snr.	1803	William Chamberlayne.
1766	John Hordel.	1804	William S. Rose.
1767	Edward Hooper.	1805	Rt. Hon George Rose.
1768	Joshua S. Jeans.	1806	Thomas Beckley.
1770	Edward Hooper.	1807	William Chamberlayne.
1771	Joseph Gibbs.	1808	Thomas Mewin.
1772	Joshua S. Jeans.	1809	Thomas Beckley.
1773	Thomas Mews Jnr.	1810	Thomas F. Hearthcote.
1774	Edward Hooper.	1811	Thomas Beckley.
1775	Thomas Mews Snr.	1812	Thomas Beckley Jnr.
1776	Joshua S. Jeans.	1813	Thomas F. Heathcote.
1777	John Cook.	1814	Thomas Beckley.
1778	William Jackson.	1815	Thomas F. Heathcote.
1779	John Cook.	1816	Rt. Hon George Rose.
1780	Edward Hooper.	1817	George Eyre.
1781	John Cook.	1818	William Smith.
1782	Charles W. Wapshare.	1819	Thomas Beckley Jnr.
1783	John Cook.	1820	Thomas Beckley.
1784	William Dean.	1821	George Eyre.
1785	Saint Alban Roy.	1822	Sir Harry Neale.
1786	John Cook.	1823	Charles Lyell.
1787	Saint Alban Roy.	1824	Thomas Beckley.

1825 William S. Rose.	1862 Charles Hicks.
1826 Charles P. Rose.	1863 John Lennon.
1827 George Eyre.	1864 John Lennon.
1828 Sir John P. Dalrymple.	1865 John E. Holloway.
1829 Charles P. Rose.	1866 John E. Holloway.
1830 John C. Compton.	1867 James Druitt.
1831 John Spicer.	1868 William Tucker.
1832 John Hannaford.	1869 George Ferrey.
1833 Arthur Quartley.	1870 Charles Hicks.
1834 John Goddard.	1871 George O. Aldridge.
1845 Ambrose Tucker.	1872 Francis E. Williams.
1836 Arthur Quartley.	1873 Nicholas S. Newlyn.
1837 Arthur Quartley.	1874 Nicholas S. Newlyn.
1838 Arthur Quartley.	1875 Henry T. H. Mead.
1839 Joseph Hannaford.	1876 Samuel Bemister.
1840 Benjamen Ferrey.	1877 Samuel Bemister.
1841 John Baker.	1878 George Ferrey.
1842 Henry T. Jenkins.	1879 Henry Pain.
1843 Arthur Q. Palmer.	1880 James Kemp Welch.
1844 Abraham Pike.	1881 James Kemp Welch.
1845 John Newman.	1882 Nicholas S. Newlyn.
1846 George Ferrey.	1883 Samuel Bemister.
1847 William W. Humby.	1884 Edward Aldridge.
1848 Richard Collins.	1885 Samuel Bemister.
1849 James King.	1886 James Kemp Welch.
1850 James Druitt.	1887 John E. Holloway.
1851 Abraham Pike.	1888 James Druitt.
1852 Arthur Q. Palmer.	1889 John King.
1853 Arthur Q. Palmer.	1890 Samuel Bemister.
1854 George Ferrey.	1891 William Tucker.
1855 William Ferrey.	1892 Elias Lane.
1856 Edward S. Elliott.	1893 Samuel Bemister.
1857 Henry T. Jenkins.	1894 Henry W. Jenkins.
1858 Arthur Q. Palmer.	1895 John Green.
1859 James Druitt.	1896 James Druitt.
1860 George Ferrey.	1897 George Marshall.
1861 Edward S. Elliott.	1898 William Tucker.

1899	Samuel Bemister.	1934	Norman Barnes.
1900	Henry W. Jenkins.	1935	Douglas Galton.
	William Tucker.	1936	Douglas Galton.
1901	Philip E. Mouckton.	1937	Henry E. W. Lapthorne.
1902	Frank A. Lane.	1938	Henry E. W. Lapthorne.
1903	Philip W. Mouckton.	1939	Thomas Markham.
1904	Philip W. Mouckton.	1940	Thomas Markham.
1905	Philip W. Mouckton.	1941	Thomas Markham.
1906	Sambrooke Newlyn.	1942	Thomas Markham.
1907	Sambrooke Newlyn.	1943	Douglas Galton.
1908	Davis Galbraith.	1944	Douglas Galton.
1909	David Galbraith.	1945	Douglas Galton.
1910	Robert Druitt.	1946	Edmund J. Slinn.
1911	Robert Druitt.	1947	Edmund J. Slinn.
1912	Robert Druitt.	1948	Edmund J. Slinn.
1913	Robert Druitt.	1949	Edmund J. Slinn.
1914	Alfred H. Searle.	1950	Mrs Eileen M. Wallis Power.
1915	Augustus H. B. Hartford.	1951	Mrs Eileen M. Wallis Power.
1916	Augustus H. B. Hartford.		
1917	William Tucker.	1952	Kenneth H. Ashcroft.
1918	William Tucker.	1953	Kenneth H. Ashcroft.
1919	John Maidment.	1954	Kenneth H. Ashcroft.
1920	Leonard Agate.	1955	Kenneth L. Smith.
1921	Leonard Agate.	1956	Kenneth L. Smith.
1922	Leonard Agate.	1957	Kenneth L. Smith.
1923	Norman Barnes.	1958	John W. Richardson.
1924	Norman Barnes.	1959	John W. Richardson.
1925	Francis E Abbott.	1960	Miss Elsie I. Padwick.
1926	Herbert J. Martin.	1961	Miss Elsie I. Padwick.
1927	Herbert J. Martin.	1962	Barrington Myres.
1928	Miss Mona Robinson.	1963	James R. Bell.
1929	Francis E. Abbott.	1964	James R. Bell.
1930	John W. Tucker.	1965	Mrs. Irene A. Stevenson.
1931	John W. Tucker.	1966	Eric N. S. Spreadbury.
1932	John W. Tucker.	1967	William A. Bridge.
	George W. Saunders.	1968	Mrs. Dorothy Baker.
1933	Norman Barnes.		

1969	Herbert R. Bourke.	1985	Mrs Norma K. Fox.
1970	John S. C. Morgan.	1986	Adrian M. Winfield.
1971	William J. Bentley. D.F.C.	1987	David J. Fox. O.B.E., D.L.
1972	Miss Caroline Sharp.	1988	Mrs. Margaret P. Pardy.
1973	Tom Staniforth. J.P.	1989	John Moss.
1974	James T. Beattie.	1990	Michael C. Kidman.
1975	John S. C. Morgan.	1991	Eric N. S. Spreadbury.
1976	Eric N. S. Spreadbury.	1992	Colin R. Bungey. J.P.
1977	John Beachamp.	1993	Mrs. June Payne.
1978	Michael A. Hodges.	1994	Edward Coope.
1979	James T. Beattie.	1995	Michael Peirce.`
1980	Kevin P. Bishop.	1996	Eric W. Wood. Ll.B.
1981	Robert C. Bruce.	1997	Colin R. Bungey. J.P.
1982	Adrian M. Winfield.	1998	John Lofts.
1983	Kenneth W. L. Gibbs.	1999	Robert J. R. McArthur.
1984	Eric N. S. Spreadbury.		

The Arms of the Borough of Christchurch.

Appendix 2.

The Deans, Priors and Vicars at Christchurch.

Over the period of about thirteen centuries that there have been priests, first at Twynham and then at Christchurch, the person in charge has held various titles. There are several lists of names, none of which is complete. Those listed below, with their dates, have been taken largely from the list compiled in 1793 by Revd. Richard Warner. F.R.S. He spent his early years in Christchurch, and was a pupil in the school in St Michael's Loft before going to Oxford University.

From about A.D. 650, when the first missionary priests came here, their leader had no official title, all the priests going under the title of Canon. The spelling of names, particularly until the 15th century, often varies considerably and the version used is but one of several that appears on different documents. The earliest record of a priest at Twynham occurs in the second Saxon Charter of A.D. 985. He is Sulfric, though his position is unknown. The names of priests next appear in the Domesday Record.

Their leader was: Godric.

Other priests mentioned were: Alnod.
                                Alsi.
                                Godwine.

The first title given to the leader of the priests was that of Dean - a title that the records state was not previously known in Twynham. The list of Deans reads:-

   c. 1090   Ranulph Flambard. (Consecrated Bishop of Durham 1094).
   1128   Gilbert de Dousgunels.
   1135   Peter de Oglander.
          Ralph.
   1140   Hilary. (Consecrated Bishop of Chichester 1147).

With the establishment of the Order of Augustinian Canons Regular in 1150, the head of the Convent took the title of Prior. Because part of the Priory Church was also the parish church, one of the canons held the office of Vicar, having the cure of the souls of the people of the burgh.

The list of priors, some of whom had previously been the sub-prior, reads:-

1150	Reginald.
1161	Julian.
1186	Ralph.
1195	Peter.
1225	Roger.
	Richard.
	Nicholas de Wareham.
	Nicholas de Sturminster.
1272	John de Abingdon.
1272	William de Netheravon.
1286	Richard Maury. (May.)
1302	William Quintin. (13th April.)
1317	Walter Thovleshide.
1323	Edmund de Ramsbury.
1337	Richard de Busthorne. (27th March.)
1340	Robert Leighe. (21st August.)
1347	Henry Eyre. (March.)
1349	William Tyrewache. (18th March.)
1377	John Wodenham. (21st July.)
1397	John Borard. (8th November.)
1413	Thomas Talbot.
	John Morton.
1420	John Wimborne.
	William Norton.
1450	John Dorchester.
1477	John Draper I. (16th December.)
1502	William Eyre.
1520	John Draper II,
	Chaplain to Henry VIII and Bishop of Neapolis.

During this time there would have been a succession of vicars to minister to the needs of the parish. In 1359, the salary for the vicar and his servant amounted to £10.14s.6d and benefits in kind equal at least to the same amount. The names of only a few vicars are presently known, though study of the Borough's documents may reveal others.

So far, the following names have been discovered:-

  1262   Robert.
  1351   John.
  1387   Henry Baker.
  1416   John Brym (chaplain).
  1438   Walter Hyder.
  1520   John Pope.
  c.1530   John Smith.

There are also records of men being ordained and probably joining the Augustinian Convent as canons. Ordained at Marwell were:-

  1306   Cordray. - an acolyte.
         Nicholas Prewert. - priest.
         Robert de Wareham. - priest.
         Thomas de Bere. - priest.

Ordained at Braemore were:-
  1307   Thomas. - first tonsure.
         William Hulcote. - priest.
         Thomas Gardyn. - canon.
  1308   Richard de Cranborne. - applied 3 times to be a canon.
  1309   Aden Plote de Neyrbuns. - canon.
  1319   Stephen de Staplebrigge. - an ex-Templar who received the first tonsure and seems to have been under supervision.
  1351   John Calors. - canon.

The ancient Conventual Seal

The 'Visitation' of the Priory in 1501 listed in addition to the Prior, John Draper I, the following ten the canons, giving the offices they held:-

William Eyre. - sub-prior
John Warner. - steward
Richard Cogin. - third Prior
Nicholas Bryght. - precentor
John Baker. - almoner
John Gravy. - cellarer
John Gregory. - warden of the Frater
William Beaver. - warden of St Mary's Chapel
Walter Lodge. - master of the Works
Robert Godewyn. - sub-deacon

The remaining 13 canons were not named.

The 1539 document surrendering the Priory to Henry VIII, lists in addition to the Prior, John Draper II, the following 18 canons:-

Robert Beverey — probably the sub-prior.

Reginald Bennett.
Richard South. — These five probably
William Clerke. — held senior offices.
Robert Merifelde.
Thomas Hancock.

John Pope.
Walter Churche.
John Poppett.
Willliam Marten.
Walter Mathewe.
William Keyte.
John Stone.
Thomas Andrewes.
John Tulse.
John Drover.
Thomas Cooke.
Anthony Pitteman, probably a novice.

John Smith is not mentioned because he was the vicar of the parish.

After the suppression of the Priory by Henry VIII in 1539, and the return of the church to the town, the Parish of Christchurch was in the hands of vicars. They were:-

1539	William Trapnell.
	John Smith, (who may have been re-appointed when the church was returned to the town in 1540).
1549	Robert Newman.
1574	William White.
1577	William Ley.
1587	John Lee.
1616	John Marston, B.A.
1631	William Greene.
1640	John Imber.
1647	John Warner.
1660	John Imber, re-instated.
1673	Henry Goldwier.
1689	Edward Bowen, B.A.
1748	W. Batt, M.A.
1753	Charles Moody, B.A.
1757	James Talman, B.A.
1778	William Jackson, B.A.
1802	Samuel Clapham, B.A.
1830	William F. Burrows.
1871	Zachary Nash, M.A.
1884	Thomas Henry Bush, M.A.
1910	John James Cooke-Yarborough, M.A.
1915	Edgecombe Walter Leachman.
1916	Robert Raikes Needham.
1919	Walter Marshall, M.A.
1920	William Hayne Gay, M.A.
1945	Robert Peel Price, M.A.
1962	Leslie H. Yorke, L.Th.
1976	Basil H. T. Trevor-Morgan, B.A.
1993	Hugh M. Williams, A.K.C.

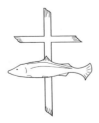

The present day Priory symbol of the Cross and Salmon.

Appendix 3.

Masters of the Leper Hospital of St Mary Magdalen.

The list of Hospital Masters is unfortunately not complete. Since the hospital was built on Priory land, in the early days the Master was probably one of the canons of the Priory. By the early 15th century, the Mayor and burgesses were having an increasing influence in the running of the hospital. Some of the Masters also became Mayors of the town. As always, the spelling of the names tends to vary in different documents. The dates against the names are when they were first known to be Master, but not necessarily the date of their appointment.

1314	Richard Wade.
1370	Richard Wade.
1394	John Boyl. (Mayor 1439.)
1439	Robert Grynston.
1498	Nicholas Guylbert.
1507	William Stamford.
1550	John Emberle. (Mayor 1536, '38.)
1551	William Maryet. (Mayor 1547 and 1554.)
1594	Thomas Sabley.
1595	John Phillips.
1596	Evan Jones.
1609	John Agar.
1646	Richard Flurey.
1674	Robert Collins.
1674	Samuel Carter.
1699	Richard Holloway. (Burgess 1694.)
1766	Thomas Mews, junior. (Mayor 1773.)
1812	Robert Reeks. (Burgess 1780.)
1825	Benjamin Ferrey.
1847	George Ferrey. (Mayor 1854, '60, '69.)
1876	John E. Holloway. (Mayor 1887.)

Since 1901, the Hospital Trust has been run by Trustees.